Tony Karbo is Executive Director of the Centre for Conflict Resolution in Cape Town, South Africa. He has worked extensively in Africa with numerous organisations working in conflict zones, facilitating training in conflict resolution and peacebuilding, and in monitoring and evaluating election processes and programmes. Karbo holds a master's degree and doctorate from the School of Conflict Analysis and Resolution at George Mason University, Virginia.

Tim Murithi is Professor Extraordinary of African Studies at the Centre for African Studies, University of Free State, South Africa and Head of Justice and Reconciliation in the Africa Programme at the Institute for Justice and Reconciliation, Cape Town. He has over 23 years of experience in peace, security, governance, transitional justice, and development in Africa, has authored over 85 journal articles, book chapters, and policy papers, and is author and editor of nine books.

'This timely book brilliantly navigates a mosaic of complexities that the African Union continues to grapple with as it searches for pertinence today. The AU has become antithetical to its foundational principles of promoting unity, solidarity and prosperity in African states. This book poses thought-provoking and unnerving questions about the continuing validity and integrity of the AU. A great reflective read for policy and decision makers, analysts and scholars of African politics'.

Professor Pamela Machakanja, Dean, College of Business, Peace, Leadership and Governance, Africa University

'This book presents a diplomatic history of the African Union and readers are treated to a rigorous analysis of Africa's peace and development prospects and challenges'.

Professor Victor Adetula, Head of Research, Nordic Africa Institute, Uppsala, Sweden

'This timely book on the African Union after 15 years has assembled leading scholars on Africa to probe the past, present, and future trajectories of African integration. The chapters reiterate the abiding message that continental unity, security, and prosperity are not only inter-generational imperatives, but they also point to the perennial obstacles in translating these lofty objectives into practice. The book provides a useful addition to the growing literature on continental integration and Africa's relationship with external actors'.

Professor Gilbert Khadiagala, Head of the Department of International Relations at the University of the Witwatersrand (Wits), Johannesburg, South Africa

THE AFRICAN UNION

Autocracy, Diplomacy and Peacebuilding
in Africa

Edited by
TONY KARBO AND TIM MURITHI

I.B. TAURIS

LONDON · NEW YORK · OXFORD · NEW DELHI · SYDNEY

Published in association with the Centre for Conflict Resolution,
Cape Town, South Africa

I.B. TAURIS
Bloomsbury Publishing Plc
50 Bedford Square, London, WC1B 3DP, UK
1385 Broadway, New York, NY 10018, USA
29 Earlsfort Terrace, Dublin 2, Ireland

BLOOMSBURY, I.B. TAURIS and the I.B. Tauris logo are trademarks
of Bloomsbury Publishing Plc

First published in Great Britain 2018
Reprinted 2020, 2021

A catalogue record for this book is available from the British Library.

A catalog record for this book is available from the Library of Congress.

ISBN: HB: 978-1-7883-1149-6
PB: 978-1-7883-1150-2
ePDF: 978-1-7867-3328-3
eBook: 978-1-7867-3328-3

Series: International Library of African Studies, volume 65

Typeset in Garamond Three by OKS Prepress Services, Chennai, India

To find out more about our authors and books visit www.bloomsbury.com
and sign up for our newsletters.

This book is dedicated to the Supreme Court of Kenya for its courageous and historic decision to nullify the Kenyan presidential elections, which were held on 8 August 2017, on the basis that the polling processes contravened key provisions of the country's constitution. This decision affirms the primacy of the rule of law and stands as a beacon of hope for other African countries, and countries around the world, particularly in this era of encroaching authoritarianism. The African Union (AU) member states should draw a lesson from this bold demonstration of judicial independence in Kenya, which has now set a precedent for the continent of Africa and future generations of its citizens.

CONTENTS

LIST OF ILLUSTRATIONS

Tables

Figure

LIST OF ABBREVIATIONS

AAF-SAP	African Alternative Framework to Structural Adjustment Programme for Socio-Economic Recovery and Transformation
ACDEG	African Charter on Democracy, Elections and Governance
ACIRC	African Capacity for Immediate Response to Crises
AEC	African Economic Community
AfDB	African Development Bank
AFISMA	African-Led International Support Mission in Mali
AGA	African Governance Architecture
AIIB	Asian Infrastructure Bank
AMIB	African Union Mission in Burundi
AMIS	African Union Mission in Sudan
AMISOM	African Union Mission in Somalia
AMU	Arab Maghreb Union
AMV	Africa Mining Vision
ANC	African National Congress
APPER	Africa's Priority Programme for Economic Recovery
APRM	African Peer Review Mechanism
APSA	African Peace and Security Architecture
ASEAN	Association of Southeast Asian Nations
ASF	African Standby Force
AU	African Union
AUC	African Union Commission
CAADP	Comprehensive Africa Agriculture Development Programme

CADSP	Common African Defence and Security Policy
CAR	Central African Republic
CATTF	China-Africa Think Tank Forum
CDS	Commission for Defence and Security
CEMAC	Central African Economic and Monetary Community
CEN-SAD	Community of Sahel-Saharan States
CEWARN	Conflict Early Warning and Response Mechanism
CEWS	Continental Early Warning System
C-FTA	Continental Free Trade Area
CNPC	China's National Petroleum Corporation
COMESA	Common Market for Eastern and Southern Africa
COPAX	Council for Peace and Security
COWARN	Early Warning System of the Common Market of Eastern and Southern Africa States
CPA	Comprehensive Peace Agreement
CPX	Command Post Exercise
CSSDCA	Conference on Security, Stability, Development and Cooperation in Africa
DDR	Disarmament, Demobilization and Reintegration
DDRCP	Disarmament, Demobilization and Reintegration Capacity Programme
DRC	Democratic Republic of the Congo
EAC	East Africa Community
EACWARN	Early Warning System of the East African Community
EASBRIG	East Africa Standby Brigade
EASF	East African Standby Force
ECCAS	Economic Community of Central African States
ECCWARN	Early Warning System of the Economic Community of Central African States
ECOSOC	Economic and Social Council
ECOSOCC	Economic, Social and Cultural Council
ECOWARN	Early Warning System of the Economic Community of West African States
ECOWAS	Economic Community of West African States
ESAMI	Eastern and Southern African Management Institute
ESF	Economic Community of West African States Standby Force
EU	European Union

FAD	Final Act of Lagos
FDI	Foreign Direct Investment
FOMAC	Central African Multinational Force
G77	Group of 77 at the United Nations
GDP	Gross Domestic Product
HIPPO	High-Level Independent Panel on Peace Operations
IEA	Institute of Economic Affairs
IGAD	Intergovernmental Authority on Development
ILO	International Labour Organization
IMF	International Monetary Fund
LPA	Lagos Plan of Action
MAP	Millennium Africa Recovery Plan
MDGs	Millennium Development Goals
MICOPAX	Central African Peace Consolidation Mission
MINURCA	United Nations Mission in Central African Republic
MINUSCA	United Nations Multi-Dimensional Integrated Stabilization Mission in the Central African Republic
MINUSMA	United Nations Multidimensional Integrated Stabilization Mission in Mali
MISCA	AU-Led International Support Mission to the Central African Republic
MONUA	United Nations Observer Mission in Angola
MSC	Military Staff Committee
NAM	Non-Aligned Movement
NARC	North African Regional Capability
NATO	North Atlantic Treaty Organisation
NEPAD	New Partnership for Africa's Development
NEWC	National Early Warning Committee
NGOs	Non-Governmental Organisations
OAU	Organisation of African Unity
OBOR	One Belt One Road
OECD	Organisation for Economic Cooperation and Development
ONUC	United Nations Operation in Congo
ONUMOZ	United Nations Observer Mission in Mozambique
P5	Five Permanent Members of the United Nations Security Council
PAP	Pan-African Parliament
PCRD	Post-Conflict Reconstruction and Development

PIDA	Programme for Infrastructure Development in Africa
PRC	Permanent Representatives Committee
PSC	Peace and Security Council
PSD	Peace and Security Department
PSOs	Planning and Conduct of Peace Support Operations
RDC	Rapid Deployment Capability
RECs	Regional Economic Communities
RECs/RM	Regional Economic Communities/Regional Mechanisms
SADC	Southern African Development Community
SADCWARN	Early Warning System of the Southern African Development Community
SAPs	Structural Adjustment Programmes
SDGs	Sustainable Development Goals
SHIRBRIG	Standby High Readiness Brigade for United Nations Operations
SSR	Security Sector Reform
STCDSS	Specialized Technical Committee on Defense, Safety, and Security
TICAD	Tokyo International Conference on Africa's Development
UN	United Nations
UNAMID	United Nations–African Union Hybrid Operation in Darfur
UNAMIR	United Nations Assistance Mission in Rwanda
UNAMSIL	United Nations Mission in Sierra Leone
UNDP	United Nations Development Programme
UNECA	United Nations Economic Commission for Africa
UNIDO	United Nations Industrial Development Organization
UNMEE	United Nations Mission in Eritrea and Ethiopia
UNMIL	United Nations Mission in Liberia
UN-NADAF	United Nations New Agenda for the Development of Africa
UNOAU	United Nations Office of the African Union
UNOMSIL	United Nations Observer Mission in Sierra Leone
UNOSOM	United Nations Operation in Somalia
UN-PAAERD	United Nations Programme of Action for Africa's Economic Recovery and Development
UNSC	United Nations Security Council
UNTAG	United Nations Transition Assistance Group

US	United States
WHO	World Health Organization
WTO	World Trade Organization

LIST OF CONTRIBUTORS

Kasaija Phillip Apuuli is Associate Professor of Political Science in the Department of Political Science and Public Administration at Makerere University, Kampala, Uganda. He holds a doctorate in International Law from the University of Sussex in Brighton, United Kingdom. He has also served as an adviser for conflict prevention, management and resolution at the Intergovernmental Authority on Development (IGAD) secretariat in Djibouti; an assistant to the facilitator for Somalia peace and national reconciliation in Addis Ababa, Ethiopia and a programme manager for conflict prevention and risk analysis at the Institute for Security Studies in Addis Ababa. He was a British Academy visiting fellow at the University of Oxford (2010) and a Fulbright scholar-in-residence at the Stetson University School of Law, Gulfport, Florida. He is a visiting professor of Global Politics at the Uganda Peoples' Defence Forces Senior Command and Staff College and at the Rwanda Defence Force Command and Staff College and a member of IGAD's Standing Mediation Team representing Uganda. He has published journal articles, book chapters and monographs on the International Criminal Court's role in the situation in northern Uganda; on regional integration with a focus on the East African Community; on conflict management and resolution in the Great Lakes region and the Horn of Africa and on the African Peace and Security Architecture with a focus on the African Standby Force and the East African Standby Force.

Molefi Kete Asante is Professor and Chair in the Department of African American Studies at Temple University in Philadelphia. He is also president of the Molefi Kete Asante Institute for Afrocentric Studies. Asante is a guest professor at Zhejiang University, Hangzhou, and a professor extraordinary at the University of South Africa. Asante has published 83 books; some recent publications include *Revolutionary Pedagogy* (2017), *The History of Africa* (2007), *An Afrocentric Manifesto* (2007), *The Afrocentric Idea* (1987), *As I Run Toward Africa* (2011), *African Pyramids of Knowledge* (2015) and *Facing South: An African Orientation to Knowledge* (2014). Asante has published more than 500 articles and is considered the most published African American scholar as well as one of the most distinguished authors in the world.

Adonia Ayebare works as a senior adviser to the African Union Permanent Observer Mission to the United Nations (UN) in New York, where he coordinates the peacebuilding and peace and security with the UN. He has extensive conflict prevention and mediation experience, having served as a principal adviser and special envoy to the Burundi peace process, where he worked closely with South African and Tanzanian mediators, as well as with Burundian president Pierre Nkurunziza and his predecessors, and other Burundian stakeholders. Ayebare also worked as a mediator between Presidents Yoweri Museveni and Paul Kagame to restore ties after clashes in the Democratic Republic of the Congo. He holds a bachelor's degree in Mass Communication from Makerere University in Kampala, Uganda, two master's degrees, from Long Island University in New York and the Fletcher School of Law and Diplomacy, Tufts University, in Medford, Massachusetts, respectively, and a doctorate in Global Studies from Rutgers State University in Newark, New Jersey.

Ulf Engel, trained as a political scientist, is a professor of Politics in Africa at the Institute of African Studies, Leipzig University. He was director of the German Research Foundation (DFG)-funded PhD research training programme Critical Junctures of Globalization, and is co-director of the DFG special research programme Adaptation and Creativity in Africa and director of the graduate programme of the DFG collaborative research programme Processes of Spatializations Under the Global Condition. Engel is also a visiting professor at the Institute for

Peace and Security Studies at Addis Ababa University, Ethiopia, a professor extraordinary in the Department of Political Science at Stellenbosch University and a fellow at the Stellenbosch Institute of Advanced Studies, South Africa.

Afeikhena Jerome is currently consulting on policy for the Food and Agriculture Organisation's Sub-Regional Office of Southern Africa, Harare, Zimbabwe. He is also a professor of Economics at Igbinedion University, Okada, Nigeria. An accomplished economist and governance practitioner, he served with the United Nations Development Programme and the secretariat of the New Partnership for Africa's Development as pioneer coordinator for economic governance and management for the African Peer Review Mechanism secretariat, Midrand, South Africa, from 2006 to 2011. He has held distinguished positions at the International Monetary Fund, the World Bank, St Anthony's College (Oxford) and the Research Group on African Development Perspectives at the University of Bremen, Germany.

Tony Karbo is Executive Director of the Centre for Conflict Resolution in Cape Town, South Africa. Karbo has served as director of the Karamoja Cluster Project and managing editor of the *Africa Peace and Conflict Journal* at the University for Peace, Africa Programme. As part of its mandate in the Africa Programme of the UN Mandated University for Peace, Karbo taught in universities across the Great Lakes region, the Horn of Africa and in Eastern, Southern and Western Africa. He is a former senior lecturer at the Institute of Peace, Leadership and Governance at Africa University in Zimbabwe. He has worked extensively in Africa with numerous organisations working in conflict zones, facilitating training in conflict resolution and peacebuilding, and monitoring and evaluating election processes and programmes. Karbo served as the Southern and Eastern Africa representative for the Institute of Multi-Track Diplomacy, a peace-building organisation based in Washington, DC. He is a member of the Board of Trustees of the *Journal of Peacebuilding and Development* and an associate director and trainer of the South-North Center for Peacebuilding and Development. Karbo holds a master's degree and doctorate from the School of Conflict Analysis and Resolution at George Mason University, Virginia.

Chris Landsberg is Professor and SARChI Chair of African Diplomacy and Foreign Policy at the University of Johannesburg (UJ), and Senior Associate, UJ School of Leadership. He is the former Head of Politics and International Relations at UJ. Landsberg was educated at Rand Afrikaans University (now University of Johannesburg); Rhodes; and Oxford, and holds MPhil and DPhil international relations degrees (Oxon). He studied as a Rhodes Scholar at Oxford, and is a former Hamburg Fellow, Stanford University, USA. He was previously Director of the Centre for Policy Studies (CPS), Johannesburg, and co-founder and former co-director, Centre for Africa's International Relations, University of the Witwatersrand, South Africa. He is a co-editor of seven books, including *From Cape to Congo: Southern Africa's Emerging Security Challenges* and *South Africa in Africa: The Post-Apartheid Era*. He is the author of *The Diplomacy of Transformation: South African Foreign Policy and Statecraft* and *The Quiet Diplomacy of Transition: International Politics and South Africa's Transition*.

Kuruvilla Mathews has been Professor of International Relations at Addis Ababa University, Ethiopia since 2003. He was Professor of African Studies at the University of Delhi, a visiting research fellow at the University of Oxford and an associate professor of Political Science at the University of Nigeria and at the University of Dar-es-Salaam, Tanzania. He has over 100 publications to his credit, including books, chapters and peer-reviewed articles. He received a doctorate in International Relations from Jawaharlal Nehru University, New Delhi and is the founding president of the African Studies Association of India.

Khabele Matlosa is Director for Political Affairs at the African Union Commission. He is also Visiting Associate Professor in African Diplomacy and Foreign Policy at the University of Johannesburg, South Africa.

David Monyae is co-director of the University of Johannesburg Confucius Institute. An international relations and foreign policy expert, he holds a doctorate in International Relations from the University of the Witwatersrand, South Africa. He has served as section manager, international relations policy analysis, at the South African Parliament, providing strategic management, parliamentary foreign policy formulation and monitoring and analysis services. Prior to that he served as policy analyst at the Development Bank of Southern Africa (DBSA), where he undertook extensive research on Africa's regional economic communities, with a special focus on infrastructure investment opportunities for the DBSA. He also designed and launched the DBSA's policy briefs and working papers, and represented the bank on major infrastructure projects in Africa; as well as forming part of the South African academic delegations at meetings of the India, Brazil and South Africa Dialogue Forum in 2010 and the Brazil, Russia, India, China and South Africa summits in Beijing in 2011, New Delhi in 2012 and Durban in 2013. For nine years prior to that, he lectured on South African foreign policy and African international relations at the University of the Witwatersrand. He has published widely and is a respected political analyst, featuring in national and international media.

Tim Murithi is Professor Extraordinary of African Studies at the Centre for African Studies, University of Free State, South Africa and Head of Justice and Reconciliation in the Africa Programme at the Institute for Justice and Reconciliation, Cape Town. He was previously the Claude Ake visiting professor, Department of Peace and Conflict Research, Uppsala University and Nordic Africa Institute, Sweden. He has over 23 years of experience in peace, security, governance, transitional justice and development in Africa, and has held posts at the Department of Peace Studies, University of Bradford, United Kingdom; the Institute for Security Studies, Addis Ababa; the Centre for Conflict Resolution, University of Cape Town and the United Nations Institute for Training and Research, Geneva, Switzerland. He has served as an adviser and consultant to the African Union, the Southern African Development Community, the United Nations Development Programme, the United Kingdom's Department for International Development and German GiZ. He is on the international advisory boards of the *Journal of Peacebuilding and Development*, the *African Journal of Conflict Resolution*, *African Peace and Conflict Journal* and the journal *Peacebuilding*. He has authored over 85 journal articles, book chapters and policy papers, and is author and editor of nine books. This includes *The African Union: Pan-Africanism, Peacebuilding, and Development* (2005) and *The Ethics of Peacebuilding* (2009); he is co-editor of *Zimbabwe in Transition: A View from Within* (2011) and *The Politics of Transitional Justice in the Great Lakes*

Region of Africa (2016) and editor of *The Routledge Handbook of Africa's International Relations* (2014).

Charles Mutasa is an independent development policy consultant. He is the editor for *Civil Society and Constitutional Reforms in Africa* (2014) and *Africa and the Millennium Development Goals: Progress, Problems, and Prospects* (2015). His interests include governance and civil society. He is the former executive director of Mwelekeo wa NGO and of the African Forum and Network on Debt and Development, and former head of programme policy at Christian Aid's Africa division. He was the first deputy presiding officer of the African Union Economic, Social and Cultural Council, and was also a representative for the Southern Africa region. He is a graduate of the University of Washington (LLM), Nelson Mandela Metropolitan University (MA) and the University of Zimbabwe (PhD, MS and BS).

Dawn Nagar is a senior researcher at the Centre for Conflict Resolution in Cape Town, South Africa. She works on the political economy and security issues of Africa's regional integration, African politics, South Africa's foreign policy, as well as economic and security challenges, international organisations and conflict resolution and mediation. She is co-editor of the books *Region-Building in Southern Africa: Progress, Problems, and Prospects* (2012), *Region-Building in Africa: Political and Economic Challenges* (2016) and *Africa and the World: Bilateral and Multilateral International Diplomacy* (2017). She holds a doctorate of Philosophy in International Relations from the University of the Witwatersrand, South Africa, having obtained her master's degrees in Philosophy from the University of Nelson Mandela (formerly the University of Port Elizabeth), and in Politics and International Relations from the University of Cape Town.

Fritz Nganje is Lecturer in the Department of Politics and International Relations at the University of Johannesburg. He was previously a postdoctoral research fellow with the South African Research Chair in African Diplomacy and Foreign Policy at the same university, after working as a researcher in the Africa Programme of the Pretoria-based Institute for Global Dialogue. He holds a doctorate in Political Studies from the University of Johannesburg.

Hesphina Rukato is an associate lecturer for good governance at the Thabo Mbeki Leadership Institute, University of South Africa in Pretoria. She is also the board chair for Great Dyke Investments, Zimbabwe, and a board member of National Parks and Wildlife, Zimbabwe, as well as a Technical Committee member of the Tana Forum on Peace and Security in Africa. Previously, Rukato was the deputy chief of staff at the Bureau of African Union Commission Chairpersons, and a consultant for the African Union Commission and for the Institute of Peace and Security Studies, University of Addis Ababa. She was a coordinator at the Tana Forum; the deputy chief executive at the New Partnership for Africa's Development (NEPAD) secretariat and a NEPAD adviser on environment and tourism. She also worked as a policy director of the World Summit on Sustainable Development, and has experience with the Zimbabwean government and in the international non-governmental organisation sector. She holds a doctorate in Environmental Management Standards from the University of the Witwatersrand, South Africa, a master's degree in Environmental Policy and Planning from the University of Zimbabwe and a bachelor's degree (honours) in Politics and Administration.

Amos Sawyer is Chair of the Governance Commission of Liberia. He has served as president of the Interim Government of Liberia (1990–4), chair of the Panel of Eminent Persons of the African Peer Review Mechanism (2012–13), co-director of the Ostrom Workshop in Political Theory and Policy Analysis, Indiana University (2005–7) and dean of the College of Social Sciences and Humanities, University of Liberia (1981–4). A political scientist, he has published extensively and is active at both regional and international levels in addressing issues of peace, security and democratic governance in Africa and developing countries worldwide.

ACKNOWLEDGEMENTS

The editors, Tony Karbo and Tim Murithi, are grateful to all the contributors to this book and to all the CCR staff, who, in their different ways, have made the publication of this book possible.

Here we would like to mention Germaine Habiyaremye, who coordinated the interaction between the editors, the chapter contributors and the publishers. We are also grateful for the support provided to the publication process by Tefo Mosienyane, Maria Nantege and Liliane Limenyande (all CCR staff) and we would like to thank former CCR Executive Director Adekeye Adebajo, whose ideas inspired this book.

Most importantly, we are indebted to the Embassy of the Kingdom of Norway, who provided the funding for this publication. In addition, we are grateful to the people and the government of Sweden, through its development arm Sida, for their consistent support of the work of the CCR.

INTRODUCTION

THE AFRICAN UNION:
A DECADE AND A HALF LATER

Tony Karbo and *Tim Murithi*

The African Union (AU), established in 2002, has developed a broad range of treaties, protocols and norms relating to peace, security, gender issues, governance, trade, education and economic development, to guide the conduct and behaviour of its member states. In the 15 years since its transformation from the Organisation of African Unity (OAU), the AU has attempted to play a continental role in crafting policy frameworks to improve the livelihood of its citizens, through continental interventions and international engagement.[1] In January 2017, to mark the 15th year since the organisation was formally launched, the AU Assembly of Heads of State and Government adopted a report titled *The Imperative to Strengthen Our Union*, containing recommendations for institutional reform of the African Union.[2] This report was compiled by President Paul Kagame of Rwanda, with the collaboration of a panel of senior African leaders, in response to a decision 'on the need to conduct a study on the institutional reform of the African Union' that emerged from a retreat of heads of state and government, ministers of foreign affairs and ministers of finance held in Kigali, Rwanda, on 16 July 2017.[3] The Kagame Panel report observes that 'as unprecedented challenges multiply and spread across the globe at a dazzling pace, new vulnerabilities are increasingly laid bare, in rich and poor nations alike'.[4] In particular, the report identifies climate change, violent extremist ideologies, disease pandemics and mass migration as among the key issues that urgently need to be addressed by 'focused and effective regional organisations'.[5] The Kagame Panel report laments: 'the unfortunate truth is that Africa today is ill-prepared to adequately respond to current events, because *the African Union still has to be made fit for purpose*'.[6] This is a forthright and honest appraisal of the state of the African Union 15 years after it was launched with much fanfare and great expectations in 2002 in Durban, South Africa.

The purpose of this book is to interrogate the current state of the African Union, and its policy frameworks, continental interventions, and institutional partnerships, at this point in its 15-year history. The intention of this book is also to critically interrogate the AU's internal challenges with a view to determining how it can enhance its governance processes, so that it can become 'fit for purpose' in addressing the continent's challenges as well as in strengthening Africa's assertiveness in the international sphere. The 15th year of the African Union's existence also marked the arrival of a new leadership team at the AU Commission, when in March 2017, Moussa Faki Mahamat, the former Chadian foreign minister, assumed the position of chairperson of the AU Commission, and Kwesi Quartey, the distinguished Ghanaian diplomat, became deputy chairperson. It is promising that Moussa Faki and his team of commissioners are approaching their historical mission at the AU with a degree of pragmatism about the constraints and possibilities they face. Specifically, on 14 March 2017, during his first public address as the AU Commission chairperson, Moussa Faki outlined six priorities, including the need 'to reform the structures' of the organisation to make it 'a tool capable of translating into reality the vision of our leaders and aspirations of our peoples'.[7] In addition, Moussa Faki emphasised the need to address the continent's conflicts and enhance the participation of women and young people in promoting peace, development and the revival of the continent. Moussa Faki also identified the promotion of economic integration with a specific focus on 'increasing inter-African trade and free movement of people so that Africans can finally cease to be foreigners in their own continent'. He argued for the revitalisation of Africa's private sector in order to enhance wealth and job creation, and for strengthening Africa's engagement in international relations. The academic chapters in this book speak to all of these, and other, issues, making it a relevant and timely volume at this juncture of the AU's 15-year history. Prior to examining the outline and structure of the book, it is necessary to further elaborate on some over-arching themes that have informed the research and analysis contained here.

Pan-Africanism and a Global Order in Transition

The prevailing global order is currently in a state of flux, with a significant amount of uncertainty injected into international relations due to the rising tide of right-wing fascist populism in Europe and the United States (US). More specifically, this is evident in the anti-immigrant and anti-Muslim ideologies of political formations that are ascending to power, and in some instances are co-governing a number of countries in the so-called global North. The ascendancy of Donald Trump to the American presidency and the rejection by a section of the British population of its membership of the European Union, now caricatured by the word 'Brexit', speak to a bigger problems of growing nationalistic and xenophobic trends in America and Europe and around the world. These processes should, in an ideal world, not be of any significant concern for Africa and for the AU, but given the historical and contemporary penetration of Africa by Europe, during colonialism, and the US, during the Cold War, this period of global transition is in fact a significant turning point for the African continent. The liberal international order that America and Europe created, and sustained by overt and covert co-optation and coercion, is now collapsing, providing a unique opportunity for Africa to break free from the geo-political, economic and socio-cultural clutches of its erstwhile patrons and exploiters. However, even as Africa seeks to break from its exploitative relationships with the West, global actors from the East, notably China, Russia and India, are already positioning themselves to feed from the African trough by means of the unbridled extraction of natural resources to their own advantage and at the expense of African people. Africa therefore stands on the precipice of either allowing itself to once again become a neo-colonial carcass for these Eastern forces to feed off, or becoming an autonomous agent of its own destiny and self-determination. The former condition will prevail unless the continent can revive the spirit of Pan-Africanism, defined by solidarity and self-determination, to assert its agency as a self-defined actor that will in fact contribute towards remaking the global order.

The African continent is still confronted by deep-seated Western civilisational agendas that infiltrated and were uncritically adopted by a sector of Africa's political and economic elite to frame the governance and socio-economic systems of their countries. In fact, the majority of African countries are more aptly defined by their degree of colonial continuity. This persistence of the colonial logic is particularly evident in the systems of governance that dominate the African landscape, as well as in the adoption of neo-liberal economic models that have fed the external 'extraction' agenda and singularly failed to ensure distributive processes that can improve the livelihood of the majority of people on the continent. Consequently, the 15th year of the AU's existence is also an opportunity for the African continent to assume the responsibilities of self-determination and redefine its governance and economic models to ensure that it creates functional polities across the continent that will respond to the basic needs of its people in terms of peace, security, accountability and improved livelihoods.

The African Union and the Quest for Improved Governance, Security and Development

The African Union has made some initial practical efforts to address continental challenges and to function as an international actor. The major problem facing the AU is the lack of integrity among some of the leaders of African countries who, though they have committed themselves to principles, norms and values of human rights and democratic governance, continue to practice suppression, dominion and exploitation of their own people. In terms of limitations, not all of Africa's heads of state and government are taking the African Union seriously. The norms and values they have signed up to should be enough to encourage them to change their behaviour. However, many leaders are behaving as though the AU does not exist, by continuing to act in an autocratic manner in their own countries by committing human rights atrocities with impunity. These malpractices and misrule in turn fuel the escalation of political tension and conflict, further retarding the continent's efforts to address its security, governance, development and trade challenges.

The AU has already elaborated a robust policy framework to address a broad range of continental challenges, including those relating to security, governance and development. For example, the principles of the 2002 protocol to establish the AU's Peace and Security Council (PSC) stipulate a commitment to promoting the 'peaceful settlement of disputes and conflicts' as well as ensuring 'respect for the rule of law, fundamental human rights and freedoms'.[8] Subsequently, when the PSC was established in 2004, it was mandated to coordinate peacemaking, peacekeeping and peacebuilding efforts on the continent. The PSC protocol delineated the African Peace and Security Architecture (APSA), which includes a Panel of the Wise, composed of eminent African personalities. As part of APSA, the AU authorised the establishment of an African Standby Force (ASF), and a Military Staff Committee to provide advice on deployment and security requirements. The PSC protocol also established a Continental Early Warning System (CEWS) and an AU Peace Fund. Specifically, as the over-arching coordinating institution, the PSC has the mandate to authorise AU interventions in member states. Indeed the Council has demonstrated its ability to draw attention to crisis situations in Africa, and will continue to function as one of the most important and powerful organs of Africa's evolving peace and security architecture. However, the Council still has a lot to do to adopt a culture of prevention and proactive interventionism in situations of potential mass atrocities.

The African Union Commission's strategic plan for 2009–12, approved by the AU Assembly of Heads of State and Government, provided the AU Commission with a mandate 'to achieve good governance, democracy, human rights'.[9] In February 2010, the 14th ordinary session of the AU Assembly committed the Union to establishing a Pan-African governance architecture, subsequently established as the African Governance Architecture (AGA). The intention was not to create a new institution, but to enhance coordination among AU organs and institutions with the formal mandate to promote governance, democracy and human rights. However, the emphasis in creating this architecture was that member states would continue to 'have the primary responsibility of building and consolidating governance' based on the recognition that 'a strong and effective AGA requires solid, functioning and accountable national structures'.[10] Subsequently, the AU established the AGA Platform with a secretariat within its Department of Political Affairs as 'the central coordinating mechanism for monitoring compliance and implementation of agreed governance standards as embodied in the African Charter on Democracy, Elections and Governance'.[11] The way in which the AGA Platform was conceived and structured as a coordinating mechanism, rather than an executing mechanism, means that, out of necessity, it must foster greater collaboration and synergy between the AU's institutions that have a formal mandate to promote governance, democracy and human rights.

A security approach is necessary, but not sufficient, for the gradual stabilisation of societies and regions across the continent.[12] The challenging work of winning the hearts and minds of local populations through the transformation of societies through governance is an equally important and a vital complement to the security initiatives in these war-affected regions. The cyclical nature of conflict points to the critical need to move beyond the temporary stalemates and ceasefires, peacekeeping deployments and military operations that are so common in this era, towards a regional policy informed by intentionally confronting the underlying grievances that have fuelled decades of animosity and violence on the continent.

Despite the AU having been operational for 15 years, there is a troubled nexus between peacekeeping, peacebuilding, governance and development at the institutional level within the Union. This phenomenon also replicates itself at the United Nations (UN), so it is not unique to Africa. Specifically, there is a lack of *effective* institutional interface at the level of decision making. While all African Union staff members sing from the same song sheet of inter-departmental collaboration, and despite efforts to initiate concrete activities to operationalise this rhetorical harmony, the effects on the ground in terms of APSA and AGA interventions do not yet translate into a coordinated strategy to deliver to the victims of war and injustice.

This lack of effective APSA and AGA interface reveals the perils of actualising inter-departmental collaboration on the ground. Well-intentioned platitudes at the policy and decision making levels, about the urgency of promoting synergy between peacekeeping, peacebuilding and governance processes, have become routine and banal. Consequently this creates a silo effect when it comes to the interventions, with AU peacekeepers, peacebuilders and governance and development practitioners operating in virtual isolation from one another, even when they are in the same vicinity. Paradoxically, implementing effective peacebuilding processes is a necessary pre-requisite to any exit strategy for a military intervention.

Africa and its External Partners

The African Union has a dual role of forging unity among its member states and advocating for their interests internationally. The AU's role as an international actor is complicated by the difficulty of promoting consensus among African states and then maintaining that consensus in the face of often divergent national interests. There are a selection of issues in which the AU has served as a rallying vehicle for Africa's interests, particularly in the field of peace and security, on development and trade issues, as well as on climate change. While the AU is emerging as an increasingly influential international actor, it has not yet become effective at asserting its will and projecting its power in order to secure the African continent's collective interests.

A key constraint in the AU's ability to assert itself on the international stage is its reliance and dependency on donors to pay salaries and finance its operations and programmes. The former chairperson of the AU Commission, Nkosazana Dlamini-Zuma, who served from 2012 to 2016, was consistent during her tenure in voicing her grave concern about the extent to which the AU system as a whole was dependent on external donors to run some of its core functions and to maintain vital staff within its departments. This has been a perennial challenge for both APSA and the AGA, and has raised questions about the true 'ownership' of Africa's institutions. In July 2016, the AU Assembly of Heads of State and Government adopted a decision on financing of the Union to institute a 0.2 per cent levy on eligible imports.[13] The importance of this decision was subsequently reiterated in a report titled *Securing Predictable and Sustainable Funding for Peace in Africa*, compiled by Donald Kaberuka, the AU High Representative for the Peace Fund.[14] This decision represents the first genuine attempt to wean the Union and its institutions off its donors, particularly in the sphere of promoting peace. Such initiatives should be encouraged in order to avoid insinuations that the AU is not 'owned' by Africa.

Structure of the Book

This book is divided into three parts. Part I, comprising three chapters, interrogates the notion of Pan-Africanism. Kuruvilla Mathews argues for a re-interpretation of Pan-Africanism in a manner that enables it to respond to the challenges of the twenty-first century. Molefi Asante complements Mathews's chapter by discussing the role of the African Diaspora in advancing the Pan-African agenda. And Adonia Ayebare concludes this part with a chapter assessing the efforts and challenges of the Africa Group of ambassadors at the United Nations in New York.

Part II, comprising six chapters, assesses the challenges of governance, security and development that continue to confront the work of the African Union. Khabele Matlosa assesses the AU's evolving governance architecture. Hesphina Rukato then interrogates the AU Commission's internal capacity challenges. Next, Amos Sawyer and Afeikhena Jerome interrogate the African Peer Review Mechanism and the constraints it has encountered. Kasaija Apuuli analyses the African Peace and Security Architecture through a discussion of the peace operations the AU has conducted, as well as the limitations of its interventions. Charles Mutasa deliberates on the Economic Social and Cultural Council's role in promoting the socio-economic agenda across the continent. Dawn Nagar and Fritz Nganje conclude this part with a chapter examining the relationship between the AU and Africa's regional economic communities, with a focus on the prospects for enhancing economic and security cooperation across the continent.

The final and third part of the book has three chapters dealing with the relationship of the AU with external actors with a focus on the posture of some of the African continents hegemonic players. Chris Landsberg's chapter assesses South Africa's self-defined status as a gateway to Africa, with an assessment of its relationship with international groups such as BRICS. Ulf Engel interrogates the AU's efforts to craft an international partnership with the United Nations in the sphere of peace and security, and David Monyae interrogates the AU's relationship with China, with an emphasis on the asymmetrical nature of this relationship, proposing a number of suggestions as to how a more collaborative partnership can be developed going forward.

Finally, in concluding the book, Tim Murithi assesses the challenges facing the continent, with a focus on Africa's leadership deficit, and provides a forward-looking assessment of how the AU can sustain its momentum in order to continue to pursue and achieve its objectives of guiding the continent's people towards a peaceful and prosperous future.

Notes

1. Tim Murithi, 'The African Union at Ten: An Appraisal', *African Affairs* 111, no. 445 (2012), p. 663.

2. Paul Kagame, *The Imperative to Strengthen Our Union: Report on the Proposed Recommendations for the Institutional Reform of the African Union* (Addis Ababa, 29 January 2017).

3. African Union (AU), *Decision on the Institutional Reform of the African Union*, Assembly of Heads of State and Government, Assembly/AU/Dec.606 (XXVII), Retreat of Heads of State and Government, Ministers of Foreign Affairs and Ministers of Finance (Kigali, Rwanda, 16 July 2017), p. 1.

4. Kagame, *The Imperative to Strengthen Our Union*, p. 1.

5. Ibid.

6. Ibid.

7. Moussa Faki Mahamat, *The African Union Commission Priorities* (Addis Ababa, 14 March 2017), www.au.int (accessed 20 June 2017).

8. AU, *Protocol Establishing the Peace and Security Council of the African Union* (Addis Ababa, 2002), Principles, art. 4.

9. AU, African Governance Platform, *Draft Implementation Strategy and Action Plan: 2013–2017* (Addis Ababa, 2013), p. 2.

10. Ibid., p. 7.

11. AU, African Governance Platform, *Draft Implementation Strategy and Action Plan*, p. 5.

12. Tim Murithi, The Eastern DRC Conflict and the UN-Mandated Force Intervention Brigade: Insights for Africa's Framework for Responding to Crisis', in Festus Aboagye (ed.), *A Comprehensive Review of African Conflicts and Regional Interventions* (Addis Ababa: African Union and African Peace Support Trainers Association [APSTA], 2016), pp. 155–68.

13. AU, *Decision on Financing of the Union*, Assembly of Heads of State and Government, Assembly/AU/Dec.605 (XXVII), July 2016.

14. Donald Kaberuka, *Securing Predictable and Sustainable Funding for Peace in Africa* (Addis Ababa: African Union Peace Fund, July 2016), para. 39.

PART I

PAN-AFRICANISM:
FROM THE OAU TO THE AU

CHAPTER 1

THE AFRICAN UNION AND THE RENAISSANCE OF PAN-AFRICANISM

Kuruvilla Mathews

As the twenty-first century progresses, there is growing optimism about the future of Africa. One of the most important developments in this direction has been the establishment of the African Union (AU) in Durban, in July 2002, and the adoption of the New Partnership for Africa's Development (NEPAD) in Abuja, Nigeria, in October 2001. These initiatives represent the revival and re-emergence of Pan-Africanism under the general rubric of an African Renaissance with a vision for an integrated, prosperous and peaceful Africa that will be a dynamic force in the global arena driven by its own citizens.[1] This chapter accordingly discusses the renaissance of Pan-Africanism and the challenges and prospects of continental integration under the African Union.

The Concept of Pan-Africanism

Pan-Africanism, as Ogba Sylvester and Okpanachi Anthony express it,[2] signifies a set of shared assumptions expressing the desire for political and psychological liberation and the unity of all Africans, whether on the continent or those in the Diaspora. It locates its origins in the liberation struggles of African-Americans and the aspirations of people of African descent everywhere around the nineteenth century at the height of slavery and at the dawn of colonialism. Pan-Africanism with its many forms of expression was not only a movement that brought together people of African origin. It was also a strategy for social solidarity, as well as cultural, political and economic emancipation.[3]

Pan-Africanism is also an ideology with a shared vision of what is desirable for the future of all Africans in Africa and in the Diaspora, rather than what actually existed. The key conceptual themes emerging from Pan-Africanism have been the 'redemption of Africa' and 'Africa for Africans'.[4] As Timothy Murithi notes, 'essentially Pan-Africanism is a recognition of the fragmented nature of the existence of Africans, their marginalization and alienation whether in their own continent or in the Diaspora'.[5]

Pan-Africanism has historically consisted of four key themes: a clear expression of the pride and achievement of Africans; the idea of returning to Africa, a notion mainly promoted by Africans in the Diaspora; the liberation from colonialism and all forms of oppression; and the promotion of African unity as a primary objective in the struggle for liberation from European colonialism.

Pan-Africanism has so far passed through three major phases.[6] The first phase denotes the five Pan-African Congresses held between 1900 and 1945. It was at the fifth Pan-African Congress, held in 1945 in Manchester, where Pan-Africanism was advanced and directed to the decolonisation of the African continent. The second phase ascended with the inauguration of the OAU in May 1963. Forty years later, the third phase followed with the creation of the African Union in 2002.

The Case for Pan-Africanism

The quest for continental unity has always been timely. Most African nations have a low population density, small internal markets, limited infrastructure and porous borders. African economies are also highly vulnerable to fluctuating world prices. Following the independence of most African countries, 'no African state is economically large enough to construct a modern economy alone. Africa, as a whole, has the resources for industrialization'.[7] Without access to a larger market area that could be created through economic integration, it was impossible for these small countries to grow economically and develop. Indeed, the balkanisation of Africa remains the most enduring of the colonial legacies. Economic and political integration, therefore, become essential in the development of Africa.[8]

A united Africa would command more respect in the world on account of its larger market and greater economic potential. Regional unity increases comparative advantage when it comes to negotiating in international forums. Undoubtedly, prospective investors would be more inclined to invest in a united Africa, particularly if they can be ensured access to larger markets. A united Africa would also have access to more human and material resources.

Another argument in favour of a united Africa is that it would be able to mount a credible defence force to guard African interests against internal and external attacks. Individual African states spend a significant amount of their resources on defence systems. So, perhaps Kwame Nkrumah rightly noted that 'it is ridiculous, indeed suicidal, for each state separately and individually to assume such a heavy burden of self-defense'.[9]

The OAU and Pan-Africanism

Following the Manchester Pan-African Congress in 1945, Pan-Africanism became 'Africanised' as such Africans in exile as

Kwame Nkrumah and Jomo Kenyatta took the baton from such leading proponents in the Diaspora as W.E.B. Du Bois and Marcus Garvey. Nkrumah and Kenyatta were later joined by other radical Pan-Africanists such as Modibo Keita of Mali, Ahmed Sekou Toure of Guinea, and Gamal Abdul Nasser Hussein of Egypt to form the Casablanca Group (Ghana, Guinea, Mali, Morocco, Egypt, Libya and Algeria), which, called for the immediate unification of independent African states. Their radical proposal for an immediate continental unity was met with opposition from moderate progressives that formed the Monrovia Group (Liberia, Nigeria, Somalia, Sierra Leone, Togo, Senegal, Ethiopia and Libya). Mediated by Ethiopia's Emperor Haile Selassie, the two groups in 1963 compromised their polarised positions and created the Organisation of African Unity as the institutional manifestation of Pan-Africanism on the continent.

The OAU was tasked mainly with leading the struggles for decolonisation and end of apartheid in the rest of Africa, and facilitating the gradual unification of the continent. With the liberation of Namibia in 1990 and end of apartheid in South Africa in 1994, the OAU achieved one of its goals – to end colonialism and racial rule in the continent.[10] Despite this, the continental organisation proved ineffective in meeting peoples' expectation for united and prosperous states. As the OAU wound up, Africans were not only the world's poorest people, but also poorer than they had been at the dawn of independence, with their former colonial masters merely replaced by their own blood tyrants. Independent Africa found itself paradoxically to be the epicentre of poverty, bad governance, political instability and conflicts, economic retardation, the HIV/AIDS pandemic and preventable or curable diseases.[11]

At the heart of the OAU's dysfunction in addressing those challenges was its doctrine of non-interference in the internal affairs of its member states, which made it difficult to articulate and analyse the problems facing each and every member state in their respective countries. Most of the member states in the aftermath of their decolonisation fell under nationalist dictators who paid lip service to Pan-Africanism and refused to subordinate sovereignty to a higher political entity. The doctrine of non-interference therefore provided those 'leaders' with the impunity to run their countries' affairs without regard to good governance, peace and development.[12] The assertion of nationalism undermined the OAU's effort to 'promote the unity and solidarity of the African states' as outlined in Article 2(a) of its charter.[13] Soon afterwards, the harmony demonstrated during the years following the establishment of the OAU began to dissipate. Those who heralded the founding of the OAU as the dawn of a new era soon realised that it was nothing more than a weak compromise organisation that stood more for safeguarding and consolidating the independence, sovereignty and territorial integrity of its member states than facilitating their eventual unity, as the rhetoric for its creation suggested.[14]

The OAU's weak position and evident incapacitation allowed sub-regional organisations to gain ground and occupy the space that would have otherwise been held by the continental organisation. Pan-Africanism may have accelerated the achievement of political independence for Africans, but external economic dependence remained the crucial problem. The quest for addressing this dependency led African leaders to adopt the Lagos Plan of Action (LPA) in 1980 as a blueprint for 'collective self-reliance' on the continent. This was reinforced in 1991 by the signing of the Abuja Treaty, which established the African Economic Community (AEC) with the goal of increasing economic self-reliance and promoting an endogenous and self-sustained development. None of those initiatives, however, tangibly materialised.

The Case for 'New' Pan-Africanism and the African Union

As we entered the twenty-first century, Pan-Africanism demanded a re-interpretation in terms of the need not only for political independence and regional integration, but also for throwing off the yokes of economic bondage and democratic stagnation that had for so long reversed the short-lived prosperity of the independence era.[15] Along with this demand for a 'new' Pan-Africanism[16] emerged a new generation of Pan-Africanists. Dubbed by Gilbert Khadiagala as the 'renaissance coalition', these leaders underlined the need to stop blaming donors and called for Africans to take control of their affairs.[17] This was expressed initially at the 30th session of the OAU's Assembly of Heads of State and Government, in Tunis, Tunisia, in 1995, where former South African president Nelson Mandela noted Africa's ascent into a 'new era of renaissance' based on Africans' own efforts to transform the continent's social, economic and political conditions for the better. This renascent generation also recognised the indispensability of good governance, democracy, human security, stability and international cooperation for Africa's development. As Chris Landsberg notes, the new Pan-Africanists also became keen to address the post-independence taboos of non-intervention, and articulate new norms of intervention and democratic governance.[18] By the end of the 1990s, multi-party elections were taking place in more than 30 countries in Africa. Some of the African leaders who championed the new Pan-African agenda included South African's Thabo Mbeki, Nigeria's Olusegun Obasanjo, Senegal's Abdoulaye Wade, Mozambique's Joachim Chissano, Mali's Alpha Oumar Konaré and Algeria's Abdulaziz Bouteflika.

Africa's new generation of leaders accordingly articulated Pan-Africanism afresh in the form of a comprehensive set of new norms, values, and principles of democracy, good governance, peace and security, development and partnership-based cooperation. In a fast-globalising world economy,

Pan-Africanism and the African Renaissance demanded hastening Africa's integration into a powerful united entity that could set its own agenda and effectively play a leading role in world affairs. Between 2000 and 2001, those leaders laid the crux of the new African architecture with decisions to formally incorporate the Conference on Security, Stability, Development and Cooperation in Africa into the OAU's machinery for conflict prevention, management and resolution; merge the Millennium Africa Recovery Plan (MAP) with the OMEGA Plan for Africa and launch the New Partnership for Africa's Development (NEPAD) as a new Africa-wide development initiative; and transform the OAU as an obsolete institution into the African Union to live up to the demands of the new Pan-Africanism's human-centred norms, values and principles and hasten continental integration and eventual unification. With this, Pan-Africanism was transformed into a development blueprint and a mobilising force.[19] 'African Renaissance' soon became the buzzword for the emerging generation of African leaders, the 'new' Pan-Africanists. They started using the term as a way of comparing the past 'Old Africa' with the 'New Africa' in order to chart the path to a future of genuine continental change. This sent a message of optimism about Africa's future that reverberated in many other quarters.[20]

The African Union came into being at the Durban summit of heads of state and government in July 2002, modelled on the European Union. It was a qualitative transformation of the institutional framework for realising the Pan-African vision and mission – from what some critics regarded as a mere 'talking shop' (the OAU) to an action-oriented forum.[21] In Desmond Orijiako's words, the AU 'is a political, economic and social project aimed at creating a democratic space across Africa, promoting economic development, and for reflecting a common African identity'.[22] This gave the AU a vastly expanded mandate from that of the OAU, including the principles and goals in the OAU charter as well as those of the

Abuja Treaty. The AU's proclaimed vision is for 'an integrated, prosperous and peaceful Africa, driven by its own citizens and representing a dynamic force in the global arena'. Highlighting its prime focus on enhancing' the well-being of Africans, the AU adopted NEPAD as its development program. The AU's vision has been subsequently detailed and elaborated in its *Agenda 2063: The Future We Want for Africa*, adopted at the OAU/AU's Golden Jubilee Anniversary in 2013. Composed purportedly of seven aspirations and 20 goals of the African people, *Agenda 2063* sets a definite timeframe – consolidated into five ten-year action plans – for realising Pan-Africanism's ultimate objective of creating a united, prosperous and peaceful Africa by 2063. By adjusting itself to new demands and new generations, Pan-Africanism therefore asserts its relevance and continues its attraction as a source of hope, inspiration and conviction for both Africans in Africa and their descendants in the Diaspora.

Since the AU's inauguration on 9 July 2002, the establishment and operationalisation of its institutions have moved at a relatively rapid pace. The Peace and Security Council (PSC), which is central to the AU's objectives, was inaugurated in May 2004.[23] The establishment of the PSC was recognition by the AU that, without peace and security, there can be no economic development. The PSC is composed of 15 members and is complemented by other institutions such as the Continental Early Warning System, the African Standby Force (ASF) and the Peace Fund. The AU also adopted a pact on non-aggression and common defence in 2005.

Breaking with the Past

Unlike the OAU, the AU espouses a progressive agenda geared towards breaking away from the decades-old regime of non-interference, non-intervention and obsession with national sovereignty.[24] To help meet its founding objective of promoting peace, security and stability on the continent, the AU created the African Peace and Security Architecture (APSA), which asserts AU primacy in peace and security in Africa and devolves power jointly to the AU Peace and Security Council and the chairperson of the AU Commission to undertake peacemaking and peacebuilding functions to resolve conflicts.[25]

Interference and intervention in the domestic affairs of member states rest on such grave instances as war crimes, genocide, crimes against humanity, instability in one country that threatens broader regional stability and unconstitutional changes of government. The AU also rejects impunity, political assassination and acts of terrorism. In cases of genocide or other grave human rights violations, Article 4(h) of the AU's Constitutive Act allows the launch of a military mission by the ASF, even against the wishes of the government of the country concerned, upon approval by the AU Assembly. Since its inception, the AU has non-militarily intervened in support of constitutionality in Togo, protesting Faure Gnassingbé's unconstitutional seizure of the presidency in the footsteps of his deceased father in 2005 in a military coup; in Mauritania, suspending the country's membership twice following coups in 2005 and 2008; in Côte d'Ivoire, following President Laurent Gbagbo's refusal to concede his electoral defeat and hand over power between 2010 and 2011; in Mali, in response to the military coup staged when an alliance of Touareg and Islamist forces conquered the north of the country in 2013; and in the Central African Republic (CAR), after the Seleka rebels ousted President François Bozizé in 2013. The AU, mainly through the secondment of the continent's regional economic communities (RECs), has also militarily intervened in Darfur/Sudan since 2004; in Somalia since 2007; in Anjouan, Comoros, in 2008; and in Gambia in 2017. The AU has also played a key supportive role to the United Nations (UN) in the Democratic Republic of the Congo

(DRC). As of 2013, the AU in tandem with RECs had served as partners for crisis prevention and conflict management in 28 of the continent's 38 countries where violent conflicts erupted in the preceding five years. With all their notable short-comings, those interventions have been commendable proof of the increasing seriousness of African governments to accept their mandate for ensuring peace and security on the continent.

The AU is also tasked with ensuring respect for democratic principles, human rights, the rule of law and good governance. Its endeavours have been enhanced by the coming into effect of the Charter on Democracy, Governance and Elections in 2012. In this new Pan-Africanism, democratic governance is seen as indispensable for political stabilisation on the continent. This is evidenced, for example, in *Agenda 2063*, which recognises democratic and inclusive governance and justice as necessary preconditions for a peaceful and conflict-free Africa.[26] NEPAD similarly bases the realisation of its economic development, cooperation and integration objectives on the underlying principles of commitment to good governance, democracy, human rights and conflict resolution; and recognises the centrality of maintaining these standards for the creation of an environment conducive to investment and long-term development.

Further underscoring the primacy of human security and democratic governance in the new Pan-Africanism, NEPAD was supplemented in 2002 with the Declaration on Democracy, Political, Economic and Corporate Governance. The declaration commits AU member states participating in NEPAD to 'believe in just, honest, transparent, accountable and participatory government and probity in public life'. It demands their commitment to enhance such democratic values and principles as the rule of law; the equality of all citizens before the law; individual and collective freedoms; the right to participate in free, credible, and democratic political processes; and adherence to the separation of powers, including protection for the independence of the judiciary and the effectiveness of parliaments. It also commits participating states to accede to the African Peer Review Mechanism (APRM).

The APRM came into effect as an AU specialised agency with the adoption of a memorandum of understanding by the NEPAD Heads of State and Government Implementation Committee in 2003 in Abuja, Nigeria. The APRM is a tool that AU member states voluntarily use to self-monitor all aspects of their governance and socio-economic development. This is an African-owned and managed process that assesses levels of democracy and political governance, economic governance and management, corporate governance and socio-economic development. By subjecting all branches of government as well as the private sector, civil society and the media to this self-assessment, it 'gives member states a space for national dialogue on governance and socio-economic indicators and an opportunity to build consensus on the way forward'.[27] To date, 33 countries have agreed to subject themselves to review. The existence of the APRM is in a sense a manifestation of Pan-Africanism in action.

As part of the moves to ensure African peoples' voice and representation in Pan-African endeavours, the Pan-African Parliament was formally launched in 2004, consisting of 202 representatives from 36 member countries.[28] The parliament has a vital role to play in the implementation of the objectives and principles enshrined in the AU's founding Constitutive Act, particularly with regard to the protection of human rights, consolidation of democratic institutions and promotion of good governance.

Under the AU, Africa's agency on the world stage has notably increased. AU member states have been able to develop common positions on issues of aid effectiveness, climate change and the post-2015 development agenda. This has precipitated emerging and traditional economies to collectively engage with African states through partnership frameworks. Among them are the

Forum on China-Africa Cooperation (FOCAC), the India-Africa Forum Summit, the Tokyo International Conference on Africa's Development (TICAD), the Africa-EU Partnership, the US-Africa Business Forum, the Brazil-Africa Forum, the Korea-Africa Forum, the Turkey-Africa Partnership, the Africa-Singapore Business Forum, the Malaysia-Africa Business Forum and the Taiwan Africa Summit. The AU, in partnership with the United Nations Economic Commission for Africa (UNECA), also spearheaded the adoption of the Africa Mining Vision (AMV) by African heads of state and government in 2009. Purportedly extracted from several sub-regional, continental and global initiatives and practices, the AMV presents a comprehensive blueprint for putting Africa's ample resources at the centre of its industrialisation and sustainable development.

Challenges

Despite the seeming proliferation of Pan-African treaties, declarations, policies and strategies over the past two decades, there still is more verbosity and rhetoric than the realisation of these commitments. Africa's political landscape is bedevilled with a compliance deficit with marked policy-compliance gaps. Most of these progressive documents for governance and development have been so far hardly incorporated into the domestic laws of most African states. According to Freedom House, only 9 out of the 49 sub-Saharan African countries, constituting just 12 per cent of the region's population, are rated as 'free'; the picture gets more dire in North Africa, which, together with the Middle East, is ranked as the worst-performing region in the world.[29] It has also become a common trend among African leaders to extend their term limits through contentious and at times violent constitutional amendments. Among them in the recent spotlight are Rwanda's Paul Kagame, Burundi's Pierre Nkurunziza and the

DRC's Joseph Kabila. Stringent legislations and resource constraints hamper civil society organisations from engaging the AU and its continental architectures in promoting the democratic values and principles that heightened the expectation of Africans for better and freer life in recent times. NEPAD's hailed infrastructure and development projects are still incomplete even ten years after it was criticised for inefficiency and profligacy by one of its founders, former Senegalese President Abdoulaye Wade; none of its seven flagship continental projects have yet been completed. The AU has also been largely passive, notably having failed to establish its presence and control in North Africa during the uprisings and upheavals of the Arab Spring. Regional integration is still staggeringly low, with intra-Africa trade accounting for just ten per cent of the continent's total trade.[30] Most African countries still maintain strong cliental relations with their patron erstwhile colonial powers, and give lip service to creating the legislative and infrastructural facilities for cross-border mobility; as a result, intra-Africa movement remains among the most arduous in the world.

Unlike the European Union (EU), built on the foundation of its predecessor's strong institutional capacity, the AU must grapple with a largely inefficient, ineffective and obsolete institutional foundation, without adequate implementation lessons to learn from. The AU is also constrained by the formidable capacity limitations of its member states, which have poor track records of policy implementation. Despite their clichéd rhetoric for a strong Pan-African bloc, member states still exhibit a long-standing culture of not honouring their financial obligations to the continental body. Only 19 out of the 54 member states fully met their obligations as of 2015. Of these countries, Algeria, Egypt, Libya, Nigeria and South Africa finance 65 per cent of member states' contribution to the AU's operational budget – each with an equal contribution of US$16.2 million. With the AU's key bankroller, Muammar Qaddafi, ousted, and Egypt in economic hardship following the Arab Spring, the share of AU member states' overall contribution to the its operational budget has declined drastically; that is, from about 54 per cent of the total AU budget in 2009 to just about 25 per cent with the remaining 75 per cent being financed by external sources as of 2015, and 96 per cent of this total external financing of the AU budget came from just the European Union and United States in that year. This has left the AU understaffed and heavily dependent on external funding. The EU, the USA, China, the World Bank and Turkey similarly cover most of the AU's hefty peacekeeping operation costs.[31] Such a 'godfather syndrome', as Chris Landsberg and Lesley Masters rightly call it,[32] compromises the AU's ownership of its agenda and reflects member states' lack of commitment.[33] The fact that this drastic decline in membership contribution occurred during Africa's decade-long high-growth period, and that most AU members do not falter in their dues to the UN and other international organisations,[34] at best signals their unwillingness to empower the AU as a supra-national body, and at worst exhibits their perplexing self-mockery.

The Way Forward

In May 2004, the African Union Commission provided a grand vision for the full integration of the continent in the short term by 2007, in the medium term by 2015 and in the long term by 2030. It has also provided a detailed action plan to speed integration of the continent. For the AU to tangibly break with the image associated with its predecessor, the OAU, it must seriously start operationalising its lofty ideals, agenda and initiatives.

There are several policies that can contribute towards the fulfilment of this vision, including strengthening the leadership role of the AU in promoting peace and security on the continent, and building a greater capacity to respond rapidly and effectively to crisis situations in Africa. Successfully implementing this new interventionism requires political commitment from member states. The AU needs to better coordinate regional peace, security and development mechanisms through Africa's eight regional economic communities – the Common Market for Eastern and Southern Africa (COMESA), the Community of Sahel-Saharan States (CEN-SAD), the East African Community (EAC), the Economic Community of Central African States (ECCAS), the Economic Community of West African States (ECOWAS), the Inter-Governmental Authority on Development (IGAD), the Southern African Development Community (SADC) and the Arab Maghreb Union (UMA).

As an expression of renewed Pan-Africanism, there needs to be an increase in support for the AU. The AU should work closely with all its member states to find innovative ways to mobilise resources for its key projects and programmes. African leaders' agreement in principle in 2015 to raise at least two-thirds of the AU's budget through new taxes on airline tickets, hotel stays and text messages is an encouraging move deserving a trial.[35]

This will require popularising the AU and making its vision widely shared. For example, the Union can mobilise AU Day (9 September) and African Integration Week (22–29 May) across the continent. The promotion of cultural Pan-Africanism can be achieved through strengthening and expanding Pan-African universities, centres of excellence, schools and other institutions. Linked to this issue is the need to develop effective infrastructure in Africa in order to facilitate the movement of persons, goods and services through continent-wide road, rail and air transport networks. The infrastructure gap across the continent is too wide for ongoing continental projects and initiatives to fill it.

To effectively stop violent conflicts, the AU and its African Peace and Security Architecture need to strengthen their early warning system and enhance their disarmament, demobilisation and reintegration capacities. Spending on arms and ammunition must be cut to below 1.5 per cent of gross domestic product, and African states must commit themselves to decrease their defence budgets during the next decade. The funds thus made available should be invested in peace and development, and in particular education and health. The promotion of democracy, human rights and good governance in all African countries should be encouraged, and African countries need to participate in, and respect, the APRM. Heightened emphasis should also be given to reforming the security sectors of almost all African countries.

First and foremost, the AU needs to facilitate the abolishment of visa requirements for African citizens entering other African countries. In a similar vein, it also needs to accelerate the granting of the Pan-African passport beyond the leaders to the citizenry. The AU also should spur momentum for the creation of the African economic community backed with an African common currency, an African central bank, an African monetary fund and an African investment bank, among others. The AU should also promote Africa's multi-faceted partnerships, not just with traditional powers such as the EU, the USA and Japan, but also with such major emerging powers as China, India, Brazil, Russia, South Korea, Australia, the East Asian Tigers and the Gulf countries.

Conclusion

Pan-Africanism is a constantly evolving ideological movement committed to the socio-economic and political emancipation of Africans and descendants of Africans in the Diaspora. While Pan-Africanism is the most emotionally resonant continental ideology, it has had little political success except perhaps in the area of decolonisation. Undoubtedly, developing the continent through integration will have payoffs in transforming Africa into a collective economic force in the global mainstream.

When Kwame Nkrumah presented his project for Pan-African unity in 1963, it seemed utopian. But it was a programme well suited to the real and long-term needs of the people of Africa. Pan-Africanism as an ideal has not lost its validity and vitality with the passage of time. On the contrary, Pan-Africanism remains the most effective vehicle for addressing the debilitating problems of Africa. Africa cannot be developed using externally imposed economic paradigms, cultures and models. Africa is in need of an African cultural renaissance. An African socio-cultural renaissance is essential not only for sustainable growth and development, but also to reverse the ongoing marginalisation of the continent in the age of globalisation. A united Africa will be able to manage its natural resources in order to become globally competitive and benefit its people.

Though the Pan-African movement surely remains necessary in the twenty-first century, it needs to be articulated clearly and practiced genuinely. The OAU was Pan-Africanist to the extent that it sought the political independence of all African countries from the yoke of colonialism. However, it was not successful in protecting African people from the excesses of state power and human rights abuses. As former chairperson of the AU Commission Nkosazana Dlamini-Zuma noted at the 28th AU Summit, held in Addis Ababa in January 2017:

> as the vision of *Agenda 2063* states, the AU should achieve a prosperous, peaceful and integrated Africa relying on the potential of the African people. The AU must instil a legitimate, binding respect for the rule of democratic governance if it wishes to see stability in the continent.

With democratically elected governments come visionary politicians and a genuine will for change.

The advantages of continental integration and unity can hardly be overemphasised. If Africa gives itself a central government, there will be no further need for individual countries to maintain expensive separate armies. Conflicts are fuelled in Africa by the ability of foreign powers with conflicting interests to support and arm different parties to a domestic or inter-state conflict. With the birth of a central government, no foreign power will be able to carry out military transactions with individual states. Once all member states reach stability and cultivate the political will, and political and economic unity, the essence of Pan-Africanism will become achievable. Africa as one federated country will be the third-largest country after China and India. The economic benefits of a united Africa are too numerous to list here.

The transformation of the OAU into AU represents the strengthening of the institutionalisation of this ideological movement. For the successful implementation of the AU's programmes, its objectives must be harmonised with national policies. This means that states must be prepared not only to surrender part of their sovereignty to the AU, but also to accept that convergence is needed on key policies such as economic integration and the free movement of people. This is bound to be a challenge, as African states throughout their post-colonial history have been very possessive about their sovereignty.[36]

The AU also offers a major opportunity for Africa to establish an effective legal and institutional mechanism to promote unity and prosperity. There are many hurdles to overcome to make the AU vision into a reality. Implementation of AU policies will pose a significant challenge. In the past, Africa had a record of poor implementation of treaty obligations. This was mainly due to resistance from countries to incorporate international treaties into domestic law and transfer powers to supra-national bodies. In order for the AU to succeed, there must be a genuine commitment to unity and strong political will to implement its plan of action.

Without creating a strong, democratic, independent and self-reliant New Africa, the continent will remain an easy prey to the penetration of external economic interests. A united Africa will be able to withstand its multitude of challenges, but if it continues to be divided, it will continue to be beset by crises. The AU has laid the foundation for progressively realising the Pan-African vision of creating an integrated, prosperous and peaceful Africa. But in today's complex and interconnected world, there are many more hurdles to overcome to make this vision a reality.

Africans have the opportunity to learn from the mistakes of the past and prepare Africa for its rightful place in the community of nations.[37] What is primarily needed is to have a clear picture of the vision and an honest conviction in its relevance backed by an unwavering commitment to its realisation. Undoubtedly, the strength of Africa lies in its unity and Pan-Africanism.

Notes

1. African Union (AU) Commission, *2004 to 2007 Strategic Framework of the African Union Commission,* (2 May, 2004), p.7.
2. Ogba Adejoh Sylvester and Okpanachi Idoko Anthony, 'Decolonization in Africa and Pan-Africanism', *Yönetim Bilimleri Dergisi*, 12:23 (2014), p. 7–31.
3. See Thandika Mkandawire, 'Re-Thinking Pan-Africanism', paper presented at the First Conference of Intellectuals of Africa and Its Diaspora, Dakar, 6–9 October 2004.
4. See Immanuel Geiss, *The Pan-African Movement* (London: Methuen, 1974), p. 3.
5. Timothy Murithi, *The African Union: Pan-Africanism, Peacebuilding, and Development* (Aldershot: Ashgate, 2005), p. 7.
6. Murithi, *The African Union.*
7. Reginald Herbold Green and Ann Willcox Seidman, *Unity or Poverty: The Economics of Pan-Africanism* (Harmondsworth: Penguin, 1968), p. 22.
8. Economic Commission for Africa, *Accelerating Regional Integration in Africa* (Addis Ababa, 2004).
9. Kwame Nkrumah, *Africa Must Unite* (New York: Panaf, 1963), p. 220.

10. Surajudeen Oladosu Mudasiru, 'Conflicts, Identity Crisis, and the Withering Away of the African Union: A Quest for a New (O)AU', in African Dynamics in a Multipolar World, Proceedings of the ECAS 2013, 5th European Conference on African Studies, Centro de Estudos Internacionais do Instituto Universitario de Lisboa (ISCTE-IUL) (27–29 June 2013).

11. Mudasiru, 'Conflicts, Identity Crisis, and the Withering Away of the African Union'.

12. Ibid.

13. African Union Constitutive Act (Lome, 11 July 2000), articles 3(a) and 3(c).

14. Kuruvilla Mathews, 'The OAU and the Problem of African Unity', *Africa Quarterly,* 23: 1–2 (1989), p. 1–26.

15. Carlos Lopez, 'Moving from Early Pan-Africanism Towards an African Renaissance', *The Former Cheetah Run: The Former Executive Secretary's Blog,* United Nations Economic Commission for Africa (UNECA) (23 August 2013), http://www.uneca.org/es-blog/moving-early-pan-africanism-towards-african-renaissance (accessed 10 May 2017).

16. Chris Landsberg and Lesley Masters, 'Twenty-five Years of Pan-African Democratic Governance Diplomacy', *Journal for Contemporary History,* 40:1 (2015), p. 197–219.

17. Cited in Landsberg and Masters, 'Twenty-five Years of Pan-African Democratic Governance Diplomacy', p. 200.

18. Chris Landsberg, 'The Fifth Wave of Pan-Africanism', in Adekeye Adebajo and Ismail Rashid (eds), *West Africa's Security Challenges: Building Peace in a Troubled Region* (Boulder: Rienner, 2002), p. 140.

19. Stephen Okhonmina, 'The African Union: Pan-Africanist Aspirations and the Challenge of African Unity' *Journal of Pan African Studies,* 3: 4 (2009), p. 85–100.

20. Fantu Cheru, *African Renaissance: Roadmaps to the Challenge of Globalisation* (London: Zed, 2002); Oyewole Simon Ogini and Joash Ntenga Moitui, 'African Renaissance and Pan-Africanism: A Shared Value and Identity Among African Nationals', *Africology: The Journal of Pan African Studies,* 9:1 (2016), p. 39–58.

21. Mudasiru, 'Conflicts, Identity Crisis, and the Withering Away of the African Union'.

22. Desmond Orjiako, 'The African Union: Our Common Home', keynote speech presented at Northeastern University, Boston (24 March 2005), p. 8.

23. See *Protocol Relating to the Establishment of the Peace and Security Council of the African Union,* Durban (9 July 2002).

24. Landsberg and Masters, 'Twenty-five Years of Pan-African Democratic Governance Diplomacy'.

25. Crisis Group, 'The African Union and the Burundi Crisis: Ambition Versus Reality', Briefing no. 122 (September 2016).

26. AU Commission, *Agenda 2063: The Africa We Want,* 2nd edn (Addis Ababa, August 2014).

27. African Peer Review Mechanism (APRM), 'History', http://www.aprm-au.org/pages?pageId=history (13 March 2017)

28. See Gumisai Mutume, 'Pan-African Parliament Now a Reality', *Africa Recovery*, 18:1 (April 2004), p. 19.

29. Freedom House, 'Populists and Autocrats: The Dual Threat to Global Democracy', in *Freedom in the World 2017* (Washington, DC, 2017)

30. This is a comparative analysis statement. It shows that, even if you count the trade between African countries as part of the volume of their overall external trade, the volume of intra-African trade constitutes just ten per cent of the volume of African countries' overall external trade, thereby depicting the staggeringly low level of regional economic integration in the continent. Plus, Africa is not a unified political entity; hence, the trade that each sovereign African country with other sovereign African countries is part of their overall external trade.

31. Christine Mungai, 'As New AU Chair Mahamat Takes Office: The African Union's Financing Headache, in Two Charts', *Africapedia* (20 March 2017). See also *Daily Mail*, 'No Strings Attached: African Union Seeks Financial Independence', 1 February 2015, http://www.dailymail.co.uk/wires/afp/article-2935107/No-strings-attached-African-Union-seeks-financial-independence.html (accessed 12 April 2015) [No city name is mentioned in the article].

32. Landsberg and Masters, 'Twenty-five Years of Pan-African Democratic Governance Diplomacy', pp. 215–16.

33. Crisis Group, 'The African Union and the Burundi Crisis', Briefing No. 122/Africa (28 September 2016), https://www.crisisgroup.org/africa/central-africa/burundi/african-union-and-burundi-crisis-ambition-versus-reality (accessed 30 September 2016).

34. Landsberg and Masters, 'Twenty-five Years of Pan-African Democratic Governance Diplomacy', p. 215.

35. *Daily Mail*, 'No Strings Attached: African Union Seeks Financial Independence'.

36. Eddy Maloka (ed.), *A United States of Africa?* (Pretoria: Africa Institute of South Africa, 2001), p. 4.

37. Mammo Muchie, 'Has the Pan-African Hour Come?', in Mammo Muchie (ed.), *The Making of the Africa-Nation: Pan-Africanism and African Renaissance* (London: Adonis and Abbey, 2003), pp. 2–11.

CHAPTER 2

PAN-AFRICANISM AND THE AFRICAN DIASPORA

Molefi Kete Asante

Pan-Africanism emerged in the twentieth century as an expression among Africans spread throughout the world because of colonisation, enslavement and voluntary migration. Pan-Africanists insist that solidarity and unity of Africans is the ultimate destiny of all African people.[1] Based on the idea that African peoples and countries are woven together in a commonality that rests upon concrete economic, social and political realities and experiences of half a millennium of historical dislocation, Pan-Africanism is on one hand an ideology and on the other a movement.

From its memic inception, Pan-Africanism was an idea promoted by Africans of the Diaspora in a quest to reconnect to the peoples and homeland lost during the European slave trade. Interestingly, there is no such movement in the literature about the descendants of the Arab slave trade of Central and East Africa. In other words, an ideology of return or common destiny does not seem to have emerged, probably for religious and social reasons, among Africans who had been taken to Arabia, Oman, India and the Baghdad caliphate. We know, of course, of the Zanj Rebellion in the tenth century in Baghdad, but have no record of any sustained movement toward a Pan-African ideology deriving from the Africans living to the east of the continent. In addition, the Arab slave traders forced Africans to become Muslims and have children with African women to confuse the descendants of Arabs and Africans until this present era. On the other hand, Europeans could be jailed or sentenced to exile or lose their positions and status in society by having sex with African women. Of course, enough of them violated all principles of restraint to produce a population of people of colour that had some of the characteristics of the Arab-produced population. Many African women were brutalised and raped during their Arab enslavement and thus were agents of the disintegration of African culture.

Thus, the current strand of Pan-Africanism found in the literature, and in actions on the continent and in the Diaspora, seems to be a singular province of Africans who descended from the European slave trade. The evidence is that the European enslavement was brutal but of a different kind in the sense that the European enslavers thought of Africans as not human, without souls, and incapable of thought and reason. With such a belief, the Europeans were loath to embrace Africans as Christians or to marry them as social equals. It is this social distance that drove Africans in the Diaspora to ache profoundly for an identity with Africa.

The Portuguese began the uprooting of Africans in the fifteenth century.[2] Perched in Ceuta since 1415, the Portuguese sailors, taking advantage of the fact that their country had claimed its freedom from the Moors in the twelfth century, began exploring the west coast of Africa. By 1441, Portuguese sea captains Antão Gonçalves and Nuno Tristão had captured 12 Africans in Cabo Branco (modern Mauritania) and had taken them to Portugal, where they were enslaved.[3] Three years later, on 8 August 1444, Lançarote de Freitas, a tax collector from the Portuguese town of Lagos who had organised a company to trade with Africa, landed 235 enslaved Africans, making it the largest group of Africans to be kidnapped and enslaved in Europe at the time. On 18 June 1452, Pope Nicholas V issued the *Dum Diversas*, a papal bull authorising the Portuguese to reduce any non-Christians to the status of slaves. Soon the Portuguese were working alongside enslaved Africans in sugar fields on the Madeira archipelago with such commercial success that on 1 January 1454, Pope Nicholas V issued the *Romanus Pontifex*, a bull granting the Portuguese a perpetual monopoly in trade with Africa. Nevertheless, Spanish traders, with the weakening of the hold of the Moors, started sending ships to Africa for Africans as well.[4] Soon Italy, southern France, Spain and Portugal had significant populations of Africans. The Portuguese trading fort at Arguin in Mauritania was completed in 1462, giving Portugal a head start on other European countries. By the end of the European enterprise, from Africa to the Americas, millions of Africans had been forcibly transported across the Atlantic.[5]

The world created by the distribution of Africans because of colonisation and enslavement was a very different one than the world prior to the Columbian adventures to the Americas. After Columbus's voyages, the accelerated slave trade of ships leaving Europe for Africa and then the Caribbean and the Americas competed with the insatiable thirst for new bodies to fill the sugar cane fields of Santo Domingo, Martinique, Guadeloupe and South America. By the time the British entered the trade, with ships landing in Barbados, Jamestown, Savannah, Charleston, Philadelphia, Boston and New York with their cargoes of human flesh, Africans in South America and the Caribbean had already become the dominant numerical and economic force in many lands. Consequently, the idea of the unity of Africans or the commonality of Africans had taken root in the revolts, plots, rebellions and resistance movements of groups of Africans from different ethnic and linguistic backgrounds who fled to the swamps and mountains of their new lands.

Indeed, there were hundreds of liberators who struck for a united and collective freedom, some successfully and others unsuccessfully, but their names were whispered in the cotton fields, on the sugar cane plantations, in the deep copper and gold mines and the liberated areas in mangrove swamps. Their names were Mackandal, Boukman, Dessalines, all of Haiti; Yanga of Mexico; Nat Turner of Virginia and Harriet Tubman of Maryland and Zumbi of Palmares in Brazil; and thousands of other defenders of African people whose names have dropped from history.

With more than a hundred African ethnic groups forced into enslavement over the four-century cross-Atlantic experience, it is important to appreciate the gallantry of those who sought to create instruments of social transformation by uniting African languages and creating simplified creoles and pidgins so that various groups of Africans could speak with each other.[6] Without such an appreciation of the resilient creativity of the enslaved, it is impossible to discover a path forward to Pan-Africanism. The African languages they created were perhaps the most significant contributions of the early Africans in the Americas. Speakers of Yoruba, Wolof, Ewe, Bamun, Kongo, Akan and a hundred other languages could craft ways to communicate across linguistic differences. Thus, while we are inclined to see Pan-Africanism in a contemporary sense, perhaps as a twenty-first century or twentieth century phenomenon, it is now clear that the idea of the unity of African people did not originate in the twentieth century but rather before, during the creation of common ways of speaking, merging of cultural ideas, forms of syncretism and cultural dynamism.[7]

Any analysis of African revolts in the United States, for example, will show that most of them, such as the rebellions of Gabriel Prosser in Richmond, Virginia, and Denmark Vesey in Charleston, South Carolina, although unsuccessful, had participants who were from different African ethnic groups.

Africans in the Americas and the Caribbean recognised their African identity much earlier than the institutionalisation of the Pan-African conferences and congresses energised by the work of Trinidadian Henry Sylvester Williams, Haitian Antenor Firmin and African American W.E.B. Du Bois. In effect, they were operating on a long tradition of working together with Africans of various ethnicities. Williams left Trinidad to study in New York but could not find work and then moved to Halifax, Nova Scotia, Canada. After leaving Nova Scotia he went to Britain, where in 1897 he formed the African Association to confront imperialism, racism and white domination of Africans. The organisation was to promote and 'protect the interests of all subjects claiming African descent, wholly or in part, in British colonies and other places, especially Africa, by circulating accurate information on all subjects affecting their rights and privileges as subjects of the British Empire, by direct appeals to the Imperial and local Governments'.[8]

The African Association morphed into the Pan-African Association and in 1900 the 31-year-old Williams organised the first Pan-African Conference, held at Westminster Hall in London. After the conference, he went to South Africa to practise law, becoming the first black person to be admitted to the bar in the Cape Colony.

The history of Pan-Africanism cannot be fully written without an understanding of the role played by Haitian intellectual Antenor Firmin. It was Firmin who had attacked Joseph-Arthur de Gobineau's thesis on the inequality of the human races with his powerful rebuttal on the equality of the human races in 1885.[9] However, Firmin's name often drops out of the discourse on Pan-Africanism though in fact he stood alongside Henry Sylvester Williams and fellow Haitian Benito Sylvain as an important figure at the Pan-African Conference in London. Firmin's intellectual abilities and devotion to Pan-Africanism must be seen in the same context as those of

Williams and Du Bois. Williams died in March 1911 and Firmin in September of the same year. However, Du Bois, who was a year older than Williams, was also in attendance at the conference and was given the role of drafting the general report. That conference brought together for the first time the leading Pan-Africanists of the English-speaking and French-speaking diasporas. The London conference may be seen as the launching of the Pan-African movement.

Pan-Africanism is an ideology grounded in a moral and political desire for the unity of all African peoples to usher in a rise in African consciousness. Thus, it seeks to create the conditions for unity among African people. It is grounded in the belief that there are certain historical and cultural relationships and objectives that are common to African people.[10] One could reasonably and with good evidence claim that the impulse towards Pan-Africanism existed before the word was used. In fact, the idea that Africans had a common identity and a common destiny was present at the earliest moments of the enslavement. Thus, there is no mystery to the establishment of syncretic expressions of spirituality in the Americas, iterations that were derived not from the thirst to combine with European versions of religion, but foremost from the desire to merge African ideals and ideas into one overarching approach to the African condition. This is often overlooked when writers try to understand the syncretic responses to situations among the early Africans in the Americas. Blending of African deities took place before any blending with Christianity. The ideas of Santería in Cuba, Vodun in Santo Domingo and Candomblé in Brazil were syncretised with Catholicism only when the practitioners were forced to conceal their spirituality. In the United States the religious practices of Africans created a collective identity as well, and served as the foundation for protest and radical politics. Nat Turner, Gabriel Prosser, and Denmark Vesey, who led attempts to overturn slavery, were religious leaders.

Ethiopianism emerged in the nineteenth century among Africans in the Caribbean and Americas. Those who had read Psalm 68:31 – 'Ethiopia shall soon stretch forth its hands unto God' – saw it as a prophecy that God would redeem Africa. Ethiopianism thus emerged initially as a form of resistance to white supremacist theologies. Actually, the Pan-Africanist work of religious groups like the African Methodist Episcopal Church, and its profoundly Pan-African bishop Henry McNeal Turner, made the church one of the engines of Ethiopianism. In South Africa the African Methodist Episcopal Church influenced Joseph Mathunye Kanyane Napo in 1888 and Mangena Maake Mokone in 1892 to leave the Anglican and Methodist Churches and establish the Ethiopian Church in 1892, which then merged with the African Methodist Episcopal Church in 1996. South Africans were recruited to black colleges in the United States, where they were indoctrinated with ideas of African equality and liberation. The 1906 Natal Zulu Rebellion has been linked to the idea of Ethiopianism. This is not an uninteresting fact given the view that without an ideology there can be no African nation, no Pan-Africanism. Nevertheless, the literature on our persistent quest suggests that a sufficient number of Africans believe in our common destiny to make Pan-Africanism a worthwhile and a viable objective.

General Movements of Pan-Africanism

There are three general movements in modern Pan-Africanism: the convening of international conferences and congresses; the creation of statist organisations such as Organisation of African Unity (OAU) and the African Union (AU); and the rise of Afrocentric Pan-Africanism.

International Conferences and Congresses

The Pan-Africanist international conferences and congresses had their beginnings with the recognised founders of the movement. However, W.E.B. Du Bois, unlike H. Sylvester Williams, called his international meetings congresses instead of conferences. The first Pan-African Congress, directed by Du Bois, was held in Paris in 1919. It represented Africa in a small way but was mainly a conference of Diasporic Africans, since of the 57 delegates from 15 countries, only 12 delegates came from 9 African countries, compared to 16 from the United States and 21 from the Caribbean. Most of the delegates already resided in France, because the United States and all the colonial nations refused to issue visas to Africans coming to the conference. The *New York Evening Globe*, on 22 February 1919, described it as 'the first assembly of the kind in history, and has for its object the drafting of an appeal to the Peace Conference to give the Negro race of Africa a chance to develop unhindered by other races.'

Du Bois initiated the second Pan-African Congress and went to work developing a platform and agenda that would attract a diverse group of Africans. The idea of Pan-Africanism having thus been established, he wanted to build a true movement. This was his second congress, but the third if we take Williams's 1900 conference into consideration. Du Bois was concerned mainly with his own congresses, and when he counted them he rarely spoke of the first conference as a part of his congresses. Nevertheless, by the time of Du Bois's second congress, the idea of Pan-Africanism had fully matured. Du Bois arranged for the second congress to meet in London, Brussels, and Paris in August and September 1921.

The third Pan-African Congress was held in London and Lisbon in 1923. Du Bois had a dispute with the Paris secretariat of the Pan-African movement and went ahead with the congress even though Paris wanted it delayed. The congress did not receive proper publicity or preparation and so the London session was small and unremarkable. However, the meeting of the congress in Lisbon was more successful. Eleven countries were represented, mainly from Portuguese Africa.

The Liga Africana, headquartered in Lisbon, was in charge. It was a federation of all the indigenous associations scattered throughout the five provinces of Portuguese-controlled Africa. The fourth Pan-African Congress was held in New York in 1927. Thirteen countries were represented, although representation of continental African was small. There were 208 delegates from 22 American states and 10 foreign countries. Representatives from the Gold Coast, Sierra Leone, Liberia and Nigeria attended from the continent. Chief Amoah III of the Gold Coast was a principal speaker at the fourth congress.

The fifth Pan-African Congress was held in Manchester, England, in 1945. An assembly of African trade union representatives who were attending a meeting in England had called for it to coincide with the number of black people meeting in England. After consultation and correspondence with several individuals, the Pan-African Federation was organised to sponsor the congress. Du Bois, George Padmore, Kwame Nkrumah, Amy Ashwood Garvey and Jomo Kenyatta were among the outstanding leaders and super-delegates. The fifth congress was the spark for decolonisation in Africa and in the Caribbean. It marked a significant advance in the participation of workers in the Pan-African cause. It demanded an end to colonial rule and an end to racial discrimination. It established the African vanguard against imperialism and for human rights. The manifesto and economic demands of the congress were keys to a new construction of the international world.

Du Bois was an active 73-year-old at the time of the fifth congress, and honorary chair of the meeting. Amy Ashwood, Marcus Garvey's first wife, presided over the first session. However, what was so powerful about the Manchester congress, coming on the heels of war in Europe, was the fact that a new generation of continental leaders were being trained and readied to take over the continent. The Pan-Africanists from the Caribbean, including George Padmore, and those from the continent of Africa, including Kwame Nkrumah, Nnamdi Azikiwe and Jomo Kenyatta, would take a vision of independence to their people with a new fire. T. Ras Makonnen of Guyana and Wallace-Johnson of Sierra Leone were present as supporters of George Padmore's leadership. Makonnen, who traced his ancestry to Tigre in Ethiopia, was already a passionate Pan-Africanist when the meeting was held. Upon his death in Nairobi, Kenya, in 1983, Pan-Africanists around the world knew that one of the great sons of Africa had passed. He was business manager and public relations officer for the 1945 Manchester congress.

However, it was Nkrumah who would soon become the major voice and organising spirit of Pan-Africanism.[11] Africans in North and South America would remain hopeful though oppressed in white-majority nations of those two continents. Men and women would arise by legions to carry on the work of the African renewal less than ten years after Manchester, resulting in the civil rights movement and the black power movement.

These classical conferences and congresses created the kind of critical masses necessary to sustain an international movement. Nothing short of brazen self-determination and ingenuity would satisfy the work of those who wanted to see the liberation of Africa. These individuals must be considered the truly passionate and genuinely political Pan-Africanists.

The OAU and AU

Ghanaian president Kwame Nkrumah and Ethiopian emperor Haile Selassie spearheaded the creation of the Organisation of African Unity on 25 May 1963. Gamel Nasser, Milton Obote, Ben Bella and Julius Nyerere were among the first supporters. Addis Ababa, Ethiopia, served as the home of the OAU and would become the headquarters of the African Union. Thabo Mbeki, president of South Africa, as the last chairperson of the OAU, disbanded it on 9 July 2002. He had declared earlier his

Pan-Africanist credentials in his great speech on the African Renaissance when he was deputy president.[12] The objectives of the OAU were to coordinate and intensify the cooperation of African states to better the quality of life for African people, to defend the territorial integrity and sovereignty of African states and to rid the continent of white settler regimes. Although there were successes, the objective of integrating the continent – bringing about African unity – was elusive.

The African Union was born at a seminal assembly of African states held in July 2002 in South Africa. Thus, a new, more dynamic organisation was brought into existence along the lines of continental unity. The Pan-African Parliament was created and situated in Midrand and Johannesburg, South Africa. However, the African Union has not been able to work its way out of the bureaucratic malaise that overcame it with the death of Muammar Qaddafi, one of the leading proponents of African unity, and the leaving of office by the first generation of African Union presidents.

Two objectives consumed the early years of the African Union: economic development and the creation of a United States of Africa. What was at stake in the creation of the Union was the authority and control of the development agenda for Africa. It was clearly understood by the member states that they had to take responsibility for the continent and not allow outside nations and forces to influence the development process. At independence, nearly all the states of Africa and their leaders were saddled with debts made by the colonial governments. This meant that they could only concentrate on defining political and social relationships between states, with great difficulty.

The African Union represents a concrete expression of the unity of the states of Africa minus Morocco. However, it is not an expression of the sentiments of Pan-Africanist originalists Henry Sylvester Williams and W.E.B. Du Bois, who saw Pan-Africanism in a much larger context than African state unity.

They wanted a Pan-Africanism with equal emphasis on
Pan and *African*. The word *pan*, derived from the Greek,
means 'all', as in Pan-Arabism, Pan-Europeanism and Pan-
Americanism, among others. For Williams and Du Bois, who
were Diasporic Africans, the idea of Pan-Africanism included
Africans born in the Americas and Caribbean. It was not
merely the union of African states. What African state is more
African than Haiti, Jamaica or the Bahamas? Furthermore,
what continental African nation has had any larger contingent
of Pan-Africanists than one finds in the United States?
In fact, during the early twentieth century and up until the
1945 Manchester Pan-African Congress, the idea was to
include Africans from any continent in the definition of
Pan-Africanism.

Afrocentric Pan-Africanism

Emerging at the start of the twenty-first century, a broad-based
Afrocentric Pan-Africanism captured the imaginations of
millions of Africans throughout the world. Afrocentric Pan-
Africanism is a modern variety of the old internationalist Pan-
Africanism that was created with the early conferences and
congresses. The aim of this new movement is trans-national,
trans-generational and communalist, with tendencies towards
the ancient cultural values of African people. One of the first
such iterations was the Afrocentric International Movement,
started in April 2012. During a long search and study of the
early movements, especially the work of Marcus Garvey, Ama
Mazama and I examined the procedural and legal documents of
the Universal Negro Improvement Association and African
Communities League in order not to repeat the errors and
missteps of the former as well as those of the Pan-African
Congresses.

Our intention was to create an organisation that would have
as its mission support for the economic, cultural and
educational elevation of African people to create cultural

consciousness that would transform the lives of ordinary Africans throughout the world. Since other movements, especially those of Williams and Du Bois, and to an extent the African Union, had avoided adding Marcus Garvey and Cheikh Anta Diop to the narrative on Pan-Africanism, we believed it was essential to integrate all the avenues of Pan-Africanism into a world movement. Therefore, we even accepted the notion that *négritude* at its core, as expressed by Aimé Césaire of Martinique, Léopold Senghor of Senegal, Léon Damas of French Guiana and Jacques Rabemananjara of the Malagasy Republic, was central to the idea of Pan-Africanism. Afrocentricity International could not be authoritarian in its character; it had to be open to the various possibilities of African methods with the objective of creating unity. Therefore, one could not speak of this idea without some ideological position that would theoretically be opened to those who accepted their identity as African and who desired to see the rise of Africans collectively worldwide. Hence we were the spiritual children of Garvey, Diop, Césaire, Guillen and the Nardal sisters. Afrocentricity International's method is Afrocentric and Pan-Africanist because it participates at national and international levels in the creation of an advanced cadre of individuals whose objective is to bring into existence an African Renaissance for the purpose of establishing a continental United States of Africa with avenues for participation of Diasporic Africans as citizens and supporters. Such a state would have to deal with the problem of African states such as Haiti and Jamaica that are not on the African continent. It would have to take on the Arab racist assaults on Africans on the continent and not ignore, as the African Union has ignored, the demeaning enslavement of black people in Sudan and Mauritania.

Afrocentricity International is led by Guadeloupean Ama Mazama, the Peraat of the organisation, and it has established chapters in Brazil, the United States, the Caribbean, Europe

and several African nations.[13] It is truly Pan-African, not
simply in the state context, but also in the sense of all-African
peoples wherever they exist. The idea is to create a United
States of Africa that could be the spiritual and cultural home of
nearly a billion Diasporic African people. The members
commit to do all that they can to bring into existence the rise
of African consciousness and to generate grassroots efforts for
the creation of the United States of Africa. Only in a
vibrant and robust community of activists committed to
African transformation based on the principles of agency and
centredness will Africa realise its potentiality, greatness and
sacredness. There can be no African unity based on any alien
ideas that degrade, decompose and destroy African spiritual
agency; all African advances must begin with an appreciation
and critique of what our ancestors have bequeathed us.
The motto of the organisation is 'Unity is our Aim; Victory is
our Destiny!'

There are two key components to the methods of
Afrocentricity International. The first is to grasp the severe
nature of the spiritual destitution of many African people
caused by exploitation, brutality, forced acceptance of alien
ideas and cultural dislocation. This is called assessment of the
spiritual, not religious, condition of the African people in a
country or region of the world. Afrocentricity International
understands the nature of this phenomenon as a paralysing
spiritual fear. This is a worldwide phenomenon directly
credited to the massive destruction of African icons, rituals,
holidays, sacred places, ancestral shrines and names of African
ancestors and gods. Beginning with Arab colonisation and
enslavement in the ninth century and continuing through
European colonisation and enslavement, the African continent
suffered an intense and spectacular loss of confidence in Africa's
destiny. Subsequently, the cultural ravages of segregation,
discrimination, racial animus and historical distortions
produced in Africans a profound hesitancy that created

reluctance to assert agency. Afrocentricity International made this analysis of the Pan-African situation and recognised that there could be no renaissance without a critical mass of people who believed deeply in the possibility of an African transformation. International conferences held in Philadelphia, Paris, Salvador, Harare and Douala underscored this work and deepened the psychological and spiritual attachment to an African vision devoid of the cataracts of misinformation, cultural inferiority and political malaise. Our findings have also been reported to several international meetings and numerous universities in Africa, the Caribbean, Europe and the United States.

The second component to Afrocentricity International's method is locational. The Afrocentric paradigm posits place as an important concept in the transformation of African people. Where is a person, phenomenon or action located? This is not mere place as in being somewhere in geography, but location historically and psychologically. To inquire into the nature of one's location is to ask questions about what one understands about the common historical facts of African people as well as the collective vision of Africans to fulfil a mission of humanising the world. Freedom is essential to location; one must be free from oppression and free to exist on one's own terms to even announce a Pan-African vision. Friction occurs when a few try to oppress the majority, and try to suppress freedom, and when this happens insanity and violence are bound to be present. The foundation for proper location – that is, location that rewards Pan-Africanism – must comprise a certain minimum amount of historical assumptions and facts. Finally, the Afrocentricity International Movement seeks to advance the idea of Pan-Africanism on the foundation of Maat.

Another movement emerging is the Pan-Federalist Movement, begun in 2015, which seeks to bring into existence a United States of Africa based on the idea that heads of state will never achieve the unity necessary to have a

Pan-African continental state. The objective of the Pan-Federalists, led by Joomay Ndongo Faye, is to rally the leading Pan-Africanist groups to force the politicians to act in the interest of the ancient objective of African unity. They see their inspiration in the works of Kwame Nkrumah, Haile Selassie, Cheikh Anta Diop, W.E.B. Du Bois and Marcus Garvey. In this respect, they are like Afrocentricity International because we share the same names of visionaries as inspirations. Pan-Federalists claim that a bottom-up approach is the only way to achieve the dream of Pan-Africanism. The intention is to critique the existing political parties wielding power in Africa as not being federalist formations. I say 'intention' because as of 2016 the Pan-Federalist group has yet to be formed on an international basis. The arguments of the Pan-Federalists, however, are formidable; they claim that the leaders of African nations did not come to power on Pan-African platforms to bring into being the United States of Africa. In fact, the Pan-Federalists claim that some of these political parties are anti–Pan-Africanist and possess a bias towards working across ethnic and regional lines. I suspect this is true, although I have not made any concrete research into this issue myself. I mention this issue because it is a heuristic that might lead to deeper analysis of the political parties in various nations of Africa. Perhaps the rampant Afrophobia that we have seen across the continent, from Côte d'Ivoire and Libya to South Africa and Somali, might be related to the lack of progressive and transformatist political parties. I say 'Afrophobia' and not 'xenophobia' because it is not the fear of strangers that is at work in the anti-Pan Africanist countries, but the fear of other Africans. In some cases, the leaders of the parties have expressed progressive tendencies, but their policies have proven to be anti-Pan-Africanist.

The aim of the Pan-Federalist Movement is to seek to win political power as a political party in every African nation.

Leaders of this movement believe that this is the only way to create a federalist union government. In effect, the Federalist Party would be an example of Nkrumah's idea that through the democratic process one could create a revolutionary people's party. The Pan-Federalists believe that they can create a cadre of people who would form political parties that would contest for political party and become the bedrock for continental unity.

As a committed Afrocentric Pan-Africanist, I believe that no conscious African can ever be against the United States of Africa or any other formation such an idea will take. We see it as part of the destiny of the continent and its people to establish a more effective union that will bring into existence the mechanisms for a fuller life for African people and a defence for African spiritual, cultural and economic integrity. All Pan-African work is useful, necessary and dynamic. The initiatives are to be applauded, but we cannot forget or ignore the numerous associations around the world that have worked or are now working in the same arena. Groups calling themselves the Council of African Affairs, Pan African Affairs Commission, Pan African Federation, the US Organisation, All African People's Revolutionary Party, Pan Africanist Congress, Ubuntu Republics, African Democratic Rally and African Unification Front have appeared and will continue to appear until we have the United States of Africa. Some of these groups that are contemporary may not have broad internet exposure but are active at local and regional levels, and some, like Afrocentricity International, have had a worldwide presence with many chapters throughout Africa, the Caribbean and the Americas. One could also speak of the World African Diaspora Union, an organisation that sees its work as taking place in conjunction with the African Union's proposal for a sixth region − the Diaspora. While the World African Diaspora Union is not, as Afrocentricity International is, an organisation seeking the United States of Africa, it possesses a collective of Pan-Africanists who are determined to see the organisation of the African Diaspora to assist the African continent. Afrocentricity International wants to see a United States of Africa, even if it is initially a union of the willing states, that recognises its Diaspora, accepts the Caribbean African states such as Jamaica and Haiti into their confidence and develops a policy for granting citizenship to Africans forced into exile by enslavement.

Afrocentricity International contends that Pan-Africanism is a mere call to action without an ideological engine. Pan-Africanism must have a narrative of struggle and a vision of victory based on common principles accepted by those who see themselves as Africans. To bring Africans at the grassroots into an international organisation where the people will put fire to the feet of those who are elected by political parties will take a commitment to several basic principles: commitment to the psychological location of Africans; the defence of African cultural elements; commitment to changing all negative and nonfactual lexical items such as terms like 'Black Africans', 'primitive Africans', 'Sub-Saharan Africa', 'jungles of Africa', or 'tigers of Africa'. One never says 'White Europe' or 'Yellow Asia'. Africa is the black continent and those who live in Africa who are not black are the descendants of recent migrations back into the continent. When Africans left the continent 70,000 years ago in the wave of *homo sapiens* crossing out of the continent they were black. Africa contains the oldest civilisations, but primitive has become a pejorative term meant to demean Africans. There is not Sub-Saharan Africa; the Sahara is Africa; this seems like a construction to separate Africa from its classical Nile Valley Civilisations and to give it to the Arabs who arrived in numbers with General El As in 739 CE. There are no tigers in Africa. We can speak of lions.

My argument is that language must be cleansed and the terminology that negates black people as Africans must be dispensed with at once. Finally, there must be a commitment to correcting the history of Africa and African people.[14] Without these minimum principles, Africa will never be able to articulate a reasonable Pan-African future. In some circles, they call these ideas bases for a national patriotism. What is to ensure that those who claim to be Pan-African will be committed to the world African project? I ask this question because the fundamental problem of African identity is integrally related to unity. One can see this with the Sudanese example, par excellence. It is true that Sudan, not Ghana, was the first African country to gain independence, but the historians record Ghana as the first country to do so because of the confused identity of Sudan. Sudan received its independence on 1 January 1956, but the leadership who took control of the country did not accept the fact that they were an African country.[15] Afrocentricity International uses the motto 'L'Unite est notre But; la Victoire est notre Destinee'.

Notes

1. Bankie Forster Bankie and Viola C. Zimunya, *Sustaining the New Wave of Pan Africanism* (Windhoek: National Youth Council of Namibia, 2011).

2. Molefi Kete Asante, *The History of Africa*, 2nd edn (New York: Routledge, 2015).

3. Hugh Thomas, *The Slave Trade: The History of the Atlantic Slave Trade, 1440–1870* (London: Picador, 1997).

4. Herbert S. Klein, *The Atlantic Slave Trade* (Cambridge: Cambridge University Press, 2010).

5. Phillip D. Curtin, *The Atlantic Slave Trade: A Census* (Madison: University of Wisconsin Press, 1969).

6. Molefi Kete Asante, *Speaking My Mother's Tongue: Introduction to African American Language* (Fort Worth: Themba Hill, 2010).

7. Ronald W. Walters, *Pan Africanism in the African Diaspora: An Analysis of Modern Afrocentric Movements* (Detroit: Wayne State University Press, 1997); Olisanwuche Esedebe, *Pan Africanism: The Idea and Movement, 1776–1991* (Washington, DC: Howard University Press, 1994); C.L.R. James, *A History of Pan African Revolt* (New York: PM, 2012).

8. Marika Sherwood, *Origins of Pan Africanism: Henry Sylvester Williams, Africa, and the African Diaspora* (New York: Routledge, 2012), p. 14.

9. Théophile Obenga, 'Hommage à Anténor Firmin (1850–1911), Égyptologue Haïtien', *ANKH* no. 17 (2008), pp. 128–45.

10. Ama Mazama, *The Afrocentric Paradigm* (Trenton: Africa World, 2003).

11. Daryl Zizwe Poe, *Nkrumah's Contribution to Pan Africanism: An Afrocentric Analysis* (New York: Routledge, 2003).

12. Thabo Mbeki, 'The African Renaissance, South Africa, and the World', speech at United Nations University, Tokyo, Japan (9 April 1998).

13. See www.dyabukam.com.

14. Molefi Kete Asante, *An Afrocentric Manifesto* (Cambridge: Polity, 2007).

15. Bankie and Zimunya, *Sustaining the New Wave*, p. 18.

CHAPTER 3

THE AFRICA GROUP AT THE UNITED NATIONS: PAN-AFRICANISM ON THE RETREAT

Adonia Ayebare

This chapter analyses the impact of divisions within the Africa Group at the United Nations (UN) on Africa's capacity to push for common positions to shape the UN's global agenda. Common positions by Africa is a major diplomatic tool that Africa has used to exert urgency in international politics and diplomacy. The Africa Group of ambassadors accredited to the United Nations in New York is the main channel through which African ambassadors proffer and pursue their collective positions on such issues as Sustainable Development Goals, the UN Security Council reforms, peacekeeping and peace building.

However, since 2015 the Africa group has been deeply divided due to differences between Morocco and some African countries over the participation of Western Sahara in meetings of the Africa Group in New York. Morocco, supported by a number of African countries has effectively blocked Africa Group meetings that normally take place at the African Union office, which has led to shifting the venue to committee rooms at United Nations headquarters. Morocco's objection is based on the argument that Western Sahara is not a member state of the United Nations and cannot therefore participate in meetings of the Africa group, which is a designated regional group at the United Nations.

The re-admission of Morocco to the African Union has not offered a solution to the stalemate in Africa group. This stalemate has led to holding of separate meetings for African Union member states that Western Sahara belongs to and Africa Group meetings in which Western Sahara cannot participate. This stalemate has slowed down the formulation and implementation of African common positions. The New Chairperson of the African Union former Chadian Foreign Moussa Faki Mahamat has pledged to help end the stalemate within the Africa group.[1]

Pan-African Origins of the Africa Group

The Organisation of African Unity (OAU) designed Pan-African institutions and other frameworks to enhance inter-state cooperation in Africa. These frameworks included African diplomatic groups abroad to promote common positions of African countries as members belonging to a common geographical region, and common political, economic, social and cultural history, as well as to promote the objectives of the OAU.

In 1961, the Africa Group in New York engaged in its first significant task when the third All-African Peoples' Conference, held in Cairo from 25 to 31 March, adopted a UN resolution calling on the independent African states to demand the re-organisation of the United Nations Secretariat and the revision of the United Nations Charter to give Africa appropriate representation on the Security Council and other bodies of the UN. In effect, this initiative by the Africa Group planted the seeds of the on-going struggle to reform the Security Council. This initiative was a precursor to the current Committee of Ten, charged with implementing the African Union's common position on reform of the Security Council, commonly known as the Ezulwini Consensus. Africa is demanding two permanent seats on the Council with veto power. The split within the Africa Group is beginning to undermine the already fledgling African common positions on Security Council reform.

In addition to the Africa Group in New York, African groups were similarly created at the various United Nations regional headquarters, in New York, Geneva and Nairobi. In addition, the Africa Group formation has also been constituted at the capitals of key international actors including Washington, Brussels at the European Union (EU) headquarters and Tokyo, which meet regularly and have some form of by-laws governing their internal procedures. One of these processes is the rotation of chairs monthly. The relationship between the African groups and the OAU and its successor, the African Union, has never been clearly defined, which is partly the cause of the current crisis of the Africa Group in New York. Prior to interrogating this issue further, it is worthwhile to examine the mandate of the Africa Group.

Mandate and Composition of the Africa Group

The Africa Group comprises all the African permanent missions to the United Nations. The membership of the group is open to all African states represented at the United Nations, making it the largest regional group at the UN and one of the most active components of the Group of 77 (G77) and the Non-Aligned Movement (NAM). The group is not structured in the form of an international institution or organisation, and has no constitutive legal contract binding its members to certain obligations.

As a political group, it also provides a platform for African states to promote their interest at the United Nations. It is an advocacy group with a mandate to articulate and promote Africa's interests at the UN and the latter's specialised agencies. To achieve these goals, the group meets weekly at UN headquarters in New York and other international forums to discuss how issues of concern affect or relate to Africa, and strives to take a common position.

The activities of the Africa Group span the whole spectrum of issues dealt with by the United Nations: political, economic and financial, social and cultural, administrative and budgetary, environmental, health, education, agriculture, humanitarian and legal. The group meets as a whole usually at the level of ambassadors and permanent representatives or other senior officers. The work of the group is coordinated by the permanent representative of the country or mission nominated each month as chair of the group. The nomination of each country or mission is based on the alphabetical order of names of African permanent missions to the UN, its specialised agencies or other inter-governmental organisations.

The chairperson of the month presides over the plenary meetings of the group. He or she represents the group in various UN meetings and forums involving regional representatives. The chairperson of the month also collaborates with the permanent observer mission of the African Union to organise and schedule meetings. He or she also works with the six committee coordinators to articulate Africa's positions on various issues on the agenda of the United Nations.

The Africa Group reviews issues concerning Africa with the purpose of articulating the continent's common positions after consultations with the six coordinators. The plenary may decide to accede or delegate some of its functions or powers to the chair or to a committee of experts or an ad hoc committee. The plenary is the supreme organ of the group and makes final decisions.

The executive committee of the group is composed of ten members elected by the group, following equitable geographical representation: three from West Africa, two from Eastern Africa, two from Central Africa, two from Southern Africa and one from Northern Africa. This committee reviews statements of the group with the view of articulating Africa's common position, taking into account the different geographical interests. It deals exclusively with issues involving consolidating positions on the submission of names of African candidates to key international portfolios. Its main purpose is to resolve and prevent disputes or disparity over Africa's nominations and candidatures at the UN and other international forums.

The group's expert committees comprise African experts nominated by their missions or states to work or follow up on the proceedings of all six main committees of the United Nations. These expert committees are made up of professionals or experts in specific fields, and only make recommendations based on technical and other considerations, which are then reviewed and adopted or endorsed by the plenary of the Africa Group at ambassadorial level.

While the plenary is a political body with decision making powers, the expert committees are technical committees that deal with technical issues. Each expert committee is headed by a coordinator, who presides over committee meetings and coordinates the work of the committee for a term of one year. The proceedings of the committees are guided by the rules of procedure of the Africa Group. The six expert committees deal with disarmament, economic affairs, human rights and gender issues, decolonisation, budget and legal matters.

Role of the African Union and its Relationship with the Africa Group

The permanent observer mission of the African Union to the United Nations serves as the secretariat to the Africa Group.

The Secretariat of the AU Observer Mission prepares the agenda of all meetings of the group in consultation with the chairperson of the month. The chairperson of the month ensures that the provisional agenda and other materials are sent to all members of the group in time for meetings. The Secretariat also prepares a summary record of each meeting and presents it to the chairperson of the month for approval. The record is distributed to all members of the group in both English and French. The AU office also provides translation services in English and French, and coordinates the work of the three African non-permanent members of the UN Security Council.

The loose and informal relationship between the African Union Secretariat and the Group and the is the root cause of the current crisis at the group in New York. One African ambassador (name withheld) described the relationship as 'a political disconnect rather than technical'. The divisions within the Africa group have persisted despite Morocco re-joining the African Union in January 2017, during the Addis Ababa Heads of States summit.

Morocco withdrew its membership from the Organisation of African Unity, the predecessor to the AU, when Western Sahara was granted independence in 1984, an issue that remains controversial in International diplomacy. The Africa Group is composed of the 54 African member states accredited to the United Nations, which technically excludes Western Sahara.

Challenges and Achievements of the Africa Group

The Africa Group is the largest regional group at the United Nations, with 54 member states, and has been effective. The main achievements of the Africa Group include lobbying for the election of two United Nations Secretaries-Generals, Boutros Boutros-Ghali and Kofi Annan. The group has also lobbied for the elections of various Africans as presidents of the United Nations General Assembly.

The Africa group in New York handles candidatures in the International system by coordinating with the candidature committee of the African Union. Africa is the only continent that presents a clean slate when it comes to candidatures at the United Nations. The example being the selection of three countries that represent Africa on the United Nations Security Council, unlike other regions that compete for the seats in the United Nations General Assembly. In the case of Africa each sub-region nominates a country to be represent it on the Council, using a rotational formula, which gives each member state a chance to serve on the council. The Africa Group in New York has negotiated for the position of president of the United Nations General Assembly, with 11 Africans having so far held the presidency, and more than twice this number having held the post of vice-presidency. Almost all countries in Africa have served at least one term on the Security Council and its presidency.

The Africa Group played a key role in advocating for the process of decolonisation and independence of African countries. In 1958, when the first conference of independent African countries was held, they were only eight independent African countries represented at the United Nations. But by 1963 the number had risen to 32, giving Africa almost one-third of the votes at the UN. By the end of the 1990s, the number stood at 53. As the summary records of the Africa Group indicate, the role of the group in achieving the independence of Zimbabwe and Namibia was pivotal. In fact, in the 1970s and 1980s, the Africa Group played a pivotal role in decolonisation and the elimination of racism and apartheid in South Africa.

The Africa Group took several actions to mobilise the United Nations and the international community to place decolonisation and the end of apartheid at the top of the agenda. It drafted statements and resolutions, and reviewed and defended Africa's position on these matters. It convened meetings at the highest levels, including special sessions at the United Nations. The Africa Group also helped to promote OAU sanctions against South Africa and boycotted activities and events in which South Africa participated. Speaking to the Africa Group in September 1982, Archbishop Desmond Tutu thanked the Africa Group for all its efforts and further requested the group to keep up the struggle to overcome apartheid in South Africa.

Today, apartheid has ended and all African countries formerly under colonial rule have gained their independence, except for Western Sahara, whose lack of independence has divided the continent and threatens the survival of the Africa Group. The Africa Group has been instrumental in ensuring that Africa's concerns are reflected in the various UN and international forums for action, including Agenda 21, the Millennium Declaration, the Beijing Declaration, the Monterrey Consensus and many others in the economic, political and environmental domains.

The Africa Group has also negotiated for and obtained top positions of other prestigious UN bodies and organs such as the Economic and Social Council (ECOSOC). Zimbabwe won the ECOSOC presidency in 2017, after Rwanda withdrew its candidature. Key African individuals who have served within the leadership of the United Nations system are shown in Tables 3.1 and 3.2.

African ambassadors at the United Nations have also held the presidency of the G77, an influential grouping that includes developing countries and China. The most recent was Ambassador Kingsley Mamabulo, former permanent representative of South Africa at the United Nations. Kenyan ambassador Kamau Macharia also chaired the UN Peacebuilding Commission; African countries on the agenda of the commission include Burundi, the Central African Republic,

Table 3.1 Africa's General Assembly Presidents

	Country	Tenure	General Assembly Session
Sam Kuresa	Uganda	2015	69th
Jean Ping	Gabon	2004–5	59th
Theo-Ben Gurirab	Namibia	1999–2000	54th
Amara Essy	Côte d'Ivoire	1994	49th
Joseph Nanven Garba	Nigeria	1989–90	44th
Paul J.F. Lusaka	Zambia	1984	39th
Salim Ahmed Salim	Tanzania	1979–80	34th
Abdelaziz Bouteflika	Algeria	1974–5	29th
Angie E. Brooks	Liberia	1969	24th
Alex Quaison Sackey	Ghana	1964	19th
Mongi Slim	Tunisia	1961	16th

Table 3.2   Africa's ECOSOC Presidents

	Country	Tenure
Lazarus Kapambwe	Zambia	2011
Martin Belinga Eboutou	Cameroon	2001
Jean-Marie Kacou Gervais	Côte d'Ivoire	1996
Manuel dos Santos	Mozambique	1986
Paul John Firmino Lusaka	Zambia	1981
Simeon Ake	Côte d'Ivoire	1976
Rachid Driss	Tunisia	1971
Tewfik Bouattoura	Algeria	1966

Guinea, Guinea-Bissau, Liberia and Sierra Leone. Rwanda and Angola previously chaired the Peacebuilding Commission.

The Africa Group has been largely successful in the political fields of decolonisation, candidatures for international organisations and convening of meetings in New York. The group has been weak in engaging civil society and the African Diaspora in a systematic manner. The Diaspora as a sixth region of the African Union would be a key constituency in addressing challenges in the economic, health and education fields that contribute to impoverishment of the continent. Africa has a disproportionate number of impoverished countries compared to other continents and regions, among the highest illiteracy rates in the world, and remains afflicted by internecine conflicts.

Since 2004 the Africa Group has facilitated the holding of a special session on causes of conflict and promotion of durable peace and sustainable development in Africa, at both the UN General Assembly and the UN Security Council. The African Union Observer mission and the office of the United Nations Special Adviser for Africa have organised Africa week in New York to highlight key challenges facing Africa especially development and trade issues. Participants in the Africa week have included academics, senior United Nations officials, World Bank representatives, New Partnership for Africa's

Development (NEPAD) officials and officials from African Union Commission headquarters in Addis Ababa.

In the recent past, the Africa Group has adopted common positions on key processes on the international agenda such as the Sustainable Development Goals (SDGs), the High-Level Independent Panel on Peace Operations (HIPPO), review of the UN's peacebuilding architecture, and development financing. By taking common positions at the United Nations, the Africa Group has been able to influence the outcomes of these processes.

Another important area where the Africa Group has been instrumental is pursuing Africa's interests at the Security Council through Africa's three representatives (A3) on the body. The activation of the A3 has significantly improved coordination between the United Nations Security Council and AU Peace and Security Council (PSC) on African issues on the agendas of both councils. The A3 submits quarterly reports to the entire Africa Group outlining trends, dynamics and recommendations to the group. The Africa Group, especially those countries on the Security Council agenda, always receive an opportunity to inform the Council's decision making process. The A3 countries also receive feedback from Africa Group members, which is crucial for their work on the Security Council.

Internal Challenges of the Africa Group

The main challenge affecting the Africa Group has been co-ordination with the capitals of African countries. In some cases, African ambassadors obtain instructions from their capital contrary to the agreed positions of the Africa Group. Non-African countries regularly lobby individual African countries to support their positions or candidates at the United Nations. Poor coordination has undermined the effectiveness of the group in New York. How to make coordination more effective has been raised several times at both the plenary and committee levels, but the Africa Group has yet to devise the sound mechanisms needed to enhance communication between the group and the African Union.

Much tension has been generated by Western Sahara's efforts to join the meetings of Africa Group, based on its argument that a member state of the African Union is entitled to attend all meetings at the premises of the African Union offices in New York, including those of the Africa Group. This development has led to the splitting of the Africa Group, comprising all 54 African countries represented at the United Nations, into pro-Morocco and pro-Saharawi camps. Repeated rounds of negotiations among members of the group have failed to yield compromise, and the matter was referred to the African Union Summit in July 2016 in Kigali, Rwanda.

The compromise over the issue of whether Western Sahara should participate in Africa Group meetings will linger due to the failure of the July 2016 summit of AU heads of state to resolve the impasse as requested by the African ambassadors in New York. Morocco's successful re-entry into the African Union has thrown a spanner in the works, especially with regards to what this means for the membership of Western Sahara.

The African Union's 50th-anniversary solemn declaration adopted by heads of state is clear on decolonisation and the Western Saharan question in particular: the AU seeks 'completion of the decolonisation process in Africa to protect the right to self-determination of African peoples still under colonial rule, solidarity with the people of African descent and in the Diaspora in their struggles against racial discrimination, and [to] resist all forms of influences contrary to the interests of the continent'. In the declaration, the AU 'reaffirm[s] of our call to end expeditiously the unlawful occupation of the Chagos Archipelago, the Comorian island of Mayotte and also reaffirm the right to self-determination of the people of Western Sahara, with a view to enable these countries and peoples to effectively exercise sovereignty over their respective territories'.[2] Consequently the AU has already committed itself to a process of self-determination for the people of Western Sahara. However, with Morocco's membership of the AU, the question of how this commitment will be fulfilled remains a conundrum.

Enhancing the Working Relationship Between the African Union and the United Nations

The Africa Group at the United Nations in New York plays a key role in promoting the relationship between the African Union and the United Nations. Promotion of common African positions at the UN is the area where the Africa Group has exercised agency in International Diplomacy. Common position on the UN Secretary General's High Level Independent Panel on Peace Operations (HIPPO), the common position on Peace Building Review and the common position on Sustainable Development Goals.

The relationship between the UN and the AU on issues of Peace and Security is work in progress. Although the United Nations charter states that the maintenance of International peace and security is a preserve of the United Nations Security Council, the charter under chapter 8 gives regional organisations like the African Union a role in maintenance of International peace and security. Despite this clear guidance from the UN charter, there is still contestation between the AU and the UN of which organisation has the mandate to act in what context.

Other concerns within the UN system about the African Union lead role include the potential for regional actors to be spoilers in ongoing peace operations. This view is dominant among Council members and UN Secretariat officials who base their concern on various reports of security council sanctions committees. Despite these concern the cooperation between the United Nations Security Council and African Union Peace and

Security Council has improved significant, the two councils hold bi-annual joint meetings in both New York and Addis Ababa. The African group in New York is the sounding board of both Councils, especially the three African members of the UN Security Council who regularly brief the whole group on developments in the Council.

The appointment of Donald Kaberuka, a former Rwandan finance minister and former president of the African Development Bank, as the high representative for the AU Peace Fund by the African Union chairperson in 2015 and his subsequent report to African Union Heads of States summit in Kigali, Rwanda, in July 2016 that proposed a 0.02 per cent levy on imports to finance African Union peacekeeping operations signalled Africa's willingness to fund 25 per cent of African Union-authorized peacekeeping operations, as agreed with key members of the United Nations Security – especially with the Obama administration.

The AU funding proposal is currently being considered by the UN system, specifically the UN Security Council and UN General Assembly. Indications are that these proposals will be subjected to scrutiny by the new United States administration that has proposed deep cuts in the UN peacekeeping budget. The role of the Africa group in New York will be key in lobbying key member states to support the AU proposal on funding peacekeeping operations, the European Union and the United states will subject the AU proposals to close scrutiny.

The UN system has for some time been concerned with the creation of a culture of dependency by regional organisations. This concern was flagged by the Security Council in its presidential statement of 26 October 2009, which explicitly stated that 'the Security Council reiterates that regional organisations have the responsibility to ensure human, financial, logistical and other resources for their organizations, including through contribution by their members and support from donors'.[3] Both the UN and the AU are financed by the same donors, which has led to competition for similar resources, with some key donors deciding to reduce contributions to both organisations.

The United Nations Security Council and African Union Peace and Security Council have attempted to coordinate their decision making processes, especially such that the Security Council can become more responsive to decisions taken by the Peace and Security Council. This has been complicated by fundamental differences in approaches to issues on their respective agendas. The African Union utilises preventive diplomacy as a conflict resolution tool, while the Security Council is more cautious, seeking to avoid meddling in internal affairs of sovereign states.

The African Union Peace and Security Council has on numerous occasions requested the United Nations Security Council to conduct joint missions in conflict areas, but these requests have been consistently rejected by the Security Council. Both councils have conducted separate field visits to conflict areas on the African continent. In a few instances, presidents of the UN Security Council have briefed the heads of AU observer missions at the UN prior to the Security Council field visits.

The two councils have fundamental differences when it comes to including a situation on their agendas. The AU Peace and Security Council stipulates that the inclusion of any item of the provisional agenda may not be opposed by a member state.[4] This contrasts with the heated contestation at the UN Security Council through when it comes to securing agreement for discussing a new issue. The electoral crisis in Gabon was a case in point: it was easy for the Peace and Security to meet and issue a communiqué, whereas the Security Council could not issue a press statement because Gabon was not on Security Council agenda.

Another significant difference in the working methods of the two councils is the involvement of interested parties or parties to a conflict in their work. The protocol that established the AU Peace and Security Council stipulates that any member of the PSC that is party to a conflict or a situation under consideration by the PSC shall not participate either in the discussion or in the decision making process relating to that conflict or situation. Though such member shall be invited to present its case to the Peace and Security Council as appropriate, thereafter that member must withdraw from the proceedings.[5]

The working methods of the two councils differ on the participation of interested parties such as regional mechanisms and civil society in their meetings. The AU Peace and Security Council is encouraged under its own mandate to hold informal consultations with parties concerned by or interested in a conflict or situation related to discussions under the PSC's consideration.[6] The UN Security Council has no such flexibility in its rules of procedure – a source of constant complaint from the UN General Assembly.

Conclusion

The divisions in the Africa Group over the presence of the Saharawi Republic (Western Sahara) have been exacerbated by Morocco's re-admission to the African Union. Prior to Morocco's re-entry, tensions between the pro-Morocco and pro-Saharawi factions within the Africa Group undermined efforts to ensure the efficiency of the body. Despite its challenges, the Africa Group remains an important diplomatic tool for Africa on the global state at the United Nations. In the current global environment, with an inward looking United States administration and Brexit, a unified African voice especially at multilateral forums will promote Africa's agency in international diplomacy.

Notes

1. Adonia Ayebare, personal interview with Moussa Faki, the chairperson of the African Union (19 April 2017).
2. The African Union 50th anniversary solemn declaration (Addis Ababa: African Union, 2013).
3. UN Security Council, *Security Council resolution 2033 (2012) {Cooperation between the United Nations and regional and subregional organizations in maintaining international peace and security}* (12 January 2012), S/RES/2033.
4. *AU, Protocol Establishing the Peace and Security Council of the African Union* (Addis Ababa, 2002).
5. *Protocol Relating to the Establishment of the Peace and Security Council of the African Union.*
6. Ibid.

PART II

GOVERNANCE, SECURITY, AND DEVELOPMENT

CHAPTER 4

THE EVOLVING AFRICAN GOVERNANCE ARCHITECTURE

Khabele Matlosa

Africa has made considerable strides in marching towards democratic and participatory governance over the years, especially since the transformation of the Organisation of African Unity (OAU) into the African Union (AU) in 2001. Today, African leaders are convinced, more than ever before, that democratic governance and durable peace are a fundamental *sine qua non* for sustainable human development. All major OAU/AU normative frameworks bear testimony to this firm conviction by Africa's leaders including, among other things, the 1981 African Charter on Human and Peoples' Rights; the 2000 Solemn Declaration on the Conference on Security, Stability, Development and Cooperation in Africa (CSSDCA); the 2000 Constitutive Act of the African Union; the 2003 African Peer Review Mechanism (APRM); the 2007 African Charter on Democracy, Elections and Governance (ACDEG); the 50th Anniversary Solemn Declaration on Pan-Africanism and African Renaissance' and the 2013 *Agenda 2063 – The Africa We Want*.

Two vivid examples will suffice at this stage to illustrate the commitment of African states to democratic, participatory and developmental governance. African leaders proclaimed in the

50th Anniversary Declaration their 'determination to anchor [African] societies, governments and institutions on the respect for the rule of law, human rights and dignity, popular participation, the management of diversity, as well as inclusion and democracy'.[1] In the same declaration, Africa's leaders affirmed their determination to achieve the goal of 'a conflict-free Africa, to make peace a reality ... and to rid the continent of wars, civil conflicts, human rights violations, humanitarian disasters and violent conflicts and to prevent genocide'.[2] Consistent with these commitments, the 2013 *Agenda 2063 – The Africa We Want* has two of its seven aspirations that are complementary, both of which resonate with the commitment to democratic, participatory and developmental governance anchored on peace and political stability.

Aspiration 3 of *Agenda 2063* envisions an 'Africa of good governance, democracy, respect for human rights, justice and the rule of law'.[3] This is the key objective pursued through the African Governance Architecture (AGA). Aspiration 4 envisions a 'peaceful and secure Africa'.[4] This is the key objective of the African Peace and Security Architecture (APSA), especially in pursuit of one of the flagship projects of *Agenda 2063* on ending all wars and silencing guns in Africa by the year 2020. It is worth noting that both aspirations 3 and 4 of *Agenda 2063* resonate with the ideals of the 2030 global agenda on sustainable development, especially Sustainable Development Goal (SDG) 16.

SDG 16 aims at promoting 'peaceful and inclusive societies for sustainable development, provide access to justice for all and build effective, accountable and inclusive institutions at all levels'.[5] These illustrations demonstrate that Africa is quite advanced in developing normative frameworks for entrenching a culture of democracy and peace. Be that as it may, developing democracy, governance and peace and security norms is one thing (the easier task), while their effective implementation at national level is yet another (the difficult task).

In respect of the evolution of norms on democracy and governance in Africa, history is the best teacher. Upon independence in the late 1950s and early 1960s, foundations for democratic governance in Africa were very weak, largely because colonialism was premised upon militarism, exploitation, coercion and domination. In the immediate aftermath of colonial rule, most African countries were governed by non-democratic regimes. Few countries operated multi-party systems predicated upon regular elections. Impunity and rampant corruption were the order of the day in many countries. Few embraced a culture of constitutionalism, rule of law and human rights. Inter-state conflicts were prevalent, most of them propelled by the Cold War. The OAU embraced the doctrine of non-interference in internal affairs of member states.

But in the post-Cold War era, which began in the late 1980s and early 1990s, a political sea-change has been under way in Africa. Since the end of the Cold War, more countries have begun embracing multi-party systems of governance. Multi-party elections have replaced military coups. In a word, increasingly ballots are replacing bullets as a method of power transfer. Although corruption is still rife, efforts are under way to curb this political cancer. Today, impunity is scorned upon as citizens constantly demand accountability from the leaders, and leaders themselves hold each other mutually accountable, for instance through the African Peer Review Mechanism. Most African countries have embraced a culture of constitutionalism, rule of law and human rights. The AU has undergone a paradigm shift from the old OAU doctrine of non-interference to the new doctrine of non-indifference to human rights abuses, mass atrocities and crimes against humanity within its member states.

This is the context within which the African Governance Architecture was established in 2010. Following these prefatory remarks, this chapter is organised into six sections.

The next section provides a conceptual-cum-theoretical discussion around governance in Africa. It is followed by a section that sets the historical context to the current state of democratic, participatory and developmental governance in Africa. The historical context is followed by a discussion of the origins and evolution of the African Governance Architecture. This is followed by a review of the operationalisation of AGA, and then analytic insights into the synergy between the AGA and the African Peace and Security Architecture. Next, complementarity between the AGA and the New Partnership for Africa's Development (NEPAD) is examined. The conclusion synthesises the debate and recaps the main findings of the chapter.

Conception/Theory of Governance in Africa

For Africa to achieve the noble goals of both *Agenda 2063 – The Africa We Want* and the 2030 global agenda for sustainable development, it must be governed in a democratic, participatory and accountable manner. This is how central governance is to Africa's integration and development agenda. To be sure, democracy and governance are pre-requisites for peace and security in Africa and vice versa. Both democracy and governance and peace and security are a *conditio sine qua non* for socio-economic development and structural transformation of the African continent. The reverse is also true: inclusive and equitable socio-economic development provides an environment conducive to durable peace and sustainable democratic governance. Be that as it may, governance neither is a new concept nor is it devoid of controversy. Since the late 1980s, when governance as a concept became in vogue, it has assumed three distinctive characterisations.

First, the concept was initially popularised in Africa by the World Bank in the late 1980s within the context of the structural adjustment programmes (SAPs) through which the Bank (together with its companion institution, the International Monetary Fund (IMF)) imposed austere macro-economic policies purportedly aimed at addressing the 'crisis of governance' in Africa. It is worth recalling that the World Bank's SAPs cost the continent two 'lost decades' of development (1980s and 1990s).

The World Bank prefers the notion of 'good governance', a codename for sound macro-economic management, effective institutions and rules that guarantee civil liberties and freedoms, private property, eradication of corruption, rule of law and sound economic policies.[6] In 1989 the World Bank published a report titled 'Sub-Saharan Africa: From Crisis to Sustainable Growth', defining the concept of 'governance' in a rather narrow and technocratic fashion simply as 'the exercise of political power to manage a nation's affairs'.

According to the Bank, 'in Africa, rent-seeking behaviour by political elites, fueled by flows of foreign aid, has undermined governmental effectiveness ... Hence the Bank has taken a technocratic approach, aiming at governance reforms and the encouragement of economic growth, rather than democratic politics ... [I]ts ... governance programme concentrates on reducing the size of government, privatising parastatal agencies, and improving the administration of aid funds'.[7] Thus for the World Bank, governance is all about governmental effectiveness for economic growth, down-sizing the state, privatising state institutions, fighting corruption and the like. In the Bank's conception, governance is a technical and depoliticised process aimed at achieving growth. Thus, the World Bank's definition of governance is narrow in that it is merely proceduralist. It reduces governance to technicalities of managing national affairs and fighting corruption.

Second, just a year after the World Bank published the report, the Ford Foundation, in its annual report of 1990, expanded the definition of governance beyond the narrow and technocratic conception of the Bank. The foundation conceived of governance as 'rooted in the belief that effective government depends on the legitimacy derived from broad-based participation, fairness, and accountability ... [strengthening] democratic institutions ... participation of disadvantaged groups ... public services responsive to the needs of the poor'.[8] The Ford Foundation's ideation of governance brought politics back in by emphasising issues of legitimacy, participation, accountability, responsiveness and strong democratic institutions. This contribution brought people to the centre of governance. Governance is the heart of politics and thus cannot be perceived as merely a technocratic issue confined to sheer management of national affairs and fighting corruption per se. The Ford Foundation's definition of governance is more substantive and political than the Bank's definition. It links governance more to citizens than does the Bank's ideation, which links governance to economic growth.

Third, seven years following the Ford Foundation's report, the United Nations Development Programme (UNDP) published a discussion paper titled 'Reconceptualising Governance', defining the concept as 'the exercise of political, economic and administrative authority to manage a nation's affairs. It is the complex mechanisms, processes, relationships and institutions through which citizens and groups articulate their interests, exercise their rights and obligations and mediate their differences. Effective democratic forms of governance rely on public participation, accountability and transparency'.[9] More than the World Bank and the Ford Foundation, it was the UNDP that placed emphasis on the need for governance to be democratic throughout all its three main realms: the state, civil society and the private sector. Furthermore, the UNDP moved the governance conceptualisation by linking it to sustainable human development. Sustainable human development not only transcends mere economic growth, but also links development directly to the people by emphasising the value of longevity of life, health and education. The distinctive contribution of the UNDP to the governance discourse is surely in the link between governance to development and through development to the people's livelihoods.

Democratic governance matters a great deal for socio-economic development and structural transformation in Africa. The UNDP's *Human Development Report* of 2002, with its focus on deepening democracy in fragmented societies, confirms this truism. Re-affirming the UNDP's definition of governance, this report proclaims that governance is all about institutions, rules and political processes that determine whether economies grow, children go to school and human development happens. Thus, 'promoting human development is not just a social, economic and technological challenge: it is also an institutional and political challenge'.[10] Development failure, in a big way, reflects governance failure, given that weak governance is primarily responsible for persistent poverty, extreme inequality, massive unemployment and devastating marginalisation and exclusion of disadvantaged social groups such as women, children, youth, people with disabilities and minorities. Governance deficits often manifest in widespread corruption, inefficient and ineffective public service, intra-state and inter-state conflicts, abuse of human rights and mismanagement of diversity. Thus, promoting democratic governance presupposes advancing some key principles of democracy including transparency, participation, accountability, responsiveness, rule of law, justice, dignity, fairness, equity, equality, consensus, human rights, gender equality, youth empowerment, equitable resource distribution, combating corruption and the like.[11] To be sure, democratic governance is not just about institutions, rules and political processes per se. It is also about citizen empowerment to ensure that state institutions and rules are accountable and responsive to citizens' needs, aspirations and demands. Thus, the UNDP sums up the meaning of democratic governance for sustainable human development aptly and succinctly as follows:

- People's human rights and fundamental freedoms are respected, allowing them to live with dignity;
- People have a say in decisions that affect their lives;
- People can hold decision makers accountable;
- Inclusive and fair rules, institutions and practices govern social interactions;
- Women are equal with men in private and public spheres of life and decision making;
- People are free from discrimination based on race, ethnicity, class, gender or any other attribute;
- The needs of future generations are reflected in current policies; and
- Economic and social policies aimed at eradicating poverty and expanding the choices that all people have in their lives.[12]

This is how the UNDP links democratic governance with sustainable human development. But democratic governance also links to durable peace. Weak institutions, rules, systems, values and practices are a breeding ground for the political instability that leads to intra-state and inter-state violent conflicts and wars. While inter-state conflicts marked the African continent during the Cold War era, these conflicts have subsided substantially in the post–Cold War epoch. However, the decline of inter-state wars has been replaced by the increased incidence of violent intra-state conflicts, some of which also have cross-border regional dimensions. Most Africa's intra-state conflicts today have at their root governance deficits. This means that democratic governance has a direct correlation with peace and security, much the same way it does with socio-economic development. Both democratic governance and peace are key pre-requisites for sustainable human development. Conversely, sustainable human development creates a conducive environment for nurturing democratic governance and building peaceful societies. In its pursuit of *Agenda 2063* and the 2030 global agenda on sustainable development, the African Union advances a three-pronged idea of a democratically governed, secure and peaceful and prosperous Africa.

Historical Context

Upon independence, the internal and external environment for the pursuit of democratic and participatory governance in Africa was inauspicious.[13] Undoubtedly, colonialism in Africa was an authoritarian and militaristic type of governance. Thus, independent Africa lacked the institutional and politico-cultural foundations to anchor democratic and participatory governance. This is not surprising, given that colonialists did not have any interest in democratising the colonies. Their main interest was to maintain stability and law and order for the sole purpose of maximum exploitation of Africa's natural resources for the benefit of Europe; hence Europe's socio-economic development became a perfect corollary of Africa's under-development. Colonial exploitation was largely achieved through repressive legislation, oppressive policies and divide-and-rule strategies. Furthermore, from the onset, independent Africa became a theatre of various wars and instability marked by both exogenous factors (e.g. the Cold War) and endogenous factors (inter-state and intra-state conflict) for the larger part of its post-independence existence. The Cold War was an imposed war on Africa involving the then-major global superpowers – the United States and the Soviet Union.

With the collapse of the Cold War and apartheid during the late 1980s and early 1990s, Africa's internal and external environment changed for the better in respect of its governance trajectory. Large-scale democratisation in Africa has a relatively short history whose momentum intensified in the late 1980s and early 1990s. It is essentially a post-Cold War and post-apartheid phenomenon that emerged as part of what Samuel Huntington calls the 'third wave of democratization' on a global scale.[14] Global and continental dynamics have had a strong bearing on approaches of the Organisation of African Unity and its successor, the African Union, towards democracy and governance on the continent.

During the heyday of the Organisation of African Unity, between 1963 and 1999, the continental inter-governmental body focused heavily on the liberation of African states and peoples from colonial domination. The decolonisation of the continent and political liberation were completed with the freedom of South Africa (the last bastion of colonial and settler domination) in 1994. It is worth noting that today the only major outstanding issue of self-determination is the Western Sahara, which remains under occupation, oppression and exploitation by Morocco. The Western Sahara issue is the main reason why Morocco pulled out of the OAU. The OAU recognised the Saharawi Arab Democratic Republic and admitted it into its fold, with 23 members voting in favour.[15]

The OAU pursued five main goals: promote the unity and solidarity of African states; coordinate and intensify their cooperation and efforts to achieve a better life for the peoples of Africa; defend the sovereignty, territorial integrity and independence of African states; eradicate all forms of colonialism from Africa; and promote international cooperation, having due regard to the Charter of the United Nations and the Universal Declaration of Human Rights.[16] Despite the numerous challenges it faced, the OAU pursued these objectives and registered major achievements, especially in ensuring the completion of the continent's decolonisation. Besides its contribution to decolonisation and political liberation of the continent, the OAU also played a key role in preventing major internal conflicts in Africa, including the Algeria–Morocco border war of 1963, the Ethiopia–Eritrea border dispute of the late 1990s, and the crisis in the Comoros in the late 1990s and early 2000s.[17] Given its doctrine of non-interference in the internal affairs of its member states, codified through the 1964 Cairo Declaration on the sanctity of colonial boundaries, the OAU was constrained in advancing democratisation and a culture of human rights. This declaration and the doctrine of non-interference reinforced narrow national sovereignty, which, left on its own, could hamper efforts towards continental unity and integration.

The OAU was transformed into the African Union in 2001 and officially launched in Durban, South Africa, on 9 July 2002. Now comprising 54 member states, the AU has a much broader mandate compared to the OAU. Beyond decolonisation and liberation, the AU pursues a three-pronged continental agenda including democracy and governance, peace and security and socio-economic development and structural transformation, all geared towards continental unity and integration. The 2000 Constitutive Act sets out the key objectives of the AU, which, while ensuring continuity from the OAU, also go a long way in introducing a new dynamic for continental integration in Africa. The AU's new doctrine of non-indifference to abuse of human rights within member states places democratisation at the centre of its major priorities. This new doctrine also empowers the AU to intervene within its member states in cases of grave circumstances including massive human rights abuses, crimes against humanity and genocide, in line with Article 4(h) of the Constitutive Act. Thus, the AU, in contrast with the OAU, is better poised to advance democratic and participatory governance in Africa. With the collapse of the Cold War and apartheid, authoritarian governance is no longer attractive. Besides, African citizens have actively demanded more legitimate, accountable, responsive and transparent governance since the onset of the third wave of democratisation. Ideally, for the notion of non-indifference to be implemented more effectively, two important pre-conditions are required:

a paradigm shift from narrow national sovereignty to pooled sovereignty; and gradual evolution of the AU from a mere inter-governmental body into a supra-national entity.

Within the context of *Agenda 2063 – The Africa We Want*, the AU is pursuing the agenda of peace and security, democracy and governance and socio-economic development and structural transformation, with greater impetus and resolve compared to its predecessor, the OAU, which as mentioned was constrained by a plethora of both internal factors (including inter-state and intra-state conflicts) and external factors (including the Cold War). It is during the current AU era that several organs and institutions mandated to promote democratisation were established, including the Pan-African Parliament (PAP); the Economic, Social and Cultural Council (ECOSOCC); the AU Board on Corruption; the African Committee on the Rights and Welfare of the Child; and the African Court on Human and Peoples' Rights. Although the African Court on Human and Peoples' Rights was established in 1986, it has become much more dynamic during the AU era of non-indifference. To reinforce the work of these institutions with a clear mandate on democracy, governance and human rights in Africa, currently three architectures have been put in place to drive the AU's three-pronged integration agenda. These are the African Peace and Security Architecture (APSA), the African Governance Architecture (AGA) and the New Partnership for Africa's Development (NEPAD) and the latter's governance offshoot, the African Peer Review Mechanism. The APSA is a coordination mechanism for advancing peace and security on the continent; the AGA is meant to advance the continent's democracy and governance agenda; and NEPAD and the APRM are aimed at promoting the continent's socio-economic development under conditions of democracy, peace and political stability. While the AU has put in place the normative framework and institutional architecture for advancing democratic and participatory governance in Africa, the challenge is to translate these norms into policy practice that affects lives of ordinary Africans in a positive manner.

The African Governance Architecture (AGA): Origins and Evolution

The historical evolution of the AGA is traceable to both internal and external political developments that have occurred since the end of the Cold War and collapse of apartheid in South Africa, and the embrace of democratic governance worldwide. The combination of democratisation and the peace dividend following the demise of Cold War and apartheid created an auspicious environment for the OAU/AU to explicitly craft its own governance initiative. Furthermore, the transition from non-interference to non-indifference accorded the AU space to address governance issues. The AGA therefore is traceable to the 2009–12 Strategic Plan of the African Union Commission (AUC), which introduced, as one of the pillars of the AU Agenda for continental unity and integration, the notion of shared values. Through its shared values pillar, the AUC committed itself to achieve participatory governance, democracy, human rights and a rights-based approach to development including social, economic, cultural and environmental rights. In this regard, based on existing institutions and organs, the AUC committed to promote and facilitate the establishment of an appropriate architecture for the promotion of democratic and participatory governance.

In January 2010, the 16th Ordinary Session of Executive Council recommended that the theme of the 2011 summit to focus on shared values in Africa, the putting in place of its Pan-African Architecture on Governance. On 2 February 2010, the 14th Ordinary Session of the AU Assembly endorsed this decision of the Executive Council by approving the theme of the 2011 summit devoted to shared values in Africa, the putting in place of the Pan-African Architecture on Governance.

During the same summit, the AU Assembly adopted yet
another important decision – 'Prevention of Unconstitutional
Changes of Government and Strengthening the Capacity of the
African Union to Manage Such Situations' – which, among
other things, implored all AU member states to sign, ratify,
domesticate and implement the African Charter on Democracy,
Governance and Elections as well as revitalise the mechanisms
for structural prevention of unconstitutional changes of
government. In the same decision, the Heads of State and
Government requested the AU's Peace and Security Council
(PSC) 'to examine regularly progress made in the democratisation processes, based on a report prepared by an independent
Rapporteur to be appointed by the Chairperson of the
Commission, who will be given the necessary support in
terms of personnel and expertise'.[18]

In January 2011, the 18th Ordinary Session of the Executive
Council adopted a decision[19] in which it endorsed the
strengthening of the African Governance Architecture through
the launch of the Governance Platform as a 'mechanism to
(a) foster the exchange of information; (b) facilitate the
elaboration of common positions on governance; [and]
(c) strengthen the capacity of Africa to speak with one
voice'. The same Executive Council decision also called for the
AUC to ensure greater synergy and coherence between the
African Governance Architecture and the African Peace and
Security Architecture.

The AU Assembly of January 2011 adopted a declaration on
the theme of the summit: 'Towards Greater Unity and
Integration Through Shared Values',[20] which re-affirmed the
importance of establishing the Pan-African Architecture on
Governance as a 'framework for dialogue between various
stakeholders'. In that declaration, African leaders re-affirmed
the need for the full implementation of all shared values
instruments, including the African Peer Review Mechanism
and relevant national plans. The declaration further called on

the AUC to ensure greater synergy between peace and security matters and governance and democracy by ensuring that developments in the terrain of shared values feature prominently in the Peace and Security Council. The declaration reiterated the importance of strengthening the African Governance Architecture and establishing the African Governance Platform as a 'basis for facilitating harmonization of instruments and coordination of initiatives in governance and democracy'. Consequently, the African Union Commission launched the African Governance Platform in Lusaka, Zambia, in June 2012. Significantly, the launch of the platform happened during the year declared by AU policy organs as the Year of Shared Values.

The year 2013 was declared by the AU policy organs as the Year of Pan-Africanism and African Renaissance to mark the 50th anniversary of the OAU/AU. Two important documents came out as part of the celebration of the Golden Jubilee of the OAU/AU: the 50th Anniversary Solemn Declaration and *Agenda 2063 – The Africa We Want*. Both documents re-affirmed the commitment of African leaders towards entrenchment of democratic, participatory, and developmental governance. The 50th Anniversary Solemn Declaration commits African leaders to 'anchor their societies, govern-ments and institutions on respect for the rule of law, human rights and dignity, popular participation, the management of diversity, as well as inclusion and democracy'.[21] To achieve this noble goal, African leaders committed themselves to:

- 'Strengthen democratic governance including through decentralised systems, the rule of law and capacities of our institutions to meet the aspirations of our people;
- Reiterate our rejection of unconstitutional change of government, including through any attempt to seize power by force but recognize the right of our people to peacefully express their will against oppressive systems;

- Promote integrity, fight against corruption in the management of public affairs and promote leadership that is committed to the interests of the people;
- Foster the participation of our people through democratic elections and ensure accountability and transparency.'[22]

Agenda 2063 places a major premium on democratic, participatory, and developmental governance for Africa to achieve sustainable socio-economic development and durable peace as vividly demonstrated by aspirations 3 and 4, which dovetail neatly into Sustainable Development Goal 16, as discussed earlier. The first ten-year implementation plan for *Agenda 2063* has already been developed, covering the period 2014–23, which means it is already in full swing. In fact, one of the flagship projects of *Agenda 2063* is silencing guns and ending all conflicts in Africa by 2020. In this regard, the success of *Agenda 2063* will be measured by the considerable reduction of protracted violent intra-state and inter-state conflicts in Africa by 2020. The operationalisation of the AGA is therefore critical for the effective implementation of *Agenda 2063*.

Operationalisation of the African Governance Architecture

The primary mandate of the African Governance Architecture is to advance the gains that Africa has made thus far in building democratic, participatory and developmental governance as an integral part of the AU vision of an integrated, united, prosperous, and peaceful continent driven by its citizens and playing a dynamic role in the international arena.[23] The specific objectives of the AGA include:

- Deepening popular participation and citizen engagement in democracy, governance and respect for human and peoples' rights;
- Promoting African shared values (AU norms and standards);
- Fostering effective implementation of decisions and norms of

the AU and member states on democracy, elections, human rights, good governance and humanitarian affairs;

- Deepening synergy, coordination and cooperation among AU organs, institutions and Africa's regional economic communities (RECs) on democracy, governance and human rights;
- Enhancing the capacity of AU and REC organs and institutions to support member states in strengthening governance and consolidating democracy;
- Facilitating monitoring and evaluation of compliance and implementation of AU norms on governance and democracy, review of state reports as envisaged by Article 49 of the African Charter on Democracy, Elections and Governance in Africa;
- Generating knowledge and data as well as communicating, sharing and disseminating comparable lessons and resources to improve governance and democracy in Africa; and
- Facilitating joint engagement in preventive diplomacy, conflict prevention and post-conflict reconstruction and development associated with governance challenges in Africa.

The AGA has four main components. First, the vision, norms and standards constitute the shared values pillar. This includes all the shared values instruments of the AU and the RECs aimed at promoting democratic and participatory governance on the continent. Particularly central to the evolution of the AGA is the 2007 African Charter on Democracy, Elections and Governance, which provides for the establishment of a mechanism to monitor its full implementation under the coordination of the African Union Commission.

Second, AU organs and institutions that constitute the African Governance Platform constitute the institutional pillar. These are all the AU organs with the democracy, governance and human rights mandate. They include the African Commission on Human and Peoples' Rights; the African Court on Human and Peoples' Rights; the Pan-African

Parliament; the African Peer Review Mechanism; the Economic, Social and Cultural Council; and the Peace and Security Council. Within the framework of the African Governance Platform, these institutions are supposed to work together and deliver as one on the AU democracy and governance mandate.

Third, the African Governance Platform constitutes the dialogue pillar. The platform is coordinated by the African Union Commission and its functions are to: evaluate mechanisms for the implementation of the African Charter on Democracy, Elections and Governance; facilitate harmonisation of instruments and coordinate initiatives in democracy and governance; convene the annual high-level dialogue on democracy, governance and human rights; enhance greater engagement and participation of African citizens including women, youth and civil society in all relevant initiatives of African Governance Platform members; and facilitate the establishment and operationalisation of the AGA clusters.

Fourth, and finally, the African governance facility or the governance fund constitutes the resource mobilisation pillar. Presently, the AU depends overwhelmingly on external sources of funding for its programmes. This situation is not sustainable. If the Union is to be more effective in driving its own democracy and governance programme, it needs to explore alternative sources of funding with emphasis on domestic mobilisation of resources, with external development partners simply complementing such efforts. The proposals on alternative sources of funding for the AU provide a glimmer of hope. Because of its recent decision, the AU has committed to continue funding 100 per cent of its operational costs, 75 per cent of all its programmes and 25 per cent of all its peacekeeping operations. Additionally, during the AU Summit held in Kigali, Rwanda in 2016, the AU policy organs have adopted a new policy introducing a 0.2 per cent levy on a selected import items as one of the alternative sources of financing the Union, with a view to reducing external dependency. It is within this framework of alternative sources of financing that the African Governance Facility is envisioned.

The AGA has five clusters. The public service, decentralisation, urbanisation, and human settlements cluster covers public service and administration, decentralisation and local governance, urban development and human settlements, combating corruption and natural resource governance. The democracy cluster covers election observation, technical support to election management bodies, support to political parties, civil society, media, parliaments and the like. The human rights and transitional justice cluster covers human rights promotion, protection and observance; advancing transitional justice in post-conflict situations; supporting national human rights institutions; human rights observation; and the like. The constitutionalism and rule of law cluster covers constitutional amendments; combating unconstitutional changes of government; inculcating a culture of constitutionalism; promoting rule of law; separation of powers/checks and balances; and supporting key rule-of-law institutions such as the police, judiciary, correctional services, and the like, as well as rule-of-law watchdog bodies such as the ombudsmen, auditors-general and anti-corruption bodies. The humanitarian assistance cluster deals with displacement of people due to either natural disasters, large-scale development projects or protracted violent conflicts. It covers support to refugees, internally displaced persons, returnees, stateless persons and the like. It also deals with aspects of migration, especially AU efforts towards free movement of persons on the continent whose vision is to strive towards a visa-free Africa and the introduction of the African Passport aimed at encouraging African citizenship within the framework of *Agenda 2063*. Besides these five clusters, there is a functioning AGA secretariat, based at the African Union Commission within the Department of Political Affairs that coordinates the work of clusters and supports the AGA bureau and its platform. All said and done, the effective operationalisation of the African Governance Architecture requires its synergy with African Peace and Security Architecture.

Synergy Between the African Governance and Peace and Security Architectures

The strategic value of the African Governance Architecture is its main mandate of structural prevention of conflict in Africa, with focus on strengthening an effective, accountable and responsive state. For the AGA to be effective, it needs to work in complementarity with the APSA, especially in conflict prevention, conflict management and conflict transformation. It is now becoming abundantly evident that the major challenges for continental unity and integration in Africa are traceable to governance deficit, political instability and development failure. Thus, the AGA will not be successful in driving the AU democracy and governance agenda on its own. It must build synergies and complementarities with other AU architectures to make meaningful impact. The AGA has to develop strong synergies with the APSA with its five pillars: the Continental Early Warning System (CEWS), the Peace and Security Council, the Panel of the Wise, African Standby Force (ASF) and the Peace Fund. Opportunities for AGA-APSA synergy are greater within the context of the 2006 AU Post-Conflict Reconstruction and Development (PCRD) policy. The effective implementation of this policy presents a platform for synergy between the AGA and the APSA.

The PCRD policy is a comprehensive peacebuilding framework of the Union aimed at assisting member states and the regional economic communities to ensure sustainable peace and socio-economic development within the overall goal of continental unity, integration and prosperity. The key objective of the policy is to improve timeliness, effectiveness, efficiency and coordination of activities in post-conflict countries and to lay the foundation for social justice and sustainable peace. It aims to consolidate peace and prevent relapse into political violence; help address the root causes of conflict; encourage planning and implementation of post-conflict reconstruction activities; and enhance complementarities and coordination between and among diverse actors engaged in post-conflict reconstruction and development. The policy has six main pillars.

The PCRD's first pillar, on security, has as its key objective the creation of 'a secure and safe environment for the affected state and its population, through the re-establishment of the architecture of the state, including the elements of judicial statehood and controlled territory, responsible and accountable state control over the means of coercion and a population whose safety is guaranteed'.[24]

The PCRD's second pillar, on political governance and transition, aims at equitable distribution of power and authority, and establishing transformative and visionary leadership in countries emerging from protracted violent conflict, with a view to consolidating peace and deepening democratic governance. This involves, among other things, inclusive and participatory politics, political pluralism, building strong governance institutions, managing diversity constructively, promoting gender equality and inculcating a culture of constitutionalism and peaceful elections.

The PCRD's third pillar, on human rights, justice and reconciliation, focuses on the protection and promotion of human rights, given that 'human rights abuses in the form of policies of marginalisation, identity-based discrimination and perceptions of injustice can trigger or perpetuate conflicts'.[25] This pillar also emphasises the importance of balancing restorative with retributive justice and implores AU member states to 'allow for opportunities to invoke traditional mechanisms of reconciliation and/or justice, to the extent that they are aligned to the African Charter on Human and People's Rights'.[26]

The PCRD's fourth pillar, on humanitarian/emergency assistance, focuses on dealing with forced displacement and other consequences of violent conflict. These include redressing the plight of refugees, returnees, ex-combatants, internally displaced persons and other war-affected populations, especially women and children.

The PCRD's fifth pillar, on reconstruction and socio-economic development, aims at placing post-conflict countries on a sustainable path for socio-economic development. It aims to integrate emergency relief (short-term relief) with sustainable human development (long-term rehabilitation). Its principal aim is to 're-orient ... the war economy for peaceful ends and promote reconstruction and modernisation of infrastructure and the economy. And because [socio-economic] inequalities are often ... the root causes of conflicts, sustainable peace must be based on fair and equitable distribution of resources'.[27]

The sixth and final PCRD pillar, focusing on gender equality, recognises that in situations of violent conflict, men and women are affected disproportionately. Often, women and girls suffer more from political violence than do men and boys. Theirs becomes a double jeopardy: women and girls are already marginalised by patriarchal ideology even in times of peace, a situation aggravated during war when cases of gender-based violence intensify as protagonists consider rape as war by other means.

To be sure, the synergy between the African Governance Architecture and the African Peace and Security Architecture is only part of the story. The other part relates to the complementarity between the AGA and the AU's development architecture, especially the New Partnership for Africa's Development. The AGA does not have to complement

NEPAD in all its programmes. In like manner, NEPAD does not have to complement the AGA in all its five clusters. The most appropriate platform for seamless synergy between the AGA and NEPAD is the African Peer Review Mechanism.

Complementarity Between the AGA and NEPAD

NEPAD was launched in 2001 in Lusaka, Zambia, as a continental development blueprint of the OAU. NEPAD came about against the backdrop of the 1980 Lagos Plan of Action and within the context of the 1991 Treaty Establishing the African Economic Community (commonly known as Abuja Treaty). NEPAD was pioneered by five African states: Algeria, Egypt, Nigeria, Senegal and South Africa. Just like the Abuja Treaty, the NEPAD base document rightly states that conditions for Africa's development include peace, security, stability and democracy. NEPAD programming therefore involved the following:

- Peace and security initiatives;
- Democracy and political governance initiatives;
- Economic and corporate governance initiatives; and
- Sub-regional and regional approaches to development.[28]

During the inaugural AU Summit in Durban, South Africa, in 2002, the NEPAD Declaration on Democracy, Political, Economic and Corporate Governance was adopted. The declaration further commits AU member states to work together in policy and action in pursuit of the following objectives: democracy and good political governance; economic and corporate governance; socio-economic development; and the APRM. The following year, the APRM was established in Abuja, Nigeria. The APRM is a voluntary platform for self-assessment and peer review of governance policies, procedures and institutions by African Union member states aimed at institutionalising and consolidating democratic governance.[29]

A country that accedes to the APRM commits itself to being reviewed periodically in terms of its policy frameworks, institutional architecture, systemic setup and practices around four clusters of governance (known as 'thematic areas'): democracy and political governance; economic governance and management; corporate governance; and socio-economic development. Upon acceding to the APRM, a state commits itself to periodic reviews that are meant to take place every two to four years (although, in practice, this timetable has not been met and no country has completed a second review). Conversely, in some instances, participating NEPAD heads of state and government could be driven by signs of an impending socio-economic or political crisis or turmoil to call for a review in a given country 'in a spirit of helpfulness to the government concerned'.

For some years, the APRM experienced a hiatus that constrained its effectiveness due largely to internal institutional arrangements and external challenges related to political commitment of the APRM countries. Under the new leadership, with Eddie Maloka at the helm as the new chief executive officer, the APRM is currently undergoing internal reforms and revitalisation aimed at its 'restoration, reinvigoration, and renewal'.[30] As part of this revitalisation, the APRM is poised to play a very proactive role in both the African Governance Architecture and the African Peace and Security Architecture. The African Union policy organs have also made a firm decision that the APRM should be given an additional task to monitor and review implementation of both *Agenda 2063* and the 2030 global agenda for sustainable development. For the first time, the APRM has developed a five-year strategic plan, covering 2016–20, in which its focus will be on eight main areas: shared values advocacy and communication; review and implementation of the APRM core mandate;

resource mobilisation and financial management; human resource capacity development; development of monitoring and evaluation frameworks and systems; enhancement of research and development capacity and improvement of operational tools; intra-APRM coordination and harmonisation; and APRM integration into the AU, universal accession and enhanced support to Africa's integration agenda.[31]

In 2007, four years after the establishment of the APRM, the AU adopted the African Charter on Democracy, Elections and Governance, which came into force in February 2012 following its ratification by 15 AU member states. This year, 2017, therefore marks the tenth anniversary of the ACDEG since it was adopted. The charter is the expression of the commitment of the AU and its member states to nurture and consolidate democratic and participatory governance on the continent. The driving impetus for the development and adoption of the ACDEG is traceable to various instruments on democratic governance, constitutionalism, rule of law, human rights and elections that have evolved within the framework of the 1963 Charter Establishing the OAU and the 2000 Constitutive Act of the AU. So far, 47 AU member states have signed it, yet only 29 of these have ratified it.

The rationale behind, and justification for, the ACDEG is not difficult to understand.[32] First, for Africa to achieve the AU vision of unity, integration and prosperity, three important pillars for such success are peace, democracy and development. The charter proposes a framework that assists the AU in achieving these three goals simultaneously. Second, the ACDEG brings various previous OAU/AU commitments together in a consolidated and legally binding document, through which member states will build solid institutional and cultural foundations for sustainable democracy and durable peace. Third, the ACDEG was developed and adopted at a time when the scourge of military coups was threatening democratic gains and peace and security on the continent.

It is a much more robust response to unconstitutional changes of government in Africa. While the incidences of military coups have receded substantially, they remain a lingering democratic deficit in Africa, as witnessed by the 2009 military coup in Mauritania, the 2012 experiences of Mali (March) and Guinea-Bissau (May), and the 2013 unconstitutional change of government in the Central African Republic (CAR). Current developments taking place in Burundi since 2015 are a major cause for concern, including an abortive military coup, a perceived unconstitutional change of government, political violence, assassinations, massive forced displacement of Burundians within the country and refugee flows into neighbouring Rwanda, Tanzania, the Democratic Republic of the Congo (DRC) and Uganda. The ongoing civil war in Somalia and resurgence of civil war in South Sudan since 2013 constitute one of the stumbling blocks to continental efforts towards inculcating and entrenching a culture of democracy and peace. Fourth, a new challenge that has come to confront progress on the democratisation front in Africa is the manipulation of constitutions by incumbents to prolong their tenure in power, without recourse to their constitutionally defined popular mandates. The ACDEG warns against this trend, which if not reversed may become toxic for the nurturing and consolidation of democracy on the continent. The abortive manipulation of the constitution in Burkina Faso by former president Blaise Compaoré with a view to prolonging his tenure in office is one clear case in point. But the popular protests that blocked Compaoré from manipulating the constitution played a key role in forestalling this move. National efforts in protecting the Burkinabe constitution were mounted by the Economic Community of West African States (ECOWAS), the African Union and the United Nations, among others. Fifth, the ACDEG has emboldened the hand of the AU, through its Peace and Security Council, in dealing with all forms of unconstitutional change of government, including rebellions, such as the most recent one that toppled the government in the Central African Republic in March 2013. The CAR was subjected to sanctions by the AU until the country held its general election in 2016 aimed at restoring constitutional order following years of transition.

Conclusion

Like elsewhere in the world, building democratic, participatory and developmental governance in Africa remains work in progress. Democratic governance is always under construction, even in industrialised countries. Democratic governance is always in a state of flux: it is constructed, at times deconstructed, and other times reconstructed. It is never perfect. It experiences moments of progress, reversals, standstills, blockages and the like, at various historical stages. Nowhere in the world is there a fully constructed and consolidated democratic governance system, as such is simply utopia. In fact, the most vivid demonstration that democratic governance always undergoes construction, deconstruction and reconstruction is the current democratic reversals we are witnessing in industrialised countries in the form of the resurgence of populist ultra-nationalist politics triggered by inequality, poverty and unemployment and accentuated by global capitalism, which has benefited the small coterie of *nouveaux riches* while leaving the large majority of the poor wallowing in the deep sea of poverty. Democratic reversals occasioned by populist ultra-nationalist politics are well demonstrated by the ascendance of Donald Trump as the new president of the United States and the withdrawal of Britain from the European Union (commonly dubbed Brexit). Thus, building democratic governance is the hallmark of Africa's continuous political transition that ought to be marked by constant and continuous reforms. Through continuous reforms, democratic governance never becomes fully consolidated; it can only be nurtured and deepened. This is likely to remain so as the AU implements *Agenda 2063 – The Africa We Want* over the next 50 or so years and the 2030 global agenda on sustainable development over the next 15 or so years.

When Africa gained its independence, given the pre-occupation with nation state building, there was little focus on democratisation. In any case, colonialism did not build democracies, but rather authoritarianism, in Africa. The Cold War did not provide any incentives, but rather disincentives, towards democratisation in Africa. Understandably, therefore, the OAU focused its attention on peace and security issues and less on democracy and governance. The OAU did not prioritise democratisation, as its main concern was the decolonisation and liberation of the continent from colonial domination and exploitation – a mission accomplished with the liberation of South Africa in 1994, with today only Western Sahara still remaining under domination by another African country, Morocco, the only decolonisation agenda inherited by the AU from the OAU. It is under the auspices of the AU that the democratisation agenda has gathered momentum in Africa. Africa has jettisoned military rule. It has embraced multi-party democratic rule. The old OAU doctrine of non-interference in internal affairs of member states has been replaced by the new principle of non-indifference to human rights abuses within member states.

It is within this context that *Agenda 2063* has been developed. The political impetus for *Agenda 2063* was provided by the 50th Anniversary Declaration on Pan-Africanism and African Renaissance, adopted by African leaders in 2013. Both the 50th Anniversary Declaration and *Agenda 2063* place emphasis on building democratic, participatory and developmental governance in tandem with building peaceful and secure societies resilient to both internal and external shocks. The agenda recognises that democratic and participatory governance is a *condition sine qua non* for the realisation of its noble goals, starting with its first ten-year implementation plan, covering 2014–23. In addressing its own governance challenges, the African Union has conceived and established the African Governance Architecture and its Platform. This is an institutional mechanism for ensuring coordination in the implementation of the Union's democracy and governance mandate. It comprises norms and standards, institutions, a dialogue platform and a resource mobilisation facility. Its five clusters define the substantive content of the architecture and platform (governance, democracy, human rights, constitutionalism and humanitarian action). The emergence of the AGA is a vivid demonstration of the AU's efforts to change gear from a reactive mode in dealing with conflict and crisis on the continent and more and more towards a proactive mode emphasising early warning, early response, conflict prevention, mediation, dialogue and negotiations, all of which aim to balance concerns for hard state security with concerns for soft human security. The AU, through the AGA, is poised to invest much more in structural prevention of conflict without compromising on direct/operational prevention of conflict, given that structural prevention and operational prevention of conflict are mutually reinforcing. This is the critical meeting point between the AGA and the APSA: conflict prevention.

It is worth emphasising that dealing with both structural and operational/direct prevention of conflict requires the AU to ensure that the AGA is implemented in complementarity with the African Peace and Security Architecture, especially through the Post-Conflict Reconstruction and Development policy. Democracy cannot be sustained without durable peace. The PCRD presents a perfect platform for the synergy between the AGA and the APSA. But the AGA and the APSA also have to be synergised with the development architecture of the Union in the form of NEPAD, particularly through the

APRM. This is because democracy and peace are the necessary pre-requisites for sustainable socio-economic transformation as envisioned in *Agenda 2063*. The APRM presents a good entry point for the synergy among the AGA, the APSA and NEPAD. The complementarities among these three have to manifest at the continental level and cascade downward to the member-state level through the regional economic communities. In the final analysis, for the AGA, the APSA, NEPAD and the APRM to work in harmony and deliver desirable results at the national level, three major factors are required: robust and effective institutions, visionary and transformative leadership and vibrant citizen engagement and popular participation ensuring that marginalised segments of society, especially women, youth and minorities, among many others, are adequately represented in decision making structures at all levels of governance.

Notes

1. African Union (AU), *The 50th Anniversary Declaration on Pan-Africanism and African Renaissance* (Addis Ababa, March 2013), p. 5.
2. Ibid., p. 5.
3. AU, *Agenda 2063 – The Africa We Want* (Addis Ababa, 2015), p. 2.
4. AU, *Agenda 2063*, p. 2.
5. United Nations (UN), *Transforming Our World: The 2030 Agenda for Sustainable Development*, General Assembly Resolution 70/1 (New York, 2015), p. 14.
6. Muna Ndulo and Mamoudou Gazibo (eds), *Growing Democracy in Africa: Elections, Accountable Governance, and Political Economy* (Cambridge: Cambridge Scholars Publishing, 2016).
7. Michael Bratton and Donald Rothchild, 'The Institutional Basis of Governance in Africa', in Goran Hyden and Michael Bratton (eds), *Governance and Politics in Africa* (Boulder: Rienner, 1992), p. 265.
8. Bratton and Rothchild, 'The Institutional Basis of Governance in Africa', p. 265.
9. United Nations Development Programme (UNDP), 'Reconceptualising Governance', Discussion Paper no. 2 (New York, January, 1997), p. 9.
10. UNDP, *Deepening Democracy in a Fragmented World: Human Development Report* (Oxford: Oxford University Press, 2002), p. 65.
11. See David A. Booth and Diana R. Cammack, *Governance for Development in Africa* (London: Zed, 2013), p. 9.

12. UNDP, *Deepening Democracy in a Fragmented World*, p. 65.
13. Khabele Matlosa, 'Pan-Africanism, the APRM, and the ACDEG: What Lies Ahead?', in Steven Grudz and Yarik Turianskyi (eds), *African Accountability: What Works and What Doesn't* (Johannesburg: South African Institute for International Affairs, 2015), pp. 8–38.
14. S. Huntington, *The Third Wave: Democratization in the Late Twentieth Century* (Norman, OK: University of Oklahoma Press, 1991).
15. Olayiwola Abegunrin, *Africa in Global Politics in the Twenty-First Century: A Pan-African Perspective* (New York: Palgrave Macmillan, 2009), p. 149.
16. Organisation of African Unity (OAU), *The OAU Charter* (Addis Ababa, 1963), p. 3.
17. Musifiky Mwanasali, 'From Non-Interference to Non-Indifference: The Emerging Doctrine of Conflict Prevention in Africa', in John Akokpari, Angela Ndinga-Muvumba and Tim Murithi (eds), *The African Union and Its Institutions* (Johannesburg: Fanele, 2008), p. 46.
18. AU, 'Decision on the Prevention of Unconstitutional Changes of Government and Strengthening the Capacity of the African Union to Manage Such Situations', Assembly/AU/Dec.269(XIV) (Addis Ababa, 2010), p. 3.
19. AU, 'Executive Council Decision on the Report of Member States Experts Consultations on the Theme of the Sixteenth Ordinary AU Assembly "Towards Greater Unity and Integration Through Shared Values"', EX.CL/Dec.635(XVIII) (Addis Ababa, January 2011).
20. AU, 'Declaration on the theme of the Summit: Towards Greater Unity and Integration Through Shared Values', Assembly/AU/Dec.1(XVI) (Addis Ababa, January 2011).
21. AU, *The 50th Anniversary Declaration*, p. 5.
22. Ibid., p. 6.
23. See also George M. Wachira, 'Consolidating the African Governance Architecture', in Steven Grudz and Yarik Turianskyi, *African Accountability*, pp. 39–44.
24. AU, 'African Union Policy on Post-Conflict Reconstruction and Development' (Addis Ababa, 2006), p. 8.
25. Ibid., p. 14.
26. Ibid., p. 15.
27. Ibid., p. 18.
28. See Matlosa, 'Pan-Africanism, the APRM, and the ACDEG', p. 19.
29. African Peer Review Mechanism (APRM) Secretariat, *Strategic Plan, 2016–2020* (Midrand, 2016), p. 1.
30. APRM Secretariat, *Strategic Plan*, p. 1.
31. Ibid., p. 3.
32. See Matlosa, 'Pan-Africanism, the APRM, and the ACDEG', p. 23.

CHAPTER 5

THE AFRICAN UNION: REGIONAL AND GLOBAL CHALLENGES

Hesphina Rukato

This chapter explores how the Addis Ababa-based African Union Commission (AUC) can be capacitated to drive the agenda of the Union more effectively. To do so effectively, it is important consider the following:

- The mission of the AU, as articulated in its Constitutive Act of 2000, with a historical reflection on its predecessor, the Organisation of African Unity (OAU).
- The functions of the AUC as articulated in the Statutes of the AUC of 2002.
- Other organs of the AU, and the role of the AUC in their work.
- The functions of the AUC chairperson, deputy chairperson, commissioners and other staff members, and the manner in which they are elected and recruited.
- The funding of the AU in the context of the Statutes of the Commission.
- The working definition of capacity (capacity to do what?), as well as current capacity challenges.

Mission of the African Union

The launch of the African Union in 2002 presented the dawn of a new era in Africa. It was a demonstration of the leadership of the time to ensure that Africans took responsibility for their destiny. The launch was followed from 2003 onwards by the establishment of the organs of the AU. The launch of the New Partnership for Africa's Development (NEPAD) in 2001, with its far-reaching promises of sustainable development, good governance and economic development, added to the euphoria that accompanied the launch of the AU. The AU Commission started its work in 2003.

The 14 objectives of the African Union are set out in Article 3 of the AU's Constitutive Act of 2000, as outlined in Table 5.1.

Article 4 of the Constitutive Act outlines 16 principles aimed at guiding the African Union in its work, including:

- Sovereign equality and interdependence among member states.
- Peaceful resolution of conflicts among member states.
- Respect for borders as they exist upon a country's achievement of independence.
- Participation of the African peoples in the activities of the Union.
- Establishment of a common defence policy for the African continent.
- Respect for democratic principles, human rights, rule of law and good governance.
- Promotion of gender equality.
- Rejection of unconstitutional changes of power.

The objectives of the Constitutive Act are many, given the many needs and aspirations of the continent at the time the act was adopted in 2001. However, a decade-and-a-half since the inception of the AU, it is becoming increasingly clear that there

Table 5.1 Objectives of the African Union

1. Achieve greater unity and solidarity between the African countries and the peoples of Africa.
2. Defend the sovereignty, territorial integrity and independence of its member states.
3. Accelerate the political and socio-economic integration of the continent.
4. Promote and defend African common positions on issues of interest to the continent and its peoples.
5. Encourage international cooperation, taking due account of the Charter of the United Nations (UN) and the Universal Declaration of Human Rights (UDHR).
6. Promote peace, security and stability on the continent.
7. Promote democratic principles and institutions, popular participation and good governance.
8. Promote and protect human rights in accordance with the African Charter on Human and Peoples' Rights and other relevant human rights instruments.
9. Establish the necessary conditions to enable the continent to play its rightful role in the global economy and in international negotiations.
10. Promote sustainable development at the economic, social and cultural levels as well as the integration of African economies.
11. Promote cooperation in all fields of human activity to raise the living standards of African peoples.
12. Coordinate and harmonise the policies between the continent's existing and future regional economic communities (RECs) for the gradual attainment of the objectives of the African Union.
13. Advance development of the continent by promoting research in all fields, particularly science and technology.
14. Work with relevant international partners to eradicate preventable diseases and promote good health on the continent.

Source: Adapted from Article 3 of the AU's Constitutive Act of 2000.

needs to be better prioritisation, implementation and coordination of activities if the AU is to succeed in achieving its mission.

A critical area in the achievement of the AU's mission is its institutional architecture. Are the AU's institutions, especially its Commission – as the secretariat of the Union – configured to effectively deliver on the AU's mission? Is there appropriate coordination and complementarity between the Commission and these institutions? Is there rivalry and competition?

Institutions of the African Union

The central location of the AUC in the Union's institutional milieu has implications for what the Commission can do, and how it does it. Article 1 of the AU's Constitutive Act spells out the nine organs of the Union:

(1) Assembly of the Union
(2) Executive Council
(3) Pan-African Parliament (PAP)
(4) Court of Justice
(5) African Union Commission
(6) Permanent Representatives Committee (PRC)
(7) The Specialised Technical Committees
(8) Economic, Social and Cultural Council (ECOSOCC)
(9) The Financial Institutions

Each of these organs has specific roles and responsibilities with respect to the overall mission of the Union. With respect to the AUC, Article 20 of the Constitutive Act says merely the following:

(1) There shall be established a Commission of the Union, which shall be the Secretariat of the Union.
(2) The Commission shall be composed of the Chairman, his or her deputy or deputies and the commissioners. They shall

be assisted by the necessary staff for the smooth functioning of the Commission.

(3) The structure, functions and regulations of the Commission shall be determined by the Assembly.

The functions of the Commission are outlined in the 2002 Statutes of the Commission, with the general provision that: 'The Commission shall be the Secretariat of the Union and shall act as such in conformity with Articles 5 and 20 of the Constitutive Act'.[1]

The AU Commission

Functions

Broadly the Commission is mandated to carry out the functions assigned to it under the Constitutive Act (including the functions specified in the protocols to the act), as well as facilitating the implementation of the decisions of the AU Assembly. More specifically, the Commission must adhere to a list has of more than 30 'shalls', ranging from representing the African Union and defending its interests, to 'implementing decisions taken by other organs, acting as the 'custodian of the Constitutive Act, its protocols, treaties, legal instruments, as well as decisions adopted by the Union and those inherited from the OAU',[2] to coordinating and monitoring implementation of the decisions of other organs of the Union in collaboration with the PRC and the Executive Council. For a detailed list of these functions, see Appendix 1 of this chapter.

Obligations

Article 4 of the Statutes spells out the obligations of Commission members and staff, stipulating that they 'shall not seek or receive instructions from any government or other authority external to the Union'. Commissioners and staff are also required to act in ways that do not bring the Commission into disrepute. They may not engage in any other occupation. A breach of these obligations may result in disciplinary measures being applied. Member States are obliged to 'respect the exclusive character of the responsibilities of the Members of the Commission and the other staff, and shall not influence or seek to influence them in the discharge of their responsibilities'.[3]

Election of Members

Another process that is critical to the functioning and performance of the Commission is the election its members. The Statutes specify that election of Commission members be governed by the procedural rules of the Assembly, the Executive Council and the Statutes; that the region from which the chairperson and the deputy chairperson are appointed be entitled to one commissioner each, with all other regions entitled to two commissioners; and that at least one commissioner from each region be a woman.[4]

Functions and Responsibilities of the Chairperson

Article 7 of the Statutes deals with the functions and responsibilities of the Commission chairperson, who is the chief executive officer of the Commission and is directly responsible to the Executive Council. The chairperson is the legal representative of the African Union (but not the Commission itself), and is the accounting officer of the Commission.[5]

Article 8 stipulates the functions of the chairperson, of which there are 26. These include chairing meetings of the Commission; promoting and popularising the objectives of the African Union; building relations with other organisations; participating in and keeping records of Assembly deliberations; preparing budgets and financial reports; assuming overall responsibility for the administration and finances of the Commission; liaising closely with the organs of the African Union to guide, support and monitor its performance to ensure conformity and harmony with agreed policies, strategies, programmes and projects; and carrying out other functions as may be determined by the Assembly or Executive Council. The chairperson may delegate any of his or her functions to the deputy chairperson of the Commission.[6] For a detailed list of the functions of the chairperson, see Appendix 2 to this chapter.

Functions of the Deputy Chairperson

Article 9 of the Statutes stipulates the functions of the deputy chairperson of the Commission, who is accountable to the chairperson in the discharge of the chairperson's duties. In addition, the functions of the deputy chairperson include assisting in the discharge of any other functions delegated by the chairperson; overseeing the administration and finance of the Commission; and acting as chairperson in the absence of the chairperson, including temporary incapacity or death (in the case of death, a commissioner may act in capacity of the deputy chairperson, after consultation with the chairperson of the African Union).[7]

The Commissioners

The commissioners are responsible for implementation of all decisions and programmes in the portfolios they are elected into. All commissioners are accountable to the chairperson. The Commission comprises eight portfolios:

(1) Peace and security (conflict prevention, management, and resolution, combating terrorism etc.).
(2) Political affairs (human rights, democracy, good governance, electoral institutions, civil society organisations, humanitarian affairs, refugees, returnees and internally displaced persons etc.).
(3) Infrastructure and energy (transport, communications, tourism etc.).

(4) Social affairs (health, children, drug control, population, migration, labour and employment, sports and culture etc.).

(5) Human resources, science and technology (education, information technology communication, youth, human resources etc.).

(6) Trade and industry (customs, immigration etc.).

(7) Rural economy and agriculture (food security, livestock, environment, water and natural resources, desertification etc.).

(8) Economic affairs (economic integration, private sector development, investment and resource mobilisation etc.).

Gender-related objectives and concerns are within the chairperson's portfolio, due to the crosscutting nature of the issues involved.

Appointment of other Staff

The Statutes acknowledge the need to have a pool of 'suitably qualified, experienced and well-motivated senior administrative, technical professional and technical staff' to assist the commissioners in discharging their duties. The Statutes also lay out a recruitment process for Commission staff that includes:

- The role and establishment of a recruitment board, including its composition.
- The role of the Advisory Sub-Committee on Administrative, Budgetary and Financial Matters of the PRC.
- The need for transparency and objectivity.
- Upholding the principles of equitable geographical representation following a quota system.
- Upholding principles of competence, efficiency and integrity.

In addition, nationals from member states that are under sanctions for defaulting in payment for a period of more than two years, or for failure to comply with decisions of the African Union, are not eligible for appointment. The Commission is also required to ensure a competitive remuneration package and conditions of service similar to those of international organisations and private sector organisations of similar status, as a means to attract and retain a suitable calibre of staff on the Commission.

Finances of the African Union

Article 20 of the Statutes articulates the financing process of the African Union, which includes delineation of budget items, budget timeframes, the submission process (through the PRC), contributions to be made by member states based on the scale of assessments, estimated incomes, the status of all AU funds and communicating with member states regarding their contributions. In addition, the chairperson is required to submit to member states a quarterly statement on contribution payments and outstanding contributions.[8]

What Capacities for the AU Comission?

Reflections on the Mission of the African Union

For the AUC to be effective, there is a need to review and revise the Constitutive Act to focus on fewer, achievable priorities. Another area that needs review and revision is the coordinating function of the Commission with respect to other organs of the AU, given that these organs see themselves as having direct access to the Assembly even though the Commission is supposed to coordinate their work. The essence of such coordination is currently not clear, and leads to what may seem like ineffectiveness of the Commission, when in fact the other organs are trying to demonstrate their 'independence' from the AU Commission.

Reflections on the Functions of the AU Commission

As can be seen in Appendix 2 to this chapter, the functions of the AU Commission are too many for one institution to handle, especially given the limited human, financial and technological capabilities at its disposal. Functions of the Commission that could better be handled at the member-state level include:

- Control of pandemics.
- Disaster management.
- International crime and terrorism.
- Environmental management.
- Negotiations relating to external trade.
- Negotiations relating to external debt.
- Population, migration and refugees and displaced persons.
- Food security.
- Socio-economic integration.
- All other areas in which a common position has been established.

Besides the challenge of too many functions, there is also the limited scope of leadership provided by the member states, including in resource mobilisation. Additionally, some of the functions of the Commission have implementation contradictions: either the member states want to control the Commission in delivering some functions on behalf of the African Union as per the Statutes, or the Commission wants to take a lead role where the member states may be wanting and willing to provide leadership.

In 2007 the AU Assembly established the independent High-Level Panel for the Audit of the AU. The Audit was aimed at providing an in-depth analysis of AU structures, processes, organs and programmes, with a view to making the AU system more effective. Specific to the Commission, the Audit found:

Although the Commission, as the nerve centre of the AU architecture, has lifted the profile of the Union globally, it is handicapped at 3 levels. First, there is a lack of clarity in the set-up of its leadership. Second, its activities are spread too widely for it to be effective in playing the role envisaged for it, and thirdly, the management needs to be improved.[9]

These challenges are still relevant today, and the Audit recommendations need to be considered for implementation.[10]

The Commission faces additional challenges in delivering on the AU mission more effectively. Some of the functions of the Commission either easily lend themselves to contradiction, or limit the effectiveness of the Commission:

Mobilise resources and devise appropriate strategies for self-financing, income-generating activities and investment for the African Union. The contradiction with this function is that when the AU Commission raises funds from development partners, some member states fear that the AU has been 'captured' or is being overly influenced by development partners. The slow pace of adopting the recommendations of the report of the High-Level Panel on Alternative Sources of Funding for the African Union[11] bears testimony to the lack of commitment by AU member states.[12] At the same time, member states are not contributing sufficiently to the activities of the Union and the Commission. How then can the Commission deliver on this mission by itself?

Promote integration and socio-economic development. The issue of integration has been a priority for the continent since the adoption of the Lagos Plan of Action in 1980, whereby all OAU member states pledged:

We reaffirm our commitment to set up, by the year 2000, based on a treaty to be concluded, an African Economic Community, to ensure the economic, social and cultural integration of our continent. The aim of this community shall be to promote collective, accelerated, self-reliant and self-sustaining development of Member States; co-operation among these States; and their integration in the economic, social and cultural fields.[13]

The moves towards regional integration have been less vigorous than initially envisaged. People-to-people integration is stifled by the refusal of member states to grant visa-free travel to their peoples, even though some countries and regions such as Rwanda and Ghana and the East Africa Community (EAC) and the Economic Community of West African States (ECOWAS) have made modest progress.[14] In such cases, countries and regions are taking the lead in implementation of the AU mission. Besides the role of advocacy, it is difficult to identify a practical role for the AU Commission. As such, unless member states and the regional economic communities drive this agenda, integration in the economic and cultural fields remains an accomplishment on paper only, with little to progress in practice.

Ensure promotion of peace, democracy, security and stability. This is one area where the AU Commission has in fact made progress, specifically in the development of the African Peace and Security Architecture (APSA). However, the Commission can only follow the lead provided by member states. In addition, most conflict takes place within countries and among member states, who are supposed to be the champions of the AU mission. Instead of member states taking responsibility for the peace, democracy, security and stability of countries, regions and the continent, too much responsibility ends up at the doorstep of the Commission.

Reflections on the Obligations of the AU Commission. There are many challenges that the Commission will need to address in order for it to successfully meet its obligations. Some of the challenges are reflected below.

Recruitment and retention of suitably qualified staff. The Statutes lay out the recruitment process to be followed by the AU. The challenge is that the Commission does not have the culture, funding and retention policies and practices to retain the high-level staff they may have recruited. The performance culture of the Commission is also highly politicised, with suitably qualified candidates not staying for long.

Lack of performance monitoring and accountability.[15] The Statutes stipulate that staff of the Commission should undergo performance monitoring and evaluation. The Commission has tried to institute this, but more needs to be done to ensure that staff members adhere to results-based performance.

Culture of impunity. The lack of performance monitoring is also linked to a culture of impunity. There is no reward for good performance, and there is no 'punishment' for lack of performance.

Non-observance of 'obligations'. Some member states, through their embassies, intervene in the sanctioning of Commission staff in the interests of 'protecting their nationals'. Staff members of the Commission in turn share Commission information with their embassies. Both of these actions contravene the obligations of staff and of member states as stipulated in the Statutes.

In addition to sharing information with their embassies, member states share information with, and obtain advice from, states outside the AU, in part due to the Union's funding dilemma, whereby most of its programmes, through the Commission, are funded by donors. Africans may see this as interference by development partners and donors, while the partners and donors see it as the only way of ensuring accountability for the use of their funds.

Reflections on the Functions of AU Commission Staff
Commission Chairpersons Since 2002

Since the transformation of the OAU into the AU in 2002, the AU Commission has been steered by four chairpersons:

- Amara Essy (14 months) was interim chairperson from 9 July 2002 until 16 September 2003, representing Côte d'Ivoire and West Africa.

- Alpha Oumar Konaré (4 years, 7 months) was chairperson from 16 September 2003 until 28 April 2008, representing Mali and West Africa.
- Jean Ping (4 years, 6 months) was chairperson from 28 April 2008 until 15 October 2012, representing Gabon and Central Africa.
- Nkosazana Dlamini-Zuma (incumbent) has been chairperson since 15 October 2012, representing South Africa and Southern Africa.[16]

Achievements Since 2002

The AU Commission, and in turn the AU, has recorded a number of achievements since 2002. But one question that needs to be addressed when analysing these achievements is whether or not the Commission has performed under par (in relation to its functions), or just done the minimum required, or gone beyond the established expectations.

Some of these achievements have included global advocacy around the AU vision and mission, and ensuring that the African voice gains space in international debates. The Commission has also managed to ensure that African common positions are articulated and given space on international platforms. In terms of development of the AU's institutional architecture, the AU coordinated the launch of the Pan-African Parliament and ECOSOCC in 2004. In the area of peace and security, most significant was the launch of the APSA in 2001, and the establishment of the AU's Peace and Security Council (PSC) in 2003. In the area of governance, the launch of the African Peer Review Mechanism (APRM) in 2003 was a major milestone, as was the development of the African Governance Architecture (AGA) in 2010.

Challenges

The AU Assembly, the Executive Assembly and the PRC need to play a more hands-on role, through the Assembly Chairs, in ensuring that the following trends are curtailed:

Lack of Continuity. Among the challenges that the AU Commission has faced since 2002 has been a lack of continuity in both leadership and substance. Each of its chairpersons has served only one term, with the only continuity between terms coming through the deputy chairperson. However, the role of the deputy chairperson is too subsidiary to that of the chairperson, meaning that continuity through the deputy chairperson cannot provide continuity in the direction and pace of the Commission.

Individual agendas. Experience with the four chairpersons of the Commission to date demonstrates that the agenda of the AU, through the Commission, is somewhat set by the chairpersons. Each chairperson has developed new priorities per their individual strategic plans:

- Strategic Plan of the Commission of the African Union
- 2004–7 Plan of Action Programmes to Speed Up Integration of the Continent
- 2009–12 African Union Commission Strategic Plan
- 2014–17 African Union Commission Strategic Plan

Further, though Africa is faced with many immediate challenges that need immediate attention (including emergencies such as the Ebola outbreak), the Assembly has already prioritised *Agenda 2063*. How can a continent plan for the next 50 years when it cannot address urgent issues such as youth unemployment and human development in general, and the impact of climate change, especially on food security, regional integration and intra-Africa trade?

AU Commission as a Stepping Stone
The position of chairperson of the AU Commission is obviously a high-level one. However, given the many needs of the continent, the position should be seen as one of leadership in service of the continent. The challenge now is that the position is largely seen by serving chairpersons a

stepping stone to higher-level positions back in their home countries, thereby weakening their concentration on serving the African Union. For example, former chairperson Jean Ping has run for the presidency in Gabon,[17] and incumbent chairperson Nkosazana Dlamini-Zuma is reported to be running for the presidency in South Africa.[18]

Regarding election of the commissioners, there have been calls to tighten the procedures as outlined in the Statutes, to ensure that the Commission obtains the best-qualified commissioners for the respective portfolios, instead of the most politically palatable. There have also been calls for appointment rather than election of commissioners. This would help prevent an obvious dilemma for commissioners, as even though the Statutes are clear on the lines of accountability, there have been cases where commissioners pay more attention to the constituencies of their home regions (who elected them) than to the chairperson, who is the accounting officer of the Commission. The tension this dilemma creates in practice also cascades to lower levels of staff, thereby breeding a culture of fear and suspicion, particularly based on regional and linguistic lines.

Capacities Required for the AU Commission to Deliver More Effectively on the AU Mission

To better understand the capacities required for the AU Commission to deliver more effectively on the AU mission, we should examine the necessary conditions rather than specific technical capacities such as computers, training or additional staff. Rather than a focus on the AU Commission alone, we should take a broader, systematic approach – to conditions that need to be delivered holistically and sequentially.

- **Value-based leadership.** There is a need for leadership based on a common set of African values. These values – which should be shared by all Africans, at all levels – must form the foundation to drive Africa where it needs to be in the next 50 years. These values will also determine the route to this desired (and defined) destination.

- **Priorities.** A set of priorities on which all other development pillars can be based must be developed. Jumping from one strategic plan to another will not get Africa to its desired destination. Africa cannot do everything at once. A proper sequence must be followed.
- **Accountability of AU Commission leadership and staff.** There is a need to ensure that the AU Commission leadership are accountable to a committed AU Assembly who will ask the hard questions. We must also ensure that there are consequences for non-delivery (there is a long-running joke among Africans that no one gets fired from the AU for non-performance). If the chairperson of the Commission and the commissioners are elected rather than appointed, it will be more difficult to hold them accountable.

Some key recommendations for the future of the AU Commission

- Review the Constitutive Act to make its objectives more practical and doable at the Commission level.
- Implement the recommendations of the AU Audit report of 2007.
- All technical capacities at the continental level of the AU Commission hinge on the capacity of the superstructure to drive change first at the national level first, and then at the regional level. The AU Assembly cannot ask the Commission to do what Member States do not do or fail to do at the national level, be it in management or results-based performance.
- There is also a need to rationalise the work of all the organs of the AU in order to simplify the coordinating role of the Commission, and make that role complementary to the organs rather than supervisory. The tension created by

the current supervisory role of the Commission debilitates the organs in their ability to implement their mandates.

- There is a need to change the political culture approach to the work of the Commission, and make it more developmental and economic, because that is the direction the continent needs to be going. The OAU dealt with most of the politics.
- The AU Commission needs to be more proactive, and more of knowledgeable, so that it can advise the AU Assembly accordingly. This requires gathering evidence on emerging issues and how they will impact the continent, as well as developing strategies to counter emergencies and to enable the necessary agility to harness opportunities.
- The AU Assembly needs to take a committed and practical approach to mobilising resources for Africa's development. It is impractical to expect partners to fund its industrialisation strategy, for example.
- Some objectives need to be delegated to the member states and regional economic communities, to better enable the AU Commission – the continent's apex body – to focus on the fundamentals of attaining the AU vision: 'an integrated, prosperous and peaceful Africa, driven by its own citizens and representing a dynamic force in the global arena'.[19] In addition, there is a need for more demonstrable commitment and action by member states in all areas, including governance, poverty eradication, conflict resolution and promotion of gender equality.

Appendix 1: Functions of the AU Commission

1. The Commission shall carry out the functions assigned to it under the Constitutive Act, those specified in Protocols thereto, decisions of the Union as well as those established in these Statutes.

2. The Commission shall:

2.1.   Represent the Union and defend its interests under the guidance of and as mandated by the Assembly and the Executive Council;

2.2.   Initiate proposals for consideration by other organs;

2.3.   Implement the decisions that are taken by other organs;

2.4.   Organise and manage the meetings of the Union;

2.5.   Act as the custodian of the Constitutive Act, its protocols, the treaties, legal instruments, decisions adopted by the Union and those inherited from the OAU;

2.6.   Establish, on the basis of approved programmes, such operational units as it may deem necessary;

2.7.   Coordinate and monitor the implementation of the decisions of the other organs of the Union in close collaboration with the PRC and report regularly to the Executive Council;

2.8.   Assist Member States in implementing the Union programmes and policies, including CSSDCA [Conference on Security, Stability, Development and Cooperation] and NEPAD;

2.9.   Work out draft common positions of the Union and coordinate the actions of Member States in international negotiations;

2.10. Prepare the Union's Programme and Budget for approval by the policy organs;

2.11. Manage the budgetary and financial resources including collecting the approved revenue from various sources, establishing fiduciary, reserve and special Funds with the appropriate approvals, and accepting donations and grants that are compatible with the objectives and principles of the Union;

2.12. Manage the assets and liabilities of the Union per laid down regulations and procedures;

2.13. Prepare strategic plans and studies for the consideration of the Executive Council;

2.14. Act in the domains of responsibility as may be delegated by the Assembly and the Executive Council. The domains shall include the following:

    2.14.1. Control of pandemics;

    2.14.2. Disaster management;

    2.14.3. International crime and terrorism;

    2.14.4. Environmental management;

    2.14.5. Negotiations relating to external trade;

    2.14.6. Negotiations relating to external debt;

    2.14.7. Population, migration, refugees and displaced persons;

    2.14.8. Food security;

    2.14.9. Socio-economic integration; and

    2.14.10. All other areas in which a common position has been established.

2.15. Mobilise resources and devise appropriate strategies for self-financing, income-generating activities and investment for the Union;

2.16. Promote integration and socio-economic development;

2.17. Strengthen cooperation and co-ordination of activities between the Member States in fields of common interest;

2.18. Ensure the promotion of peace, democracy, security and stability;

2.19. Provide operational support to the Peace and Security Council;

2.20. Elaborate, promote, coordinate and harmonise the programmes and policies of the Union with those of the RECs;

2.21. Prepare and submit an annual report on the activities of the Union to the Assembly, the Executive Council and the Parliament;

2.22. Prepare the Staff Rules and Regulations for approval by the Assembly;

2.23. Implement the decisions of the Assembly regarding the opening and closing of sections, administrative or technical offices;

2.24. Follow up and ensure the application of the Rules of Procedure and Statutes of the organs of the Union;

2.25. Negotiate, in consultation with the PRC, with the host countries, the Host Agreements of the Union and those of its administrative or technical offices;

2.26. Build capacity for scientific research and development for enhancing socio-economic development in the Member States;

2.27. Strive for the promotion and popularisation of the objectives of the Union;

2.28. Collect and disseminate information on the Union and set up and maintain a reliable database;

2.29. Ensure the mainstreaming of gender in all programmes and activities of the Union;

2.30. Undertake research on building the Union and on the integration process;

2.31. Develop capacity, infrastructure and maintenance of intra-continental information and communication technology; and

2.32. Prepare and submit to the Executive Council for approval, administrative regulations, standing orders and Rules and Regulations for the management of the affairs of the Union and keeping proper books of accounts.

Appendix 2: Functions of the AU Commission Chairperson

1. Chair all meetings and deliberations of the Commission;
2. Undertake measures aimed at promoting and popularising the objectives of the Union and enhancing its performance;
3. Promote cooperation with other organisations for the furtherance of the objectives of the Union;
4. Participate in and keep records of the deliberations of the Assembly, the Executive Council, the PRC, the Committees and any other organs of the Union as may be required;
5. Submit reports requested by the Assembly, the Executive Council, the PRC, the Committees and any other organs of the Union as may be required;
6. Prepare, in conjunction with the PRC, and submit the Staff Rules to the Executive Council, for approval;
7. Prepare, together with the PRC, and transmit to the Member States the Budget, Audited Accounts and Programme of Work at least one (1) month before the commencement of the sessions of the Assembly and the Executive Council;
8. Act as depository of all Union and OAU Treaties and other legal instruments of the Union and perform depository functions thereof;
9. Act as a depository for instruments of ratification, accession or adherence to all international agreements concluded under the auspices of the Union and communicate information in this respect to the Member States;
10. Receive copies of international agreements entered into between or amongst the Member States;
11. Receive the notification of Member States which may desire to renounce their membership in the Union as provided for in Article 31 of the Constitutive Act;

12. Communicate to the Member States, and include in the Agenda of the Assembly, as provided in Article 32 of the Constitutive Act, written requests of Member States for amendments or revisions to the Constitutive Act;

13. Circulate the provisional agenda of sessions of the Assembly, the Executive Council and the PRC to the Member States;

14. Receive proposals, together with explanatory notes, for the inclusion of items on the agenda of the Assembly and the Executive Council at least sixty (60) days prior to the session;

15. Receive and circulate requests which conform to the correct Rules of Procedure of the Assembly or the Executive Council, from any Member State, for the convening of an extraordinary session of the Assembly or the Executive Council;

16. In conjunction with the PRC, assess the need for branches, administrative and technical offices as may be considered necessary for the adequate functioning of the Commission, and create or abolish them as necessary, with the approval of the Assembly;

17. Consult and coordinate with the Governments and other institutions of Member States and the RECs, on the activities of the Union;

18. Appoint the staff of the Commission in accordance with the provisions of Article 14 of these Statutes;

19. Assume overall responsibility for the administration and finances of the Commission;

20. Prepare an Annual Report on the activities of the Union and its organs;

21. Carry out diplomatic representations of the Union;

22. Liaise closely with the organs of the Union to guide, support and monitor the performance of the Union in the various areas to ensure conformity and harmony with agreed policies, strategies, programmes and projects;

23. Carry out such other functions as may be determined by the Assembly or the Executive Council;

24. Supervise the functioning of the Headquarters and other offices of the Union;

25. Coordinate all activities and programmes of the Commission related to gender issues.

26. The Chairperson may delegate any of his/her functions to the Deputy Chairperson of the Commission.

Notes

1. African Union (AU), *Statutes of the Commission of the African Union* (Addis Ababa, 2002), p. 1.
2. AU, *Statutes*, pp. 4–5.
3. Ibid.
4. Ibid., p. 5.
5. Ibid.
6. Ibid., p. 7.
7. Ibid., p. 8.
8. Ibid., p. 14.
9. Audit of the African Union, *Towards a People Centred Political and Socio-Economic Integration and Transformation of Africa* (Addis Ababa, 2007), p. xxiii.
10. Even though the AU Audit was established by the AU Assembly in Ghana in 2007, the Assembly has never discussed the Audit report – yet another demonstration of the AU's lack of commitment to taking ownership and leadership of its own processes. Many of the recommendations of the 2007 report would have gone a long way to improve the effectiveness of not only the AU Commission, but the AU organs and systems as well.
11. The panel was chaired by Olusegun Obasanjo, former president of Nigeria.
12. The panel was formed in 2011, by then-chairperson Ping. The incoming chairperson, Dlamini-Zuma, took up the matter beginning in 2012 but is set to leave office in 2016. The recommendations have still not been adopted and/or implemented.
13. Organisation of African Unity (OAU), *Lagos Plan of Action for the Economic Development of Africa* (Addis Ababa, 1980), p. 99.
14. United Nations Economic Commission for Africa (UNECA), African Union, African Development Bank (ADB), Assessing Regional Integration in Africa IV, Enhancing Intra-African Trade (Addis Ababa, 2016).

15. In 2015 the African Capacity Building Foundation (ACBF) partnered with the AU Commission to develop a capacity framework for implementation of *Agenda 2063*. I was part of the team that undertook the first part of this work. Interviews were carried out with the chairperson, most of the commissioners and most senior staff at the AU Commission. Some of the insights obtained from these interviews inform my views as presented in this chapter.

16. 'Chairperson of the African Union Commission', https://en.wikipedia.org/wiki/Chairperson_of_the_African_Union_Commission (accessed April 2016).

17. *AfricaNews*, January 2016, http://www.africanews.com/2016/01/15/gabon-jean-ping-to-challenge-bongo (accessed April 2016).

18. 'Analysis: Is Nkosazana Dlamini Zuma the Woman for the Job of President? *Daily Maverick*, 13 October 2015, South Africa.

19. AU, 'Vision and Mission', http://www.au.int/en/about/vision (accessed April 2016).

CHAPTER 6

THE AFRICAN PEER REVIEW MECHANISM

Amos Sawyer and *Afeikhena Jerome*

> Ten years ago, the APRM was a bold initiative that showed the world that African leaders were ready to take action on difficult and sensitive problems of governance and democracy. Ten years on, this approach has proven its value.
>
> UN Secretary-General Ban Ki-moon, 2013[1]

The economic decline and violent conflicts that characterised the crisis of the state in Africa in the 1980s and 1990s as structural adjustment failed and the Cold War ended required of Africans a new and home-grown framework for development and democracy. The Organisation of African Unity's (OAU) principle of non-interference and the supremacy of state sovereignty over popular sovereignty could not adequately underpin frameworks and strategies for effective collective security and the promotion of democratic governance and development. New principles have been evolving because of changing global, regional and national circumstances, and new decisions are being made incrementally based on research, consultations and praxis. These together are redefining the framework for development and democracy in Africa.

The origins of the New Partnership for Africa's Development (NEPAD) and its offshoot the African Peer Review Mechanism (APRM) can be found, in part, in initiatives taken by the OAU before its metamorphosis into the African Union (AU). The adoption of the principle of constitutionalism, the rejection of unconstitutional change of government, and the strengthening of mechanisms for conflict prevention, management and resolution were among the major developments of the OAU on the road to establishing NEPAD and transforming itself into the AU.

It was in recognition of the indispensability of good governance for Africa's development that the AU's Heads of State and Government Implementation Committee proposed that the NEPAD countries should subject themselves to a voluntary self-assessment process to review progress in the achievement of mutually agreed targets and compliance with mutually agreed standards. The APRM is the instrument established by NEPAD to fulfil this purpose.

Establishment of the APRM

The creation of the institutional framework for the review process was concretised in June 2002 at the inaugural assembly of the AU in Durban, South Africa, when the heads of state and government of AU countries issued a base document on the APRM to provide for the appointment of the Panel of Eminent Persons and the establishment of an APRM secretariat and supporting services from NEPAD, strategic partners and special consultants and advisers.

NEPAD's sixth summit of the Heads of State and Government Implementation Committee, held in March 2003 in Abuja, Nigeria, adopted a memorandum of understanding on the APRM. Members of the Panel of Eminent Persons were appointed in May 2003 and commenced their task after an inaugural meeting in Cape Town in June 2003.

The APRM, which perhaps is the most visible achievement of NEPAD, is an instrument voluntarily acceded to by member states of the AU, as a self-monitoring mechanism intended to foster the adoption of policies, standards and practices that lead to political stability, high economic growth, sustainable development and accelerated sub-regional and continental economic integration through sharing of experiences and reinforcement of successful and best practices, including identifying deficiencies and assessing the needs of capacity building.[2] It is a commitment to African governance standards and the tool for implementing the codes and standards enshrined in the Declaration on Democracy, Political, Economic and Corporate Governance.

Since its establishment in 2003, the APRM has registered significant gains and demonstrated its utility as a latent tool for monitoring governance in Africa. However, its level of activity has decreased over the past several years with the weakening capacity of the APRM secretariat, shrinking financial contributions by participating countries, dwindling of strategic partners and stagnant growth of the overall presence and visibility of the APRM at the national and continental levels. Efforts to strengthen the APRM are encouraged in view of its potential to contribute substantially to enhancing the agenda for good governance in Africa.

The APRM Process

The Organisation for Economic Cooperation and Development (OECD) invented the modern peer review process in 1961. Since then, this process has been adopted by other organisations such as the International Monetary Fund (IMF), International Labour Organization (ILO), and the World Trade Organization (WTO). This process now covers a broad range of areas, including environment, trade, aid and competition policy.[3]

Peer review by its very nature is a discussion among equals, not a hearing by a superior body that will hand down a judgement or punishment. Basically, it is an examination by other states of one state's performance or practices in an agreed area, with a view towards assisting the state under review to improve its policymaking, adopt best practices, and comply with established standards and norms. The system thus relies heavily on mutual trust among the states involved, as well as their shared confidence in the process.[4]

A comparison with other peer reviews instituted worldwide indicates that the APRM is unique in both scope and breadth, with the review process extending to all levels of government, parliament and the judiciary as well as the private sector and civil society organisations.[5] The APRM also covers simultaneous evaluations around four distinct pillars: democracy and good political governance, economic governance and management, corporate governance and socio-economic development. It is designed as a mechanism whereby countries voluntarily subject themselves to be examined in governance areas within a formal structure according to established guidelines. Teams of African governance experts led by the Panel of Eminent Persons assess and critique a country's performance based on several key indicators in these four thematic areas. It is a non-adversarial learning process among peers.

The APRM is built around the duality of national processes by which countries evaluate their state of economic, political, social and corporate governance on the basis of the agreed indicators and criteria, and prepare a national programme of action on the basis of which they are peer-reviewed through an external process of validation anchored by the APRM panel with the technical support of the APRM secretariat.

The APRM consists of five inter-related stages as elaborated in the base document adopted by the heads of state and participating governments of the APRM:

- **Stage one**: The preparatory stage, comprising the establishment of national structures, sending out of the APRM questionnaire, the undertaking of the country's self-assessment and preparation of a preliminary national programme of action and the submission of these to the APRM secretariat.
- **Stage two**: A review team visits the country to undertake wide consultations with stakeholders considering findings of the country self-assessment and background report prepared by the APRM secretariat.
- **Stage three**: Drafting of the country review report by the country review team.
- **Stage four**: The APRM panel approves and, in some cases, modifies or rejects the country review team's report after consultation with the country being reviewed.
- **Stage five**: The actual peer review of the country by the APRM Forum of Heads of State and Government of Participating Countries and the subsequent publication of the report and its tabling before continental and regional forums.

The APRM has established clear institutional structures at both the continental and national levels. The overall responsibility of the APRM is vested in its forum, comprising the Committee of Participating Heads of State and Government of the Member States of the APRM. The task of conducting the assessments is delegated to a Panel of Eminent Persons appointed by the heads of state to oversee the conduct of the APRM process and ensure its integrity.

The APRM panel is supported by a secretariat, located in Midrand, South Africa, that was established in June 2003. It was envisaged as a node within the NEPAD secretariat in South Africa, but has now been established in separate premises. The APRM secretariat, led by an executive director, does the analytical and technical work underpinning the peer review processes. The APRM has also entered into special support agreements with three Africa-based partner institutions designated by its forum as APRM strategic partners: the African Development Bank (AfDB), the United Nations Economic Commission for Africa (UNECA) and the United Nations Development Programme (UNDP).

At the national level, a national commission with broad stakeholder representation is ideally in place to interact with the support mission team. A trend seems to be emerging of including a 'focal point' governing council supported by a secretariat as well as technical research institutes. While uniformity may not be easy to achieve based on the contexts of countries, national ownership and broad-based stakeholder representation are key features required for these institutions.

Participation in the process is open to all member states of the African Union. As of January 2016, 35 countries have voluntarily acceded to the APRM, while 18 of the 35 have undergone the base review.

Key Strengths

The APRM is one of the most comprehensive governance assessment tools ever developed and implemented in Africa. It is truly indigenous and locally owned, as it was designed by Africans, for Africans. Unlike what was obtainable during the OAU era, the APRM undoubtedly marks a paradigm shift in Africa and a complete reversal in attitude towards governance by prompting and instilling a culture of sustainable democracy; revitalisation of institutions for political, economic and corporate governance; and ensuring compliance with African and internationally accepted norms of good governance.

The APRM has succeeded in putting on the international agenda a new way of conducting peer review, promoting internalisation of the basic values of democratisation and good governance and extending these values to all layers of society. Hence, it has been described as showcasing African innovative thinking in governance.[6]

While gains from the APRM (especially in countries participating in the process) have yet to be evaluated, anecdotal evidence, especially in the APRM pioneer countries, indicates that the process has clearly had discernable and sizeable dividends in governance and socio-economic development. Even though direct causality cannot be inferred, there is increased and improved transparency, accountability and economic performance in APRM member countries, especially the pioneers.

Developments in reviewed countries have demonstrated the strength of the mechanism as an early warning system for emerging issues and potential crises. For example, the APRM report for Kenya had anticipated potential political unrest before ethnic related violence broke out in 2007, while the South Africa report had warned against xenophobic tensions that erupted in South Africa in May 2008.

The APRM is making it possible for countries to benchmark good governance in Africa, on shared African and international norms and standards, as well as for citizens to participate in the evaluation of how they are governed. Nigeria has taken this further by establishing a functional peer review programme for its sub-national units, the 36 states of the Nigerian Federation. Through the APRM, African countries are able to learn from themselves and sustain the best practices unveiled in the process, further aiding African technical cooperation within the continent as well as African solidarity.

The APRM is acting as an agent of change and a catalyst for policy enhancement in Africa. The process has been empowering in ways that were not envisaged when begun. The interactive and broad inclusiveness of the process has spawned and strengthened a culture of political dialogue in member countries, with active participation from civil society actors. The preparedness of African governments to engage with civil society and, more important, citizens of other nationalities, to deliberate on the challenges of governance and attempt to develop a framework for addressing them, is unheralded and profoundly significant and should be sustained as the mechanism forges ahead.

Key Challenges

As indicated earlier, peer review by its very nature is a non-adversarial learning process among peers that relies heavily on mutual trust among the states involved in the review, as well as shared confidence in the process. There are no explicit sanctions for non-performance, and this has been a major hindrance. Thus, in order for the APRM to become a catalyst for positive governance change in Africa, joining the mechanism should remain voluntary, but following up on the recommendations should become mandatory. As the post-election violence in Kenya and the xenophobic attacks in South Africa clearly demonstrate, considerable attention is needed to move from diagnosis to implementation of the APRM panel's findings.

The slow pace in completing the review cycle, from developing the country's self-assessment report to the peer review by the heads of state, has been particularly challenging. For example, Ghana and Rwanda each took 10 months to move from country support mission to country review mission, while Kenya took 14 months and South Africa 8 months. These are countries that have succeeded in putting themselves on the fast track. However, Burkina Faso took 21 months, while Uganda and Nigeria took 24 months each. Several other countries have joined the mechanism but have not undertaken even the preliminary stages.

A number of participating countries and observers consider the process to be too long. Naturally, the APRM trajectory is lengthy because of the extensive process of planning and consultations among multiple stakeholders. The 88-page master questionnaire covering the four thematic areas of the APRM, with 25 objectives, 91 standards and codes and 183 indicators on the basis of which the programmes and policies of the participating countries are assessed, has been considered by several countries as unwieldy and repetitive. This has led to efforts to revise the questionnaire.

The task of moving beyond general affirmations of the importance of governance, to pragmatic action, remains significant. An examination of the national programme of action as shown in Table 6.1 indicates that many of these actions programmes are bloated and not confined to the issues emanating from the review process. A cursory analysis indicates that only Rwanda produced a modest action programme (estimated to cost about $162 million). The cost of these action programmes as a share of gross domestic product has ranged from 0.2 per cent in South Africa and 3.4 per cent in Nigeria to 13 per cent in Benin and 21 per cent in Burkina Faso.[7]

A successful APRM process is contingent on having the experts on board. While the APRM secretariat is designed to be trim and efficient, the current level of staffing is inadequate. The secretariat remains understaffed in most of its areas of work and responsibilities. Monitoring and evaluation activities, communication with stakeholders and information dissemination through seminars and workshops have not received the priority they deserve in the APRM process. The growing APRM membership, while positive, and the need for secondary reviews in some countries, are adding further strain on the operations of the secretariat.

The APRM faces institutional and structural challenges relating to its governance. There is lack of clarity on the relationship between the APRM secretariat and other

Table 6.1 Cost of National Programme of Action in Peer-Reviewed Countries (US$)

	Democracy and Political Governance	Economic Governance and Management	Corporate Governance	Socio-Economic Development	Total
Ghana	119 million (2.4%)	235 million (4.7%)	2.768 billion (54.7%)	1.867 billion (37.3%)	5 billion
Rwanda	2 million (1.4%)	20 million (13.0%)	108 million (67.0%)	31 million (19.0%)	163 million
Kenya	9 million (0.2%)	46 million (0.8%)	4.947 billion (91.8%)	387 million (7.2%)	5.388 billion
Algeria	2.378 billion (40.5%)	936 million (16.0%)	751 million (12.8%)	1.800 billion (30.7%)	5.865 billion
South Africa	157 million (7.2%)	241 million (11.0%)	32.1 million (1.5%)	1.755 billion (83.5%)	2.186 billion
Benin	586 million (24.8%)	7 million (0.3%)	1.004 billion (42.6%)	758 million (32.2%)	2.356 billion
Uganda	102 million (2.1%)	389 million (8.0%)	324 million (6.7%)	4.035 billion (83.1%)	4.857 billion
Nigeria	5 billion (40%)	4 billion (25%)	3 billion (20%)	8 billion (15%)	20 billion
Burkina Faso	414 million (10.5%)	160 million (3.3%)	2.750 billion (56.0%)	1.583 billion (32.3%)	4.907 billion

Source: Compiled and adapted from APRM country review reports.

Notes: Percentages may not sum to 100 due to rounding.

Rows are arranged in the order of which the countries went through the peer review process.

All countries costed their NPOAs in US$, except for South Africa, which computed its POA using its national currency rand, which we translated to US$ at the prevailing exchange rate 6.36 rand to the dollar in 2005.

governing structures of the mechanism, such as the Committee of Focal Points, that report directly to the heads of states. More important, while the pioneer Panel of Eminent Persons comprised distinguished professionals (Chris Stals, Adebayo Adedeji, Garcia Machel, Betual Kiplagat, among others) whose eminence promoted a high level of respect and assisted in securing access to centres of power and authority in APRM member countries, some of their replacements seem to have come to the panel in a quest for eminence. The APRM panel has been polarised and frequently bogged down in quarrels about seating, travels, per diems and individual visibility. These squabbles also polarise an already thin and under-performing staff, with some incompetent staff seeking to manipulate panel members. Some members of the panel have sought to resolve internal squabbles by involving the Committee of Focal Points. Unfortunately, the increased role of the committee has further deepened the management crisis of the APRM. Improving the quality of the APRM panel is an important challenge for restoring the mechanism to an elevated standing. Not since 2008 has the APRM had a substantive chief executive officer, so the appointment of such an individual will also improve the professionalism and effectiveness of the body's secretariat.

There are also challenges regarding the functioning of the APRM at the country level. In several APRM member countries, national governing councils are not as inclusive and representative of the various sectors of society as they should be. Moreover, links between a capital city-centred council and sub-national levels of governance and socio-economic development are typically seasonal and weak. Nigeria is among the exceptions; the existence of APRM structures at the level of the states of the federation is a commendable practice.

The APRM also faces a challenge in mobilising funds to support its activities. Only a few members are usually up-to-date in the payment of the annual subvention, which was set at a minimum of US$100,000 in 2004. Annual payments have not been adequate to cover the operational and program costs of the APRM. A few members, such as Algeria, Egypt, Nigeria and South Africa, along with the strategic partners and other international partners, bear the brunt of the support to the APRM. In the recent past, support from strategic partners has been declining. The low level of resource support by member countries indicates a lack of commitment to the APRM as a home-grown, self-monitoring mechanism.

Perhaps the major challenge currently has been the dearth of champions especially at the forum level (heads of state). The focus of the pioneering leadership of Thabo Mbeki and Olusegun Obasanjo was largely sustained by Ethiopian prime minister Meles Zanawi. Political will and commitment to making the APRM work seemed to have been diminishing, as could be seen by the poor attendance of heads of state and government of the meetings of the APRM forum following the demise of Prime Minister Zanawi and the subsequent shift in leadership of the forum after the end of Ethiopia's leadership tenure of both NEPAD and the APRM. Some members of the APRM forum have attended scant few of its meetings since the accession of their countries to the APRM.

Among other challenges faced by the APRM are those associated with the slow pace of engagement with related institutions and programmes that are complementary to the work of the mechanism. For example, there is need to accelerate the harmonisation of its structures within the African Governance Architecture of the African Union so as to avoid unwanted duplication or unproductive competition and to develop stronger synergy with NEPAD. Engagements with the Pan-African Parliament and regional economic communities (RECs) among other bodies also need to be strengthened.

Recent Developments

A special forum of heads of state and government held in January 2016 deliberated on ways to revitalise the APRM. A high-level committee was established to review the base document and other documents, and to formulate a strategy for resource mobilisation and for repositioning the APRM to play a central role in monitoring implementation of AU's *Agenda 2063* and the achievements of the Sustainable Development Goals (SDGs). The APRM forum has also approved the appointment of a new chief executive officer and decided to fast-track integration of the APRM into the structure of the AU as an autonomous institution.

The APRM panel has also made progress recently. In collaboration with strategic partners, it will be conducting an impact assessment in reviewed countries to establish evidence-based information of outcomes, value addition and challenges. It is also exploring ways to ensure support for systematic mainstreaming of national action programmes into national development plans and medium-term expenditure frameworks. Both activities are vitally important for the APRM at the member-country level. It has now developed a knowledge management strategy that includes establishment of an e-library and a continental monitoring and evaluation system.

Conclusion

The APRM is no doubt a milestone in the continent's history of political and economic reforms. It represents a bold new approach to reform for capacity development and good governance in Africa. The unique and novel fact that African countries engage with the widest possible national consultative process with all stakeholders and seek to address together with all stakeholders their challenges through national action programmes is unprecedented in the history of the continent.

The APRM not only monitors and assesses the extent to which reforms are implemented, but also provides a platform on which policymakers and citizens can hold each other accountable. But its potential to become the main continental hub for sharing of best practices in governance reform needs to be more fully appreciated and developed.

The emergence of the APRM as an African-owned innovation for enhancing good governance has received overwhelming support from Africans and has been hailed internationally including by UN Secretary-General Ban Ki-moon. The mechanism should be fully utilised in pursuit of Africa's transformation agenda. For some time now, developments in the APRM threatened to make it a 'dream deferred' or even a grand failure. However, recent actions taken by the APRM forum enhance hope that the mechanism will be sufficiently revitalised and fulfil its mission.

Notes

1. Secretary-General Statements and Messages, SG/SM/15409-AFR/2725, 21 October 2013, https://www.un.org/press/en/2013/sgsm15409.doc.htm (accessed 6 June 2017).
2. African Peer Review Mechanism (APRM), *Base Document*, NEPAD/HSGIC/03-2003/APRM/MOU/ANNEX II (2003), para. 3.
3. Afeikhena Jerome, 'An Appraisal of the African Peer Review Mechanism (APRM)', mimeo (Oxford: St. Anthony's College, Oxford University, 2006).
4. Fabrizio Pagani, 'Peer Review: A Tool for Cooperation and Change – An Analysis of the OECD Working Method', OECD SG/LEG (2002), http://www.oecd.org/dataoecd/33/16/1955285.pdf (accessed 5 June 2016).
5. Afeikhena Jerome, 'The African Peer Review Mechanism: Odyssey and Introspection' in Grant Masterson, Kojo Busia and Adele Jinadu (eds), *Peering the Peers: Civil Society and the African Peer Review Mechanism* (Johannesburg: EISA, 2010), pp. 13–28.
6. APRM, 'The African Peer Review Mechanism (APRM): Africa's Innovative Thinking on Governance', paper prepared for the eighth gathering of the African Partnership Forum, Berlin, 22–23 May 2007.
7. Adotey Bing-Pappoe, *Reviewing Africa's Peer Review Mechanism. A Seven Country Survey* (Ottawa: Partnership Africa Canada, 2010).

CHAPTER 7

THE AU'S PEACE AND SECURITY ARCHITECTURE: THE AFRICAN STANDBY FORCE

Kasaija Phillip Apuuli

Since 2000, a new peace and security architecture for the African continent has been in the works. Previously, the principle African mechanisms for conflict management were the Organisation of African Unity (OAU) Mechanism for Conflict Prevention, Management and Resolution (hereafter OAU Mechanism); and the various initiatives pursued by some of the continent's sub-regional arrangements.[1] The limitation of the OAU Mechanism and the sub-regional initiatives became apparent when they failed to craft serious responses to, for example, the ethnic massacres in Burundi and genocide in Rwanda in the 1990s. Part of the rationale behind dismantling the OAU and replacing it with a new African Union (AU) was precisely to establish a more coherent set of conflict management mechanisms.[2] In general, the major change under the AU has been a renewed emphasis on building a continental security regime that is capable of managing and resolving African conflicts.[3] The adoption of the Constitutive Act of the African Union of 2000 marked a radical shift from the cardinal

OAU principle of national sovereignty and non-intervention in national affairs.[4] While under the AU the principle of non-interference is upheld, the organisation reserves the right to intervene in a member state in respect of grave circumstances, namely war crimes, genocide and crimes against humanity.[5] The AU's conflict prevention, management and resolution mechanism is in form of the African Peace and Security Architecture (APSA), comprising a set of institutions that are tasked with preventing, managing and resolving conflicts when they occur on the continent.

This chapter generally discusses the structure of the APSA, comprising the African Union Commission (AUC), the Peace and Security Council (PSC), the Continental Early Warning System (CEWS), the African Standby Force (ASF), the Military Staff Committee (MSC), the Panel of the Wise, the Peace Fund, the regional economic communities/regional mechanisms (RECs/RMs) and the Post-Conflict Reconstruction and Development (PCRD) policy. The APSA aims to outline the system (roles, instruments and procedures) by which the AU and the RECs/RMs can realise their conflict prevention, management and resolution mandates. The chapter specifically focuses on the establishment and development of the ASF.

Context

Since independence, many African countries have been ravaged by war. In many of these, the chief perpetrators of violence have been leaders against their own citizens. Africa's wars have cost the continent dearly in many respects: they have killed many millions of people. Most people are killed through disease and malnutrition exacerbated by displacement. In financial terms, one estimate has suggested that these wars have cost Africa well over US$700 billion in damages since 2000 alone.[6] According to Rita Abrahamsen, Africa's wars never end but spread like a viral pandemic, making quiet places the lonely exceptions.[7]

Predictions are that while violent conflicts, particularly those of an internal nature, will decline as the twenty-first century progresses, they will most likely continue in the short to the medium term and pose a great threat, if not greater than in previous years.[8] The predictions are based on a number of factors including; fragility/weakness of African states, existing and deepening inequalities among members of different groups and regions, religious and ethnic grievances, repression, lack of effective institutionalisation of good governance and democracy, decline of constitutionalism, rise of authoritarian tendencies, high levels of poverty and rise in the vulnerability of many parts of Africa to drought because of climate change.[9]

The first response strategy to Africa's wars has involved strengthening the continent's conflict management institutions, based on the idea that keeping the peace requires permanent institutions, not just ad hoc responses.[10] The Charter of the OAU, at its creation in 1963, included the Commission of Mediation, Conciliation and Arbitration, which was aimed at facilitating peaceful settlement of disputes between member states.[11] The commission, whose activities were restricted to inter-state conflicts, was additionally vested with powers to investigate and inquire into disputes brought before it. Unfortunately, the commission never became operational and was abolished.[12] Thus African leaders, in abiding strictly by the prohibition under the Charter on intervention in the domestic affairs of a state and in firmly upholding the principle of territorial integrity, watched civil wars erupt and destroy states and their populations. Underlying the leaders' refusal to involve themselves in the internal conflicts of other African states were two concerns. First, prior to the establishment of the OAU, some African states had alleged that their neighbours were supporting coups within their territory. Second, many African states were equally threatened by internal conflicts and hesitated to see the OAU become involved to the possible detriment of their own regimes.[13] According to Sam Ibok, 'the basic assertion was that ... it was not the business of the OAU to pronounce itself on those conflicts.'[14]

With the end of the Cold War, there was a change of attitude of African leadership towards the conflicts taking place on the continent. Most of the post–Cold War era conflicts in Africa have been intra-state in nature, taking place within states rather than between them. The OAU found it difficult to upgrade its systems to the standards needed for dealing with the intra-state conflicts of the post–Cold War era.[15] Nevertheless, there was the realisation by the African leadership that it is impossible for any society bedevilled by violent conflict to maximally benefit from political and economic globalisation.[16] Thus the OAU Mechanism was established following a decision by African heads of state during the 29th session of the Assembly of Heads of State and Government, in Cairo in June 1993. The OAU Mechanism sought to 'bring to the processes of dealing with conflicts in [Africa] a new institutional dynamism, enabling speedy action to prevent or manage and ultimately resolve conflicts when and where they occur'.[17] Following the mass killing in Burundi and the Rwandan genocide, and the OAU's lacklustre response, in 1995 the OAU Assembly endorsed the idea that 'ready contingents' should be earmarked within African armies for deployment on peacekeeping operations.[18]

Subsequently, the Solemn Declaration on Security, Stability, Development and Cooperation in Africa of 2000 (hereafter Solemn Declaration) adopted by the OAU Assembly highlighted the principle of 'African solutions to African problems' and the need for Africa to position itself, in cooperation with the United Nations (UN) and sub-regional organisations, as a platform for the maintenance of peace and stability.[19]

The Constitutive Act declares that the scourge of conflicts in Africa constitutes a major impediment to the socio-economic development of the continent.[20] Therefore, at the inauguration of the AU, the Assembly stressed the need for a Common African Defence and Security Policy (CADSP) in the context of the Constitutive Act. Eventually, the CADSP was adopted to 'to ensure that Africa's common defence and security interests and goals ... are safeguarded in the face of common threats to the continent as a whole'.[21] The ASF is part of the strategy to ensure the realisation of the CADSP, as it is one of the 'home grown initiatives that are meant to put the destiny of the continent into the hands of the African people'.[22]

The African Peace and Security Architecture

The urge to establish the APSA was informed by the recognition that developing a robust framework for a peace and security architecture is an imperative for Africa.[23] The APSA (see Figure 7.1) emerged out of a desire by African leaders to establish an operational structure to execute decisions taken in accordance with the authority conferred by Article 5(2) of the Constitutive Act.[24] According to Peter Arthur, the APSA is a coherent structure of norms and mechanisms to effectively and capably deal with the underlying causes of conflict and their non-conventional nature and consequences.[25] The APSA embodies and constitutes an institutional reflection of the shift to human security that is widely accepted at the continental level.[26] The APSA, as enshrined in the Protocol Relating to the Establishment of the Peace and Security Council of the AU (hereafter PSC Protocol), embraces an expanded and comprehensive agenda for peace and security that includes (direct and structural) conflict prevention, early warning and preventive diplomacy, peace-making and peace-building, the encouragement and promotion of democratic practices, as well as intervention and humanitarian action and disaster management.[27]

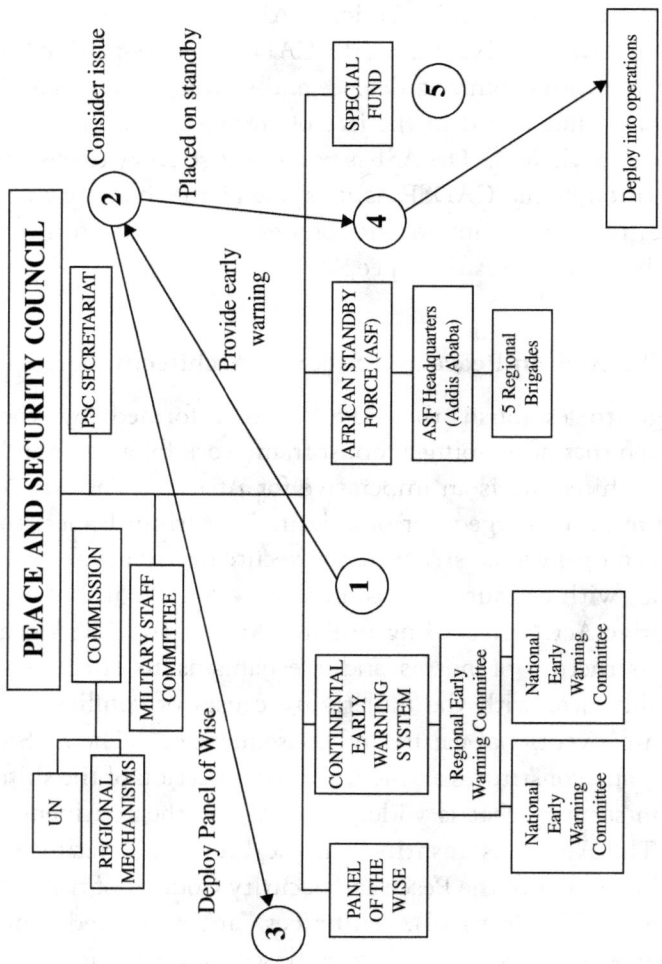

Figure 7.1 The African Peace and Security Architecture.

Source: Adapted from African Union, *African Peace and Security Architecture (APSA): 2010 Assessment Study* (Addis Ababa, 2010), p. 13.

At the heart of the architecture is the PSC as the standing decision making organ, supported by the Commission, CEWS, Panel of the Wise, ASF, Peace Fund, RECs/RMs and the PCRD policy. What ought to be noted is that all these structures are inter-dependent and work in synergy.

Pillars of the African Peace and Security Architecture

African Union Commission

The Commission (Secretariat)[28] is one of the main organs of the AU,[29] and provides the bureaucratic support – both preparatory and executive – that enables the AU to function.[30] The AU Commission is composed of the chairman, a deputy and commissioners,[31] and is responsible for the organisation's executive functions and day-to-day management.[32]

The powers of the Commission derive also from its Statutes as adopted by the Assembly in Durban in 2002 and as amended in Addis Ababa in 2007, namely: representing the AU and defending its interests under the guidance of and as mandated by the Assembly and the Executive Council; initiating proposals to be submitted to the AU's organs as well as implementing decisions taken by them; acting as the custodian of the AU Constitutive Act and AU legal instruments; providing operational support for all AU organs; assisting member states in implementing the AU's pro-grammes; working out AU draft common positions and coordinating member states' actions in international negotia-tions; managing the AU budget, resources and strategic planning; elaborating, promoting, coordinating and harmo-nising the AU's programmes and policies with those of the regional economic communities; ensuring gender mainstream-ing in all AU programmes and activities; and taking action as delegated by the Assembly and Executive Council.[33]

While the Commission has, among other things, proactively championed new relationships with China,

Japan, India and Brazil, among other countries, and informed the priorities of Africa's external partners including the Africa Health Strategy – now the point of reference for the World Health Organisation (WHO) and the newly announced International Partnerships Fund for Health – on the other hand, in the area of peacekeeping especially, it has lacked the staff and the expertise to plan and conduct missions,[34] and also has suffered from a confusing array of donor capacity-building assistance packages and schemes.[35]

Peace and Security Council

The PSC was initially not part of the Constitutive Act, but emerged out of an ad hoc process to reform the OAU Mechanism.[36] Thus the Assembly, using its power under Article 5(2) of the Constitutive Act, created the PSC. The PSC's key powers are spelled out in Article 7 of the PSC Protocol, including anticipating and preventing disputes and conflicts, as well as polities that may lead to genocide and crimes against humanity; undertaking peace-making, peace-building and peace support missions; and recommending intervention in member states in respect of grave circumstances, namely war crimes, genocide and crimes against humanity. Generally, the PSC's overarching role is to be a collective security and early warning arrangement with the ability to facilitate timely and efficient responses to conflict and crisis situations.

The PSC's membership (there are 15 members) is based on the principle of equitable regional representation[37] and rotation, whereby the North, West, Central, East and Southern regions present candidates for election.[38] The criteria for choosing the prospective members include: contribution to the promotion and maintenance of peace and security in Africa; participation in conflict resolution, peace-making and peace-building at regional and continental levels; willingness and ability to take up responsibility for regional and continental conflict resolution initiatives; contribution to the Peace Fund and/or Special Fund; respect for constitutional governance and the rule of law, and whether the prospective member is willing and able to shoulder the responsibilities of rule of law and human rights; and commitment to AU financial obligations.[39] Ten of the 15 members of the PSC are elected for a two-year term, while the remaining five are elected for a term of three years, in order to ensure continuity. Unlike the UN, there is no permanent membership on the PSC.

Since its inauguration in 2003, the PSC has been one of the most visible organs of the AU. In this regard, it has imposed sanctions against regimes that have come to power through unconstitutional means, including in Togo, Mauritania, Guinea-Conakry, Guinea-Bissau, Madagascar and Niger. It has also authorised peace support processes in Sudan (2003), Burundi (2003), Somalia (2007), Comoros (2008) and Mali (2013), among others.

Among the weaknesses of the PSC is the fact that substantively it has devoted relatively little attention to the prevention of conflict or to structural issues that encourage bad governance.[40] In other words, in its modus operandi the PSC has been reactive rather than proactive in responding to conflicts on the continent. Second, while the Council has addressed several conflicts, some have not made it onto its agenda,[41] for example the insurgence in the Delta region of Nigeria and in the Ogaden region of Ethiopia, and the continued tensions between Eritrea and Ethiopia. Third, the Council has generally devoted little attention to the non-military dimensions of security, such as environmental degradation, organised crime and disease.[42] Fourth, there is the absence of an enforcement and compliance mechanism about the implementation of the decisions made by the Council. Last, there is low-level interaction between the PSC and similar structures at the REC level.

Continental Early Warning System

The development of an early warning system at the AU level aims to provide political decision makers with timely information on emerging conflicts and corresponding policy options.[43] Early warning of violent conflicts did not become a significant issue for African organisations until the 1990s, particularly after the Rwandan genocide.[44] Subsequently, the OAU's Division for Conflict Management was created and tasked with collecting, collating and disseminating information relating to current and potential conflicts and devising response options.[45] Unfortunately, due to human and financial constraints, the initiative was stillborn. With the establishment of the AU, and conclusion of the PSC Protocol, progress was made as early warning systems were established at both continental and regional levels. While the CEWS[46] is at the Union level, regional early warning systems include the Conflict Early Warning and Response Mechanism (CEWARN) of the Intergovernmental Authority on Development (IGAD); ECOWAS Early Warning System (ECOWARN) of the Economic Community of West African States; COMESA Early Warning System (COWARN) of the Common Market of Eastern and Southern Africa States; Early Warning System of the Economic Community of Central African States; Early Warning System (EACWARN) of the East African Community; and the SADC Early Warning System (SADCWARN) of the Southern African Development Community. It has been reported that the Community of Sahel-Saharan States (CEN-SAD) is preparing a framework for the eventual establishment of an early warning system, while nothing has been heard from the Arab Maghreb Union (AMU).[47]

Today, the CEWS is technically functional,[48] comprising two parts. The Situation Room at the AU headquarters acts as a central observation and monitoring centre, collecting and analysing data on conflicts (real and potential). The second component comprises the observation and monitoring units of the regional mechanisms, which collect and process data pertaining to conflict at their level and transmit the same to the Situation Room.[49] Generally, the CEWS provides timely advice on potential conflicts and threats to peace and security in Africa to several key AU institutions, including the chairperson of the AU Commission, the PSC and the Panel of the Wise. This is done through continuous monitoring and gathering of information through the Situation Room, producing various reports, including early warning reports, situation updates, flash reports and weekly updates.[50] The Situation Room provides coverage 24 hours a day, seven days a week.[51]

The main challenges that the CEWS has faced include the weak link between early warning and early response by decision makers, inadequate gathering of relevant data due to the ever-changing nature of conflict dynamics, low connectivity between the CEWS and the early warning systems of the RECs and lack of connectivity between the national early warning systems and the regional early warning systems.[52]

Panel of the Wise

The Panel of the Wise supports the work of the PSC and the AU Commission.[53] The institution comprises five members who are highly respected African personalities of high integrity and independence, and who have made outstanding contributions to Africa in the areas of peace, security and development. The members are appointed by the AU Assembly on the recommendation of the Commission chairperson for a term of three years. Each member is drawn from one of the AU's five regions. The Panel of the Wise, which was appointed at the beginning of 2007 and launched at the end of that same year, is an integral part of the AU's preventive diplomatic framework. Among other things, it provides a communication channel between conflict parties and the PSC and the AU Commission, carrying out fact-finding missions where there is danger of armed conflict breaking out or escalating. Given its mandate to anticipate potential crisis situations and intervene in a timely fashion to prevent the escalation of a dispute or resolve existing tensions to reduce the likelihood of a return to violence,[54] the Panel of the Wise is an integral aspect of the AU's dedicated preventive diplomacy framework. As a high-level mediation panel and consultative body of the AU, the Panel not only mediates between warring groups but also has coordinated reconciliation processes in Liberia, Somalia, Guinea-Bissau, Comoros and Côte d'Ivoire.[55]

The main challenge that the Panel of the Wise has faced is that its relationship with the PSC has not been clarified, with some observing that 'relations between the two entities has so far been very limited'.[56]

Peace Fund

The special Peace Fund[57] is set up to 'fund peace and security activities'[58] and other operational activities related to peace and security. The Peace Fund is financed from the AU's regular budget and voluntary member-state contributions and from other sources within Africa, including the private sector, civil society and individuals, as well as through appropriate fundraising activities. The Peace Fund is operational and receives funds for all peace and Security Department activities.[59]

The Peace Fund is envisaged as a standing reserve on which the AU can call in case of emergencies and unforeseen priorities.[60] The 2009 AU Special Summit in Tripoli decided to gradually increase the reserve to a total of 12 per cent of the regular budget by 2012, but this was yet to be realised by 2016, as the figure stood at only 7 per cent.[61]

At the 27th AU Summit in Kigali, the AU High Representative of the Peace Fund, Donald Kaberuka, presented his report on financing the AU and the Peace Fund. As a result, the Assembly took a decision to, among other things, endow the Peace Fund with money raised through a 0.2 per cent levy on all eligible goods imported into the continent.[62] Through this mechanism, the Peace Fund will receive US$325 million in 2017, increasing to US$400 million in 2020. The money will be utilised under three thematic windows: mediation and preventive diplomacy, institutional capacity and peace support operations.

Post-Conflict Reconstruction and Development Policy

The PSC Protocol mandates the Council to undertake peace-building, post-conflict reconstruction and humanitarian and disaster management as its core activities.[63] In response to an Executive Council decision in Sirte, Libya, of July 2005,[64] the AU Commission has developed its Post-Conflict Reconstruction and Development (PCRD) policy framework. The framework was conceived as a tool to consolidate peace and prevent relapse of violence; help address the root causes of conflicts; encourage fast-track planning and implementation of reconstruction activities; and enhance complementarities, coordination, and coherence between and among diverse actors engaged in the PCRD processes.[65] The need to support sustainable peace, stability and development in countries that have emerged or are emerging from conflict through the APSA is of paramount importance.[66]

The PCRD unit in the Peace and Security Department (PSD) was created in 2011, and as of the end of 2015 the PCRD framework was only marginally operational.[67] The focus of the AU Commission has been on developing the partnerships to operationalise the PCRD policy and put into place the necessary mechanisms and consultative platforms for its implementation.[68] Under the PCRD framework the Africa Security Sector Framework has been developed for member states and RECs to formulate, implement, monitor and evaluate security sector reform (SSR) processes. The AU Commission has conducted series of SSR orientation, sensitisation and training at various levels throughout the continent.[69]

Also under the PCRD framework, the AU in 2013 launched a Disarmament, Demobilisation and Reintegration Capacity Programme (DDRCP) aimed at strengthening capacities within the AU Commission, member states, and RECs/RMs. Through the DDRCP framework, the AU helps national disarmament, demobilisation and reintegration (DDR) processes pursuant to requests made by member states.[70]

The challenges that have faced the PCRD framework include the complex nature of post-conflict issues and the level of resources the PCRD requires; lack of coordination to align PCRD efforts with other peace and security programs both at the AU and REC levels; limited financial resources; and lack of alignment of regional peacebuilding objectives to national stabilisation plans.[71]

Regional Economic Communities and Regional Mechanisms

The RECs are the building blocks of the AU and recognised in the PSC Protocol[72] as part of the overall security architecture of the AU. A memorandum of understanding on cooperation in the area of peace and security was signed between the AU, the RECs and the coordinating mechanisms of the regional standby brigades of Eastern and North Africa in January 2008.[73] The memorandum, among other things, affirms that the parties will cooperate in all areas relevant for the promotion and maintenance of peace, security and stability in Africa, including the operationalisation and functioning of the APSA.

The level of cooperation and coordination between the AU and the RECs/RMs is intensive, particularly in the operationalisation of the APSA.[74] Liaison officers to the AU from the RECs/RMs have been established, as well as AU liaison offices to the RECs/RMs. This relationship has strengthened linkages between the AU and the RECs/RMs, improving the exchange of information. Since the end of the Cold War, it has become increasingly fashionable to suggest that regional organisations should play a more prominent role in the area peace and security in accordance with the principle of subsidiarity.[75] Under the principle, sub-regional organisations should be the first resort for problems transcending national borders.[76] The PSC Protocol, when read strictly, implies that the AU and the RECs/RMs exist in a hierarchical relationship, with the former being a superior body. This has thus resulted in friction between the AU and the RECs/RMs. For example, during the Mali crisis of 2012–13, ECOWAS quickly seized the initiative by suspending the country from the activities of the REC when the Malian military carried out a coup. The AU, which was left to play 'catch up' with the action of ECOWAS, argued that the Mali problem transcended the ECOWAS border (Southern Libya was also affected by the crisis) and insisted on taking the lead. This led to both organisations losing valuable time as they jostled to take the lead instead of intervening decisively to end the crisis.[77] Nevertheless, the PSC in various communiqués has underscored the importance of building more collaboration and synergy between the AU and the RECs/RMs in the promotion of peace and stability in Africa, as envisaged in the PSC Protocol.[78]

Military Staff Committee

The Military Staff Committee is meant to advise and assist the PSC in all questions relating to military and security requirements for the promotion and maintenance of peace and security in Africa.[79] It comprises of senior military officers of the members of the PSC.[80] The idea behind the MSC was that while the ambassadors meet in the PSC, their military attachés should meet in the MSC to serve as a kind of technical advisory body to the PSC.[81] The policy framework for the establishment of the ASF urges a strong working relationship between the PSC and the MSC. It further requires that the MSC meet prior to all meetings of the PSC at the level of senior military officers, and stipulates that MSC members should attend meetings of the PSC to provide necessary clarifications and advice when invited to do so.

In practice, the MSC has been moribund. The MSC hardly meets and when it does, attendance is below 50 per cent.[82] Moreover, the PSC has not sought the MSC's input before authorising pre-deployment or deployment of troops and major military equipment to field missions. For example, the PSC did not seek the advice of the MSC before authorising the deployment of the African-Led International Support Mission in Mali (AFISMA).[83] The problem is compounded by the fact that there is confusion about the mandate and responsibilities of the MSC, and how it relates to and complements the work of the PSC.[84]

The confusion surrounding the functioning of the MSC can also be attributed to what Cedric de Coning has called 'prejudice in the African context for a military approach to peace operations'.[85] Thus the PSC has recognised that peace operations are multi-dimensional, and so it does not make sense to have an advisory body for the PSC that consists only of military officers.[86]

The African Standby Force

Kwame Nkrumah of Ghana recognised the need for some type of African regional security arrangement as early as the 1960s.[87] The Solemn Declaration outlined an action plan that among other things called for the establishment of deployable contingents. Earlier in 1995, UN Secretary-General Boutros Boutros-Ghali had called for the UN 'to consider the idea of a rapid deployment force, consisting of units from a number of member states, trained to the same standard, using the same operating procedures and inter-operable equipment, and taking part in combined exercises at regular intervals'.[88] Boutros-Ghali's call was prompted by the 19 countries that had undertaken to have troops on standby for the United Nations Assistance Mission in Rwanda (UNAMIR) failing to contribute to the mission.

In December 1996, the multi-national Standby High Readiness Brigade for United Nations Operations (SHIRBRIG) was established by Austria, Canada, Denmark, the Netherlands, Norway, Poland and Sweden.[89] The operational capability of SHIRBRIG was declared in 1999, and in November 2000 it deployed its headquarters, an infantry battalion and a headquarters company to the United Nations Mission in Eritrea and Ethiopia (UNMEE). Subsequently in 2003, the force assisted the UN and ECOWAS to plan for the peacekeeping mission to Côte d'Ivoire; and deployed 20 members to assist the UN in forming the core of the interim headquarters for the United Nations Mission in Liberia (UNMIL). SHIRBRIG ceased all operations and closed in June 2009.

The ASF is modelled on the SHIRBRIG model. According to the PSC Protocol, the ASF is to serve as a rapid reaction force, comprising 15,000 troops drawn from the regional brigades.[90] The regional brigades were later changed to regional forces: East African Standby Force (EASF) for the East; Economic Community of Central African States Standby Force (FOMAC) for Central; Economic Community of West African States Standby Force (ESF) for the West; North African Regional Capability (NARC) for the North; and Southern Africa Development Community Standby Force (SSF) for the South. It is the responsibility of the RECs/RMs to prepare their capabilities as mechanisms for the AU Commission to achieve initiatives with respect to peace, security and stability.[91] Nevertheless, 'it is the responsibility of the AU to evaluate the readiness of the regional planning elements (PLANELMs, Headquarters) and ASF regional brigades in consultation with REC PLANELMs. This involves certification which is the official recognition that the unit or force component meets the defined standards and criteria, therefore capable of performing the mandated mission'.[92] Thus, in its early incarnation in 2003, the ASF was the mechanism that provided the most hope for the provision of continental collective security, given its ability to provide the AU with a continental rapid deployment capability.[93]

In order to provide a common basis for the establishment of the ASF and to implement the provisions of the PSC Protocol, a policy framework for establishment of the ASF and the MSC was adopted by the AU Assembly of Heads of State and Government in May 2003. The policy framework defined the six different scenarios and timelines for the deployment of the ASF (see Table 7.1).

The policy framework for establishment of the ASF and the MSC, together with the roadmap for operationalisation of the ASF specifies the concept of the ASF, as well as major stages in its operationalisation. In December 2010, the third roadmap (2010–15) was adopted, aimed at building on the work and lessons from the first roadmap (June 2006 to March 2008)[94] and the second roadmap[95] (April 2008 to December 2010),[96] and 'addressing specific areas of enhancement for the ASF including advocacy and outreach, structures and management capabilities, political decision making and mission planning processes, operational concepts, logistics and legal and financial frameworks'.[97]

The policy framework and the roadmap called for establishment of a rapid deployment capability (RDC) capable of intervening, within 14 days, in cases of genocide and gross human rights abuses under the sixth ASF scenario. The RDC was framed as a part of the regional standby forces and as such would be constituted from lead elements of the regional standby forces. The third roadmap of the ASF recommended that the RDC be tested, evaluated and operationalised by 2012. This objective could not be attained within the context

Table 7.1   Conflict Scenarios and Deployment Timelines

Scenario	Description	Deployment Requirement (from Mandate Resolution)
1	AU/regional military advice to a political mission	30 Days
2	AU/regional observer mission co-deployed with UN mission	30 Days
3	Stand-alone AU/regional observer mission	30 Days
4	AU peacekeeping force for Chapter VI and preventive deployment missions (and peace-building)	30 Days
5	AU peacekeeping force for complex multi-dimensional peacekeeping missions, including those involving low-level spoilers	90 days with military component being able to deploy in 30 days
6	AU intervention (e.g. in genocide situations where the international community does not act promptly)	14 days with robust military force

Source: Adapted from African Union, *African Peace and Security Architecture (APSA): 2010 Assessment Study* (Addis Ababa, 2010), para. 106.

of the delays in meeting the timelines for the operationalisation of the ASF.

Operationalisation of the ASF

While full operationalisation of the ASF had first been slated for between 2005 and 2008, the date was pushed to 2010 as a result of serious capability gaps identified during Exercise AMANI Africa 2010. The holding of the AMANI Africa command post exercise (CPX) in 2010 was supposed to test the efficacy of the ASF idea and mark its formal operationalisation. The CPX was based on the deployment of the ASF in the context of an AU multi-dimensional peace support operation and focused on the validation of policies and processes, at the strategic level, for the employment of the ASF within the APSA framework. It provided an opportunity to identify gaps as related to the ability of the AU to plan and manage complex and multi-dimensional peace support operations as well as recommendations for addressing the challenges. Unfortunately in the course of planning for this exercise, it became too apparent that 'the ASF 2010 target was too ambitious'.[98] The evaluation report of the exercise concluded that 'the ASF was not yet operational, missing key capacity in the planning and conduct of peace support operations (PSOs) at the strategic and headquarter levels'.[99]

As a result, the AU (with the support of the European Union (EU) decided to initiate a second AMANI Africa training cycle that would culminate in a field training exercise (FTX) in 2014. The objective of the FTX would be to 'validate the capacity of the African Union to grant a mandate for the use of a RDC, as an initial operation for scenario six and lead in the process, a fully-fledged multidimensional peace operation (scenario 5)'.[100] In the end, the ministerial-level Specialised Technical Committee on Defence, Safety and Security (STCDSS) meeting in December 2010 recommended the finalisation of the third ASF roadmap, explicitly setting a new deadline of December 2015 for the full operationalisation of the force. This was the first time that a concrete deadline had been established at that level of decision making.

Between 19 October and 7 November 2015, approximately 5,400 members from the military, police and civilian,[101] participated in AA-II field training exercise. The holding of the AA-II FTX marked the final stage of a four-year exercise cycle (which included Map Exercise (MAPEX), CPX, political-strategic exercises, training and other undertakings), the cumulative outcome of which was the assessment of the state of readiness of the ASF and its RDC. The exercise's overall objective was to establish the full operational capability of the ASF ahead of the deadline of December 2015. The AA-II FTX was able to achieve the key objective of evaluating the AU's ability 'to mandate, deploy, manage, sustain and recover a RDC, and to expand the deployment by mandating a scenario 5 mission'.[102] Following the conclusion of the AA-II FTX, the AU Assembly declared the full operationalisation of the ASF in January 2016.

Challenges

Lingering Suspicions on the African Capacity for Immediate Response to Crises

The ASF policy framework stipulates that 'in an emergency, the AU should take a preliminary preventive action, while preparing for a more comprehensive action that could include the participation of the United Nations. The emphasis here is on rapid action and deployment'.[103] The RDC is a key component of the ASF, the aim of which is to enable the AU to respond swiftly to crisis situations. However, since failing to meet the 2010 deadline to fully operationalise the ASF, the AU faced several serious crises including in Côte d'Ivoire (2010–11); Tunisia, Egypt and Libya during the Arab Spring (2011); Mali (2012–13); the Central African Republic (CAR) (2013–14); and South Sudan (since 2013). While the AU engaged with each of these crises in various ways, including coordinating positions with other regional and international organisation, establishing high-level panels, conducting mediation efforts and deploying political and enforcement operations, it was generally hoped that the AU would take stronger action including mobilising the resources of the ASF. Nevertheless, the intervention of France in the conflicts in Côte d'Ivoire and Mali seems to have awoken the African leadership for the need to have rapid deployment capacity.[104] This is notwithstanding the fact that the intervention by France was welcomed by some African leaders.[105] As a result, at the conclusion of the twenty-first century AU Summit, then-AU Commissioner for Peace and Security, Ambassador Ramtane Lamamra, announced that the Assembly had decided to establish the African Capacity for Immediate Response to Crises (ACIRC).[106] The rationale for establishing ACIRC was captured by South African Minister for International Relations and Cooperation, Maite Nkoana-Mashabane, who lamented thus: 'leaders in that region (ECOWAS) say, it took them eleven meetings in eleven months polishing the decision to intervene in Mali, until one day they woke up and the rebels were now matching towards Bamako. That should not have happened'.[107] According to Lamamra, ACIRC's main aim would be to

> provide Africa with a strictly military capacity with high reactivity to respond swiftly to emergency situations upon political, decisions to intervene in conflict situations within the continent. The aim is to establish an efficient, robust and credible force, which can be deployed very rapidly, able to conduct operations of limited duration and objectives or contribute to creating enabling conditions for the deployment of larger AU and/or UN peace operations.[108]

ACIRC would be a transitional formula to expeditiously provide Africa with an urgently needed tool to enhance the continent's capacity to promote 'African solutions to African problems'.[109] Nevertheless, the decision to establish ACIRC seems to have been motivated by two main reasons.[110] First was the overwhelming dependence of the AU on funds provided by partners, affecting implementation of African solutions to African problems. Second, in the case of the armed rebellion in Mali, Africa could have moved faster and made the French intervention dispensable if it had had the appropriate tools and mechanisms. Thus, the African leadership was left to lament the unfortunate situation that after 50 years of independence,

African security was still too dependent on foreign partners. In the end, member states of the AU pledged henceforth to contribute troops and finance to AICRC on voluntary basis, to act independently.

ACIRC is premised on volunteerism by member states and the ability and capacity of states to deploy rapidly (within 15 days).[111] Other principles include continentalism rather than regionalism, as well as self-sustenance and collective security. Even though the ACIRC framework was mooted in May 2013, sadly when the crisis in the CAR escalated during that year and beyond, the capacity was not activated. This is notwithstanding the fact that an ECCAS operation – the Central African Peace Consolidation Mission (MICOPAX)[112] – was on the ground, and following political engagement between the AU and the UN this was re-hatted into the AU-Led International Support Mission to the Central African Republic (MISCA) following the adoption of UN Security Council Resolution 2127 on 5 December 2013. MISCA was transformed into the United Nations Multi-Dimensional Integrated Stabilisation Mission in the Central African Republic (MINUSCA) following the adoption of Resolution 2149 on 10 April 2014.

During the conduct of AA-II FTX, ACIRC was re-designated as RDC-2 and deployed together with the ASF's RDC. The Specialised Technical Committee on Defence, Safety and Security at its second extraordinary meeting in January 2016, recommended the dissolution of ACIRC in line with Assembly Decisions 489(XXI) and 515(XXII). This decision has not been received well by the ACIRC planning cell based at AU headquarters, which has argued that ACIRC should not be dissolved until the AU has resolved the issues bedevilling the ASF.[113] It also argues that the arrangement should not be dissolved because while ACIRC 'uses African resources to solve African problems', the ASF is 'heavily dependent on donors'.[114] Thus there is doubt on commitment of the countries contributing towards ACIRC on the establishment of the ASF.

It is not clear how the ACIRC countries will also contribute to the ASF. In the end, the fear originally expressed that ACIRC could undermine the ASF effort has come to pass.[115]

Funding and Logistics

Martin Doornbos has argued that African states, whatever their differences, share a pervasive dependence on external actors.[116] This is partly explained by dependence theory, according to which the world trading system tends to keep most developing states in a condition of economic and political bondage, resulting in a neo-imperial and neo-colonial relationship between rich and poor countries.[117] Thus the autonomy of the African state has increasingly been eroded by the international community, including through prescriptions made to national budgetary and policy processes in states that receive donor funds.[118] More recently, William Brown has found that aid affects the policy autonomy of aid-recipient countries.[119] Given the limited financial resources of African states, the role of the national government has become necessarily limited to accepting ready-made policy packages prepared elsewhere or already agreed upon by the main donors. Donor funding has been critical not only in the establishment and operationalisation of the ASF, but also generally in financing AU-originated peacekeeping and peace support missions. In fact it can be argued that without outside funding, the AU would not be able to mount any kind of peace mission. The lack of African financial independence has been lamented perennially. With specific regard to the ASF, issues of logistics and funding have been highlighted as being important in ensuring that the force becomes fully operational.

Northern Region Lagging

While the West, East, Southern and Central African regions have established their forces, the North is still lagging.

The North African Regional Capability (NARC) was created to fill a regional vacuum. However, the Arab Maghreb Union,[120] under which NARC would fall was dormant following its establishment in 1989, proved difficult to revitalise because of tensions among member states.[121] The tensions arose out of the member states of the AMU's divergent approaches to resolving the issue of Western Sahara. Thus, there was a need to create a regional mechanism to enable the North African countries to contribute to the ASF. Libya played a coordinating role in establishing the NARC, and at a meeting in Tripoli in 2008 it was agreed to locate an executive secretariat there. A memorandum of understanding on the establishment of the NARC was agreed among the members in 2008. However, constitutional and legal regulations in some member states, such as Tunisia, have delayed its ratification.[122] Thus the North African countries have fallen behind in establishing the NARC. The political upheavals that have rocked Libya since 2011 have meant that the country cannot play a meaningful role in the NARC. In its assessment on the ASF in 2013, the AU believed the 'NARC region will not be able to achieve full operational capability due to the significant disruptions that the ASF project suffered because of the Arab Spring and the ongoing uncertainty in Libya, Egypt and other countries in the region'.[123]

Opportunities

In rather a total departure from the modus operandi of the OAU, the AU has undertaken several peace support operations. These include the African Union Mission in Burundi (AMIB) (2003–4); African Union Mission in Sudan (AMIS) (2004–7); African Union Mission in Somalia (AMISOM) (since 2007); African-Led International Stabilisation Mission in Mali (AFISMA) (2012–13); and AU-Led International Support Mission to the Central African Republic

(MISCA) (2013–14). In addition to these, there is the AU Electoral and Security Assistance in Comoros (2007). All these missions have helped the AU gain valuable experience in dealing with peace and security issue in Africa. Moreover, the African forces have continued to serve in peacekeeping and peace support missions that have been taken over by the UN. This is the case of the UN-AU Hybrid Operation in Darfur (UNAMID), United Nations Multidimensional Integrated Stabilization Mission in Mali (MINUSMA) and UN Multi-Dimensional Integrated Stabilisation Mission in the Central African Republic (MINUSCA). Thus, individuals and units that make up the ASF have acquired a great deal of operational capacity and expertise in mandating, deploying, managing, sustaining and recovering peace support operations.

Second, the fact that African countries have participated in the ASF various exercises, and pledged troops and equipment to the ASF, is an opportunity that should be exploited to further build the force's capabilities. For example, the member states contributing to the EASF validated their troops in December 2014. These include motorised and light infantry battalions, reconnaissance squadrons, marine and air assets, civilians and formed police units, among others. This shows a serious commitment in the advancement of the notion of African solutions to African problems.

Third, the concept of ASF provides an opportunity for the consolidation of democratic control and oversight of the military. The ASF construct draws together elements of the military, civilians and police from different countries. The national, regional, multi-dimensional and multi-national training ensures the application of best practices, including the principle of civilian oversight of the security forces in general and military. Moreover, one of the principles that the African Charter on Democracy, Elections and Governance of 2007 establishes is the 'strengthening and institutionalizing consti-tutional civilian control over the armed and security forces'.[124]

As S.M. Makinda and Wafula Okumu observe, 'the establishment of this principle was in recognition of the negative impact of security apparatuses on the consolidation of democracy and the rule of law'.[125]

Last, during the ASF exercises, civilians, military and police work and learn together in the implementation of the prescribed mandate. Solomon Dersso has observed that 'given that ASF brigades are constituted of multidimensional contingents based in their countries of origin, cultural, material and know-how diversity, their [joint] training has resulted in standardization and institutionalization at different levels'.[126] In the context of democratic development and consolidation, the joint training in areas of human rights and international humanitarian law observance is very crucial. The networks and professional interactions established through joint training will hopefully cement within the security forces the established norm that they are subject to civilian authority.

Conclusion

The African Peace and Security Architecture is a manifestation of the AU's political principle of African solutions to African problems – essentially an issue of self-determination.[127] Most of the APSA structures/pillars that are now up and running provide Africa with ownership and a large stake in the process of resolving the problems of peace and security on the continent. A fully functioning APSA fits in with the AU's *Agenda 2020* (Silencing the Guns), which requires that the continent's mechanisms for conflict prevention, management and resolution at all levels must be functional.

The African Standby Force is supposed to provide the AU with the capacity to actualise its collective security arrangements. While several challenges remain, including logistics and funding, and the Northern region lagging, among other things, the force is advantaged for having troops, police, and civilians who have served in the various peace support missions that the AU has undertaken over the years. The declaration of the full operational capability of the ASF in 2016 provides Africa with a tool to address its peace and security challenges.

Notes

1. Paul D. Williams, *War & Conflict in Africa* (Cambridge: Polity, 2011), p. 150.
2. Ibid., p. 153.
3. Peter Arthur, 'Promoting Security in Africa Through Regional Economic Communities (RECs) and the African Union's African Peace and Security Architecture (APSA)', *Insight on Africa* 9, no. 1 (2017), p. 8.
4. African Union (AU), *Africa Peace and Security Architecture: APSA Roadmap 2016–2020* (Addis Ababa, 2015), p. 12.
5. AU, *Constitutive Act of the African Union* (Addis Ababa, 2000), art. 4(h).
6. Ibid.
7. Rita Abrahamsen, 'Introduction: Conflict & Security in Africa', in Rita Abrahamsen (ed.), *Conflict & Security in Africa* (Suffolk: Currey, 2013), p. 1.
8. Solomon A. Dersso, 'The African Standby Force: Its Role and Potential as One of the AU's Response Mechanisms', in Roba D. Sharamo and Chrysantus Ayangafac (eds), *The State of Human Security in Africa: An Assessment of Institutional Preparedness*, Monograph no. 185 (Addis Ababa: Institute for Security Studies [ISS], 2011), p. 114.
9. Dersso, 'The African Standby Force', pp. 114–15.
10. Williams, *War & Conflict in Africa*, p. 149.
11. Isaac O. Albert, 'The African Union and Conflict Management', *Africa Development* 32, no. 1 (2007), pp. 41–68.
12. Albert, 'The African Union and Conflict Management'.
13. Caroline A.A. Packer and Donald Rukare, 'The New African Union and Its Constitutive Act', *American Journal of International Law* 96, no. 2 (2002), p. 368.
14. Sam Ibok, *Conflict Prevention, Management, and Resolution in Africa* (2000), p. 5, http://unpan1.un.org/intradoc/groups/public/documents/CAFRAD/UNPAN011836.pdf (accessed 27 March 2017).
15. Albert, 'The African Union and Conflict Management', p. 49.
16. Ibid.
17. Organisation of African Unity (OAU), *Declaration of the Assembly of Heads of State and Government on the Establishment within OAU of a Mechanism for Conflict Prevention, Management, and Resolution* (Cairo, 1993), p. 13.

18. Williams, *War & Conflict in Africa*, pp. 150–1.

19. Allehone Mulugeta, 'Promises and Challenges of a Sub-Regional Force for the Horn of Africa', *International Peacekeeping* 15, no. 2 (2008), p. 173.

20. AU, *Constitutive Act of the African Union*, Preamble, para. 9.

21. AU, *Solemn Declaration on a Common African Defence and Security Policy* (Sirte, 2 February 2004), para. 4, http://www.peaceau.org/uploads/declaration-cadsp-en.pdf (accessed 28 March 2017).

22. Kasaija Phillip Apuuli, 'The African Capacity for Immediate Response to Crises (ACIRC) and the Establishment of the African Standby Force (ASF)', *Journal of African Union Studies* 2, nos. 1–2 (2013), p. 67.

23. AU, *Audit of the African Union: Towards a People-Centered Political and Social Economic Transformation of Africa* (Addis Ababa, 2007), para. 261.

24. AU, *African Peace and Security Architecture (APSA): 2010 Assessment Study* (Addis Ababa, 2010), p. 13.

25. Arthur, 'Promoting Security in Africa', p. 5.

26. Alhaji Sarjoh Bah, Elizabeth Choge-Nyangoro, Solomon Dersso, Brenda Mofya and Tim Murithi, *The African Peace and Security Architecture: A Handbook* (Addis Ababa: Friedrich Ebert Foundation, 2014), p. 21.

27. AU, *Africa Peace and Security Architecture: APSA Roadmap 2016–2020*.

28. AU, *Constitutive Act of the African Union*, art. 20(1).

29. AU, *Constitutive Act of the African Union*, art. 5(e).

30. Williams, *War & Conflict in Africa*, p. 156.

31. AU, *Constitutive Act of the African Union*, art. 20(2). The portfolios are: peace and security, political affairs, trade and industry, infrastructure and energy, social affairs, rural economy and agriculture human resources, science, and technology, and economic affairs.

32. AU, *African Union Handbook 2014: A Guide for Those Working With and Within the African Union* (Addis Ababa, 2014), p. 46.

33. AU, *Constitutive Act of the African Union*, art. 3(2).

34. Mark Malan, 'Africa: Building Institutions on the Run', in Donald Daniel, Patricia Taft and Sharon Wiharta (eds), *Peace Operations* (Washington, DC: Georgetown University Press, 2008), p. 113.

35. Malan, 'Africa: Building Institutions on the Run', p. 113.

36. Williams, *War & Conflict in Africa*, p. 158.

37. AU, *PSC Protocol*, art. 5.

38. Members are distributed as follows: Central region, three seats; Eastern region, three seats; Northern region, two seats; Southern region, three seats; and Western region, four seats.

39. AU, *PSC Protocol*, art. 5(2).

40. Williams, *War & Conflict in Africa*, p. 160.

41. Ibid.

42. This statement should be nuanced. When there was an outbreak of the Ebola disease in Guinea-Conakry, Liberia and Sierra Leone in 2013–14, the PSC

decided to deploy a humanitarian mission comprising medical doctors, nurses and other medical and paramedical personnel, as well as military personnel to help end the outbreak. *See* AU PSC, 450th meeting, communiqué, PSC/PR/COMM.(CDL) (Addis Ababa, 19 August 2014), http://www.peaceau.org/uploads/psc-com-450-ebola-outbreak-19-8-2014.pdf (accessed 18 March 2017).

43. GIZ, *APSA Impact Report: The State and Impact of African Peace and Security Architecture (APSA) in 2015* (Addis Ababa, 2015).

44. Williams, *War & Conflict in Africa*, p. 160.

45. Ibid.

46. Established under Article 12 of the PSC Protocol.

47. AU, *Audit of the African Union*, para. 281.

48. GIZ, *APSA Impact Report*.

49. AU, *PSC Protocol*, art. 12(2)(b).

50. AU, *Africa Peace and Security Architecture: APSA Roadmap 2016–2020*.

51. Williams, *War & Conflict in Africa*, p. 162.

52. AU, *Africa Peace and Security Architecture: APSA Roadmap 2016–2020*.

53. AU, *PSC Protocol*, art. 11.

54. Bah et al., *The African Peace and Security Architecture*, p. 55.

55. Alex Vines, 'A Decade of African Peace and Security Architecture', *International Affairs* 89, no. 1 (2013), pp. 89–109.

56. João Gomes Porto and Kapinga Yvette Ngandu, 'The African Union, Preventive Diplomacy, Mediation, and the Panel of the Wise: Review and Reflection on the Panel's First Six Years', *African Security* 7, no. 3 (2014), p. 191.

57. AU, *PSC Protocol*, art. 21.

58. International Peace Support Training Center (IPSTC), *Issue Briefs* no. 5 (Third Quarter) (Nairobi, 2013), p. 15.

59. AU, *African Union Handbook 2014*.

60. Bah et al., *The African Peace and Security Architecture*, p. 68.

61. Ibid.

62. AU, Assembly of the Union, 27th Ordinary Session, *Decisions and Declarations*, Assembly/AU/Dec.605-620 (XXVII), Assembly/AU/Dec.605 (XXVII) (Kigali, 17–18 July 2016), https://www.au.int/web/sites/default/files/decisions/31274-assembly_au_dec_605-620_xxvii_e.pdf (accessed 23 March 2017).

63. AU, *PSC Protocol*, arts. 3(a), 6.

64. *See* AU Executive Council, *Decision on the Report of the Chairperson of the Commission on Conflict Situations in Africa*, Doc. Ex.Cl/191 (Vii), http://www.peaceau.org/uploads/ex-cl-dec-225-vii-e.pdf (accessed 23 March 2017).

65. AU, *Audit of the African Union*.

66. AU, *Africa Peace and Security Architecture: APSA Roadmap 2016–2020*.

67. GIZ, *APSA Impact Report*.

68. AU, *Africa Peace and Security Architecture: APSA Roadmap 2016–2020*.

69. Ibid.
70. Ibid.
71. Ibid.
72. AU, *PSC Protocol*, art. 16.
73. *See* http://www.peaceau.org/uploads/mou-au-rec-eng.pdf (accessed 23 March 2017).
74. AU, *Africa Peace and Security Architecture: APSA Roadmap 2016–2020*.
75. Bjørn Møller, 'The Pros and Cons of Subsidiarity: The Role of African Regional and Sub-Regional Organizations in Ensuring Peace and Security in Africa', Working Paper no. 2005/4 (Copenhagen: Danish Institute for International Studies (DIIS), 2005), p. 3.
76. Kasaija Phillip Apuuli, 'Whither the Notion of "African Solutions to African Problems"? The African Union and the Mali Crisis (2012–2013)', Mediation Arguments no. 8 (Pretoria: Center for Mediation in Africa, January 2016), p. 10.
77. Apuuli, 'Whither the Notion', p. 11.
78. See AU PSC, 477th meeting, communiqué, PSC/PR/COMM.2(CDLXXVII) (Addis Ababa, 18 December 2014), http://www.peaceau.org/uploads/communique-of-the-477th-meeting-eng.pdf (accessed 23 March 2017); AU PSC 549th meeting, communiqué, PSC/PR/COMM.(DXLIX) (Addis Ababa, 9 October 2015), http://www.peaceau.org/uploads/psc-549-com-asf-amani-9-10-2015.pdf (accessed 23 March 2017)
79. AU, *PSC Protocol*, art. 13(8).
80. AU, *PSC Protocol*, art. 13(9).
81. Cedric de Coning, 'Africa and International Peace Operations', in Tim Murithi (ed.), *Handbook of Africa's International Relations* (London: Taylor and Francis, 2014), pp. 155–65.
82. Hallelujah Lulie, 'Towards a Functioning Military Staff Committee of the AU', *ISS Today*, 25 May 2015, https://issafrica.org/iss-today/towards-a-functioning-military-staff-committee-of-the-au (accessed 26 March 2017). The quorum of the MSC is supposed to be ten out of 15 members. *See* AU, *Policy Framework for the Establishment of the ASC and MSC (Part I)*, document adopted by the third meeting of African Chiefs of Defence Staff, Exp/ASF-MSC/2 (I) (Addis Ababa, 15–16 May 2003), p. 36, http://www.peaceau.org/uploads/asf-policy-framework-en.pdf (accessed 26 March 2017).
83. Lulie, 'Towards a Functioning Military Staff Committee'.
84. Ibid.
85. Coning, 'Africa and International Peace Operations', p. 157.
86. Ibid.
87. Terry Mays, 'African Solutions to African Problems: The Changing Face of African-Mandated Peace Operations', *Journal of Conflict Studies* 23, no. 1 (2003), p. 106.
88. United Nations (UN), *Supplement to* An Agenda for Peace: *Position Paper of the Secretary-General on the Occasion of the Fiftieth Anniversary of*

the United Nations, UN Doc. A/50/60* S/1995/1*, 25 January 1995, para. 44.

89. Gunther Grieindl, 'The Multinational Stand-by High Readiness Brigade for United Nations Operations (SHIRBRIG)', in Diplomatiche Akademie Wien, *Favorita Papers 03/2004: Peace Operations in Africa – 34th IPA Vienna Seminar* (n.d.), p. 140. Other countries that became active participants in the initiative include Finland, Italy, Ireland, Lithuania, Romania, Slovenia and Spain.

90. AU, *Audit of the African Union*, para. 283.

91. AU, *African Peace and Security Architecture (APSA): 2010 Assessment Study*, para. 105.

92. Ibid.

93. J. Warner, 'Complements or Competitors? The African Standby Force, the African Capacity for Immediate Response to Crises, and the Future of Rapid Reaction Forces in Africa', *African Security* 8, no. 1 (2015), p. 58. In my opinion, the PSC was the mechanism designed to do this, while the ASF was the mechanism whereby PSC decisions could be enforced. See also J.N. Krulick, 'Airlift in Africa: Building Operational Logistics Capability for the African Standby Force', *Army Sustainment* (January/February 2013), p. 11 (observing that the 'PSC's operational arm is the ASF').

94. The first roadmap, adopted in March 2005, resulted in the preparation and adoption of the core documents of the ASF, including on doctrine; logistics; standard operating procedures (SOPs); training and evaluation; and command and control, communications and information system (C3IS). The planning elements (PLANELMs) were also established in all the regions during this phase.

95. The second roadmap, adopted in April 2008, aimed at identifying measures to be undertaken to resolve outstanding issues from the first roadmap, and to consolidate the progress made. The second roadmap culminated in Exercise AMANI Africa, one main objective of which was the evaluation of progress and the validation of the ASF.

96. AU, *Report of the Independent Panel of Experts: Assessment of the African Standby Force and Plan of Action for Achieving Full Operational Capability by 2015* (Addis Ababa, 10 December 2013).

97. AU, *Report of the Independent Panel of Experts*.

98. Olaf Bachmann, *The African Standby Force: External Support to an 'African Solution to African Problems'?* Research Report 11, no. 67 (Sussex: Institute for Development Studies, 2011), p. 27.

99. Bachmann, *The African Standby Force*, p. 27.

100. AU, *Report of the Independent Panel of Experts*.

101. The participating countries included Algeria, Angola, Botswana, Burundi, the DRC, Egypt, Ethiopia, Gambia, Ghana, Kenya, Lesotho, Malawi, Mozambique, Namibia, Nigeria, Rwanda, Swaziland, South Africa, Uganda and Zambia.

102. AU, *Exercise Amani Africa II: 26 October–8 November 2015, Evaluation Report* (Addis Ababa, n.d.).

103. AU, *Policy Framework for the Establishment of the African Standby Force and the Military Staff Committee (Part I)*, para. 1.4(b).

104. AU, *Report of the Chairperson of the Commission on the Operationalization of the Rapid Deployment Capability of the African Standby Force and the Establishment of an 'African Capacity for Immediate Response to Crises'*, sixth ordinary meeting of the Specialised Technical Committee on Defence, Safety and Security, preparatory meeting of the Chiefs of Staff, RPT/Exp/VI/STCDSS/ (i-a) 2013, Addis Ababa, 29–30 April 2013, para. 14. The AU observed that 'the Malian crisis highlighted the need to expedite the operationalization of the RDC'.

105. For example, then-chairman of the AU, Thomas Boni Yayi, president of Benin, declared that 'he felt he was in heaven after France's intervention in Mali'. President Yoweri Museveni of Uganda welcomed the French intervention in the following words: 'I normally do not thank European countries for offering military support. But this time I thank the French president for supporting Mali because the terrorists were going to overtake the country'. He nevertheless hasted to add: 'some of the African armies go to European colleges only to get training on how to shoot and salute. To call France [support] is like a vote of no confidence in the Malian army. It is a big shame. So for me, I cannot call France or any other European country to come and support me'. See Apuuli, 'The African Capacity for Immediate Response', p. 79.

106. AU, 'The African Capacity for Immediate Response (AICRC) to Crisis is adopted', 21st AU Summit press release (Addis Ababa, 27 May 2013).

107. Olusegun Obasanjo and Greg Mills, 'Perspectives on African Security: On the State of Peace and Security in Africa from Bangui to Eastern Congo', Discussion Paper no. 3/2014 (Johannesburg: Brenthurst Foundation, 2014), p. 9.

108. AU, 'The African Capacity for Immediate Response'.

109. AU, 'Statement of Ambassador Ramtane Lamamra, Commissioner for Peace and Security', 6th ordinary meeting of the Specialized Technical Committee on Defence, Safety and Security, preparatory meeting of the Chiefs of Staff (Addis Ababa, 29 April 2013), http://www.peaceau.org/uploads/cps-29-04-2013.pdf (accessed 28 March 2017).

110. AU, 'The African Capacity for Immediate Response'.

111. Malte Brosi and Norman Sempijja, *The Africa Capacity for Immediate Response to Crisis: Advice for African Policy Makers*, Policy Insights no. 22 (Pretoria: South African Institute for International Affairs, 2015), p. 2.

112. It was deployed by the ECCAS countries in the CAR in July 2008 to play a stabilisation role in the country.

113. AU, *ACIRC Brief on the ASF and the ACIRC Challenges Towards the Implementation the Implementation of Common African Defense and Security Policy* (Addis Ababa, 13 June 2016).

114. AU, *ACIRC Brief.*
115. This debate has ably been captured by Warner, 'Complements or Competitors?', pp. 56–73.
116. Martin Doornbos, 'The African State in Academic Debate: Retrospect and Prospect', *Journal of Modern African Studies* 28, no. 2 (1990), p. 180.
117. Jack C. Plano and Roy Olton, *The International Relations Dictionary*, 4th edn (Santa Barbara: Longman, 1988), p. 122.
118. Plano and Olton, *The International Relations Dictionary*, p. 122.
119. William Brown, 'Sovereignty Matters: Africa, Donors, and the Aid Relationship', *African Affairs* 112, no. 447 (2013), pp. 262–82.
120. For a comprehensive discussion on why the AMU has been moribund, *see* Azzedine Layachi, 'Region-Building in North Africa', in Daniel H. Levine and Dawn Nagar (eds), *Region-Building in Africa: Political and Economic Challenges* (Cape Town: Palgrave Macmillan, 2016), pp. 245–63.
121. International Institute for Strategic Studies (IISS), 'AU's Regional Force Still on Standby', *Strategic Comment* 16, no. 10 (2010), p. 2.
122. IISS, 'AU's Regional Force Still on Standby', p. 2.
123. AU, *Report of the Independent Panel of Experts.*
124. AU, *African Charter on Democracy, Elections, and Governance*, art. 14 (1). Note that the charter came into force in 2012.
125. Samual M. Makinda and Wafula F. Okumu, *The African Union: Challenges of Globalization, Security, and Governance* (London: Routledge, 2008), p. 64.
126. Dersso, 'The African Standby Force', p. 137.
127. Solomon A. Dersso, 'The African Peace and Security Architecture', in Murithi, *Handbook of Africa's International Relations*, p. 59.

CHAPTER 8

THE AFRICAN UNION'S SOCIO-ECONOMIC CHALLENGES

Charles Mutasa

The African Union (AU) is facing substantial socio-economic challenges. In almost all indices of human well-being, the continent is yet to fulfil its potential. Transformation in the following areas remains an uphill task: social welfare, agriculture, education, healthcare, infrastructural development, economic and industrial development, intra-regional trade, scientific and technological know-how. For most African citizens, more still needs to be done to meet their basic human needs, especially food, housing, water, electricity, transport and communications. Despite the presence of well-intentioned development plans, from the Lagos Plan of Action of 1980 to the prevailing and ambitious *Agenda 2063,* socio-economic transformation gains have been minimal and very limited progress has been made on the continent. Much still needs to be done in terms of securing the political will of African leaders to ensure good economic governance and domesticating proposed regional development plans proposed by the Organisation of the African Unity (OAU)/AU.

This chapter discusses the current socio-economic challenges that confront the African Union, tracing the various strategies employed in the quest for socio-economic development on the continent, from the inception of initiatives by the OAU to those of the AU. The chapter also discusses the contradictions of these strategies, their implications and lessons learned, and offers recommendations on the way forward.

The Status of Socio-Economic Challenges in Africa

Africa's sustainable development has continued to be elusive and expensive, despite the five decades since the establishment of the OAU and its successor, the AU. Despite having ample natural resources, a favourable ratio of population to natural resources, good incentives for foreign investors and a strict observance of orthodox theories and prescriptions, Africa has not been able to increase its economic growth rate, self-reliance, economic dynamism and diversification. Almost 50 per cent of Africa's citizens still live below the international poverty line of US$1.25 a day per person.[1] Food insecurity and malnutrition remain serious challenges, with nearly one in four Africans deemed unable to access sufficient food.[2] Unemployment and under-employment are rife, with significant negative impact on issues related to gender and youth. Women and girls are mostly confined to the informal sector, which suffers from inadequate infrastructure, no viable income, and lack of access to capital and technology. The proportion of employed women working in the agricultural sector is as low as 20 per cent, even though they provide much of the manual labour in the fields.

Poverty is arguably the dominant problem afflicting most African countries. Associated with the problem of widespread poverty is the issue of high levels of inequality.[3] Inequality between the rich and the poor, the urban and the rural, men and women, geographical regions and other various groupings remains a significant challenge for the African continent. For instance, income and wealth distribution in South Africa is among the most unequal in the world. South Africa's inequality within the continent is followed by that of Kenya.[4] Inequality in these countries has been associated with high incidences of violence and insecurity in some of their major cities, such as Johannesburg and Nairobi.

For many sub-Saharan African countries, rapid and unsustainable urbanisation has led to increased poverty and inequality. Children and youth face challenges to their well-being due to increased vulnerability and lack of adequate social security. The phenomenon of high death rates, low life expectancy, hunger, disease, ignorance, lack of access to land, weak educational systems, energy crisis, poor road networks, poor healthcare systems and gender discrimination characterises life in most AU member states. Add to this external dependency – a situation in which the 'world's poorest region overall' is disproportionally reliant on donors. Significant hurdles to improving the livelihood of Africans persist, encompassing a range of factors, from the visible off-shoots of unstable economies, to the existence of a survivalist mentality, retrogressive cultural and traditional practices, absence of skills, presence of corruption and a lack of political will.[5]

Africa is also experiencing both an energy crisis and climate change problems. Kandeh Yumkella, former director-general of the United Nations Industrial Development Organisation (UNIDO), notes that nearly 600 million people on the continent do not have access to electricity. In addition, Africa is the world's most energy-poor region. The continent loses two to three per cent of its gross domestic product (GDP) because of this lack of reliable energy.[6] Yumkella cites the case of Nigeria, which needs 10,000 megawatts of electricity but generates only 4,500, despite the fact that it has some of the largest deposits of oil and natural gas on the continent.[7] Exacerbating this situation, climate change in Africa has meant an increase in droughts, floods and deforestation, making it difficult to boost agricultural production and food security.

Compounding these challenges, the absence of sufficient infrastructure is an additional challenge to socio-economic development of the region. Dilapidated and obsolete infrastructure hinders industrialisation efforts. Entrepreneurs in Africa 'face high transaction costs, protracted and cumbersome administrative procedures and bureaucratic bottlenecks, and poor physical and financial infrastructure'.[8] If Africa is to facilitate its own development, especially trade in goods and services, it must reduce distribution costs through improved infrastructure. The Programme for Infrastructure Development in Africa (PIDA) is the continent's comprehensive long-term plan for its infrastructure development, serving as a coherent platform for action at the national level in addition to engagement with the private sector and development partners. Based on an assessment of about 50 major infrastructure projects pre-selected under PIDA, 'it is estimated that closing Africa's infrastructure deficits will increase the continent's per capita economic growth by 2 per cent a year and increase productivity of firms by as much as 40 per cent'.[9] The infrastructure areas concerned include energy, transport and information and communication technologies. There is also need to address transparency in procurement processes, because they act as a disincentive to foreign investors. A good starting point would be to identify problems and enact and implement agreed rules and processes, including public-private partnerships, de-regulation, dispute resolution mechanisms, streamlined administrative processes and simplified procedures.

The Millennium Development Goals (MDGs) framework (2000–15) did not bring about the hoped transformation of the underlying economic, social and cultural factors that could propel genuine development in Africa. Seven of the MDGs focussed on social outcomes, with an eighth focussed on political and economic outcomes, failed to question and reverse the underlying causes of under-development. As an illustration of the limitations of the MDGs, 'the liberal model of democracy and economic governance that underpinned them ignored the crucial roles played by genuine democracy and economic growth in promoting social progress'.[10] Africa experienced uneven progress in implementation of the MDGs, with reasonable progress on only three goals: the second, achieving universal primary education; the third, promoting gender equality and empowering women; and the sixth, combating HIV/AIDS, malaria and other diseases.[11] Setbacks in agricultural production, food insecurity and malnutrition remain the most significant obstacles to solving the continent's problems. The MDGs overlooked issues of inclusion, citizen ownership, self-reliance, job creation, democracy, sustainable economic growth and equitable distribution of development dividends.

The successor framework to the MDGs, the Sustainable Development Goals (SDGs), which include a heavy dose of pro-poor, pro-women, pro-equality, pro-development targets, are expected to turn things around for Africa and revive efforts for wealth accumulation and development. The SDGs, just like the MDGs, are expected to galvanise the continent into taking action to achieve their targets. *Agenda 2063* is currently at the heart of AU leaders' desire for integration, prosperity and peace, emphasising the importance of capable, inclusive and strong states. However, the Ebola epidemic, which hit Guinea, Liberia and Sierra Leone from early 2014, will mean that West African region as a whole may suffer Ebola-related losses of US$3.6 billion per year between 2014 and 2017, due to a decrease in foreign direct investment, border closures and flight cancellations.[12] While the Sustainable Development Goals centre on poverty reduction, translating such goals into meaningful policy responses that address the needs of the poorest children and the promotion of gender equality remains a considerable challenge in many contexts.

Agricultural GDP in Africa grew 3.2 per cent a year between 2000 and 2010, compared with 3.0 per cent in the previous decade.[13] This growth contributed to reducing poverty in various African countries given the fact that more than two-thirds of Africa's population live in rural areas and are very dependent on agriculture. The Comprehensive Africa Agriculture Development Programme (CAADP) is the African Union's policy and framework to champion agricultural transformation, food security, nutrition, wealth creation and economic growth. CAADP came into existence in 2003, in Maputo, Mozambique, when the AU leadership declared it an integral part of the New Partnership for Africa's Development (NEPAD).[14] CAADP also emphasises accountability, transparency, outcome-based policy planning and implementation. Through CAADP, most AU states aim to align different stakeholder interests, such that at least ten per cent of national budget allocation goes to agriculture, to ensure that agriculture is also used to create wealth rather than just reduce poverty.

In terms of its impact, CAADP has failed to address the plight of smallholder farmers, who are the largest producers of food, especially women. The Global Harvest Initiative Africa noted that the continent is the only region in the world whose average food production per person has fallen over more than 50 years, and predicted that Africa is likely to meet only 13 per cent of its 2050 food needs.[15] CAADP seems to have made no progress in terms of generating modern jobs for the continent's expanding youth quotient. The programme relies heavily on donor funding and has failed to promote local private sector engagement and ownership. Unfortunately, most African politicians have used agriculture inputs, fertilisers and seeds as means of vote-buying during elections. Agriculture must play a fundamental role in the continent's structural transformation, given that 60 per cent of the labour force is in the sector; as such, a mammoth internal effort is needed to increase productivity and take advantage of the continent's enormous reservoir of unused arable land.[16] According to the October 2016 edition of the IMF Regional Economic Outlook for Africa, Africa's agro-based economy, which had been growing at approximately 5.0 per cent per year in 2014, fell to 4.3 per cent in 2016. To make matters worse, given falling oil and commodity prices, oil-exporting countries such as Nigeria, Africa's biggest economy, and Angola, among others, will most certainly face new economic headwinds that could complicate the poverty.[17] Africa receives only about US$52 billion of official development assistance per year, an unsustainable model for the continent's development.[18]

Africa's Strategies for Socio-Economic Transformation

The OAU/AU's common concerns about political and economic vulnerability in the global economy have inspired the design of several regional economic initiatives to tackle under-development. The OAU leadership coined five land-mark indigenous strategies for the continent's socio-economic development: the Lagos Plan of Action for the Economic Development of Africa (1980–2000) and Final Act of Lagos (1980); Africa's Priority Programme for Economic Recovery (APPER) (1986–90), which was later converted into the United Nations Programme of Action for Africa's Economic Recovery and Development (UN-PAAERD) (1986); the African Alternative Framework to Structural Adjustment Programme for Socio-Economic Recovery and Transformation (AAF-SAP) (1989); the African Charter for Popular Participation for Development (1990); and the United Nations New Agenda for the Development of Africa in the 1990s (UN-NADAF) (1991). These regional economic initiatives prioritised reversing Africa's dependence on the outside world inherited from colonialism. However, the implementation of the initiatives faced both internal and external challenges in terms of implementation, making it impossible to achieve expanded trade and investment, economic cooperation and integration.[19]

Adebayo Adedeji observed that one of the major challenges with Africa's socio-economic development agenda has been 'the ability of the international financial institutions (IFIs) with the support, or at least the connivance, of the Western donors to pooh-pooh or sabotage indigenous initiatives'.[20] Thus, Africa's socio-economic development is largely associated with the persistence of colonial and paternalistic attitudes, predominantly in the West, and the continent's subordination to programmes and economic models that are not of its own design and aspiration. Most of the indigenous development initiatives by African leaders were opposed, undermined and jettisoned by the Bretton Woods institutions, thus denying the continent the right to pave its own development path. Similarly, donors seem to have repeated this trend in the implementation of the MDGs, as they failed to fulfil their commitments under the eighth goal, developing a global partnership for development. In line with this, Claude Ake argued that development in Africa will not begin until the struggle over development paradigms, strategies and agendas is over.[21]

Debates over which development model or strategy to pursue concern the role of external actors, especially the pernicious and corrosive role of development aid. Africa is a large recipient of both Western aid as well as financial investment from the East. Some academics have attributed the continent's development problems to the conditionalities of – the strings attached to – development aid. There is a large volume of literature on the impact of foreign aid on development in Africa, yet most of this literature does not recognise all the factors that contribute to aid effectiveness or ineffectiveness. It appears most African countries are so dependent on aid that, without it, almost half of their yearly budgetary commitments cannot be fulfilled.[22] In her book *Dead Aid*, Dambisa Moyo brought out the salient issues surrounding this debate on internal versus external development strategies. She argued that aid disbursements, especially in the form of concessional loans and grants, have hampered, stifled and retarded Africa's socio-economic development.[23] In the same vein, William Easterly and colleagues raised new doubts about the effectiveness of aid even in the case of good policies.[24] It seems that aid is not meant to ensure recipients becoming more self-reliant, but rather linked to the geo-political agendas of external actors. Moyo also touched on 'the paradox of plenty', insisting that aid instigates or prolongs conflicts in Africa. If this thesis is inaccurate, then why is the same continent that receives the largest amount of aid the most conflict-ridden region in the world?[25] It is important to note that finding a correlation between development aid and economic growth is quite a complex exercise. Nonetheless, it suffices to also acknowledge that aid has some positive impact on the socio-economic development of Africa. These issues illustrate the importance of interrogating the OAU/AU's major strategies for socio-economic development, focusing on their major tenets, and points of similarity and differences. In so doing, one can also consider the merits and demerits of each of these strategies.

The Four Major Socio-Economic Policy Frameworks

The OAU/AU's four major interventions aimed at solving Africa's socio-economic development problems are the Lagos Plan of Action of 1980; the Abuja Treaty of 1991, which formed the African Economic Community (AEC); and the New Economic Partnership for Africa's Development, and *Agenda 2063*. These interventions are full of contradictions, especially regarding their ideological approach to socio-economic transformation, issues of self-reliance and dependence on external actors. The debates around which strategy works best for development have also brought questions about whether Africa needs a radical or gradual regional integration approach. What one realises despite the rhetoric is that African leaders have only paid lip service to these strategies, failing to move with unity of purpose and direction. It has not been easy for the leaders to walk their talk, and the influence of donors or former colonial masters often continues to hover over decisions made by the OAU/AU as a collective, as well as decisions by individual member states.

The Lagos Plan of Action

A seminal moment in the OAU's socio-economic agenda can be traced back to the establishment of the Lagos Plan of Action of 1980:

> [T]he Lagos Plan of Action (LPA) together with the Final Act of Lagos (FAD) were borne out of an overwhelming necessity to establish an African social and economic order primarily based on utilising to the full the region's resources in building a self-reliant economy. The other parallel objective was the establishing of an African Economic Community (AEC) by beginning of the twenty first century.[26]

The LPA was drafted in 1980 in Nigeria as a response by OAU leaders to the World Bank's Berg Report. The LPA blamed Africa's socio-economic woes solely on vulnerability to external shock, especially the oil crisis. The crafters of the LPA also considered the weakness of Africa's agriculture in the global village, food insecurity, socio-economic stagnation and the resultant poverty and malnutrition. The implementation of the LPA and FAD was the responsibility of member states, with the technical assistance of the Economic Commission of Africa and the OAU bureaucrats. It was a self-enforced failure that very few member states made strides to incorporate these strategies into their national development agendas.

The absence of an effective mechanism of implementation, monitoring and evaluation by the OAU was a primary reason that African governments did not feel any obligation to follow these development plans.[27] Another explanation for the failure of these plans could be the Cold War problems that divided Africans between those standing with the East and those standing with the West.

The African Economic Community

The African Economic Community, formed under the Abuja Treaty, which was adopted in June 1991, came into force in 1994. The treaty put forth six stages, due to be completed over 34 years, for the community to become fully operational. The AEC was to be set up through a gradual process, which would be achieved by coordination, harmonisation and progressive integration of the activities of existing and future regional economic communities (RECs) in Africa. The RECs are regarded as the building blocks of the AEC. The idea behind the treaty was to encourage OAU member states to integrate their economies into sub-regional markets that would ultimately form one Africa-wide economic union. African leaders recognised that cooperation and integration among African countries in the economic, social and cultural fields were indispensable to the accelerated transformation and sustained development of the African continent. Some of the expected results of the AEC are a continental free trade area, a customs union, an Africa central bank, a common currency and a continental parliament. It was also anticipated that with the AEC, Africa would enjoy increased intra-African trade, self-sufficiency in import demands, and consequently socio-economic progress with a reduction of poverty.[28] The AEC is an important historical framework when it comes to discussing Africa's socio-economic development, since most subsequent development plans that followed it – including the most recent vision, *Agenda 2063* – are informed by the AEC's key tenets.

After experimenting with the Lagos Plan of Action's self-reliance for decades, the results were disappointing for most Africa countries, compelling them to embrace the structural adjustment programmes (SAPs) imposed by the World Bank and International Monetary Fund (IMF) in the early 1980s. Despite African governments' openness to international trade and financial systems as advocated by the World Bank, IMF, and the World Trade Organisation (WTO), the SAPs – which emphasised export-led growth – failed to catapult Africa out of its economic malaise. Most African countries were poorer in 2000 compared to 1980 when the SAPs were launched. The only 'success' of the SAPs was their ability to align African countries to the liberal policies of the West and make the continent fertile ground for foreign corporations to generate excessive profit and then siphon out that profit with the collusion of corrupt leaders across the continent. This alignment by OAU/AU member states was not a deliberate choice; it was forced on them by the conditionalities for the loans they desperately needed from the World Bank and IMF.[29]

The architects of the New Partnership for Africa's Development assumed that if Africa were to boost its GDP growth rate to 7 per cent annually, the country would exit from poverty. NEPAD also assumed that the continent needed some US$64 billion of resource inflows every year, and that aid and trade flows into Africa would increase.[30] NEPAD has four main goals: eradicating poverty, promoting sustainable growth and development, integrating Africa into the world's economy and accelerating the empowerment of women. Several scholars have argued that there is a strong correlation between socio-economic development, good governance and democracy.[31] African countries that do well in terms of promoting accountability, transparency and citizen participation tend to be more economically viable than those that do not. The AU adopted NEPAD as a means of directly addressing governance issues, since bad governance was perceived as anti-developmental and impoverishing the continent. There was realisation that African countries that had a bad governance record were bogged down by corruption and political instability. Ghana and Botswana were regarded as good examples of how good governance gives birth to socio-economic progression.

Agenda 2063

Agenda 2063 is a strategic framework for the socio-economic transformation of the continent over the next four and a half decades. This framework builds on the vision and mission of the Constitutive Act of the African Union, the eight priority areas of AU's 50th-anniversary Solemn Declaration, the agenda's 'aspirations', and regional and continental frameworks as well as member states' national plans. More specifically, Agenda 2063 'aims to build upon the achievements and draw lessons from earlier strategic planning efforts at the regional and sub-regional levels, including the Lagos Plan of Action, the Abuja Treaty and the NEPAD, to address new and emerging issues in the continent over the short, medium and long-term'.[32]

The AU launched Agenda 2063 parallel to the post-2015 MDG processes as an ambitious effort to tackle extreme poverty through greater ownership and inclusivity of citizens in the continent's development agenda. It is a set of seven 'aspirations' that resemble the SDGs. Some of the flagship projects of Agenda 2063 include the establishment of continental financial institutions, including an African central bank, a free trade area, free movement of people with a continent-wide African passport, 'silencing the guns' by 2020, a high-speed train network, a single African aviation network and the Grand Inga Dam in the Democratic Republic of the Congo (DRC). The planned US$80 billion Grand Inga Dam, if finally constructed, will be massive, producing 40,000 megawatts of electricity when completed. It will be capable of literally lighting up the continent, providing electricity to half of African countries.[33]

The continuity between *Agenda 2063* and the previous AU socio-economic development strategies is evident in their quest to attain the following: economic transformation in Africa, industrial development, trade development, the creation of an African bank with a single currency, financing of regional cooperation, infrastructural development, acceleration of regional integration among African countries and enhanced intra-African trade among the continent's countries. As with previous policy frameworks, the jury is still out on whether *Agenda 2063* offers a pathway towards addressing Africa's socio-economic challenges. A systematic analysis and review of *Agenda 2063* would be premature at this stage due to the limited period it has been in operation.

Contradictions and Limitations of Africa's Socio-Economic Strategies

There are contradictions and limitations evident in these different major African regional economic initiatives. The Lagos Plan of Action was traditionally state-led and inward-looking, advocating collective self-reliance compared to the outward-looking, market-oriented prescriptions of the New Partnership for Africa's Development. The LPA's strategy of regional import substitution industrialisation contrasts with the option for engagement chosen by NEPAD. The two were inspired by the different historical contexts in which Africa found itself. The Lagos Plan of Action was formulated in a context where there was need to transform a global economic order troubled by the oil crisis of the 1970s, at a time when the 'dependency thesis' was fashionable, when North-South relations were unbalanced, and when the exigencies of the Cold War affected international relations and cooperation.[34]

Given its economic and governance principles, NEPAD attracted a lot of controversy among both AU leaders and technocrats. Although presented as an inward-looking and self-reliant initiative by its proponents, NEPAD's neo-liberal market orientations and paradigmatic underpinnings, especially the curtailing of the role of the state within a discredited economic paradigm, attracted much criticism and resentment from civil society. Attempts to present NEPAD as presenting both a statist and a liberal economic paradigm, or being both inward- and outward-looking, were futile. The policy shifts within NEPAD made it a challenge to implement the partnership across the entire continent, especially its African Peer Review Mechanism (APRM), which operated on the principle of voluntary participation.[35] In effect, the entire NEPAD matter became significantly much more outward-looking than inward-looking. More important, NEPAD's architects argued in several ways for the need to address the inadequacy of domestic institutions and governance to tackle under-development and poverty. Inspired by global changes of the time, NEPAD brought a shift in orientation from the LPA in that it looked at internal factors rather than blame external factors, though it did not remove the need for foreign investment and external aid as key to Africa's development. Africa's deepening debt crisis, weak bargaining position and global economic transformations, especially at the Bretton Woods institutions and the World Trade Organization (WTO), necessitated NEPAD. With the new waves of democracy, good governance, globalisation and the dominance of the liberal paradigm at the dawn of the twenty-first century, as well as sentiments of the African Renaissance with the birth of the AU, it became fashionable for Africa to embrace NEPAD and its tenets.

An analysis of the continent's development documents gives the notion that there is need for Africa to catch up with the rest of the world, meet its peoples' rising aspirations and improve on Africa's global image and investment. Africa's specific drivers and risks include its population size, which could be either a dividend or a social time bomb, its mineral resources, which could be either a blessing or a curse, and its security concerns, which could either lure or scare investors. To tackle the current and future challenges, there is need for jobs and sustained high economic growth, which are possible only through more competitive economies, transformed agriculture, managed urbanisation for growth, as well as mobilisation of and investment in natural resource beneficiation. All this calls for capable states, macro-stability, strong institutions and the rule of law among Africa's priorities.

Key Recommendations

Development experts sum up the solution to Africa's socio-economic and political problems in two words: good governance. If Africa's 54 countries were all to practice good governance, these experts say, their economies would grow, poverty would be eliminated and the continent's 1.2 billion people would enjoy their socio-economic rights. Following are some recommendations worth considering in the continent's endeavours to address its socio-economic challenges.

- For socio-economic development to become a reality, Africa still needs to take advantage of its natural resources. With new mineral discoveries, 12 per cent of the world's oil reserves, 40 per cent of its gold, about 90 per cent of its chromium and platinum, 60 per cent of its arable land, among many other sources of mineral wealth, Africa should be doing better at eliminating poverty. Africa should not be importing food to feed its citizens. For instance, Nigeria, the world's sixth-largest producer of crude oil, should refine enough for local consumption rather than spending US$8 billion a year subsidising fuel imports.[36]

- Africa needs to diversify its agro-industry and expand its export of services. The continent's economic growth and resilience during the global financial crisis were largely due to 'new mineral discoveries, rising commodity prices and the recovery of domestic demand'.[37] This growth trajectory is not sustainable because commodities are mostly exhaustible, and Africa has little control over disruptions in world demand and prices.
- Industrialisation is key to the continent's socio-economic development. There is need to consider the processing of raw materials within the continent. In today's global village, Africa needs to think of processing its own cocoa coffee, for example. Adding value to agricultural produce will unleash new opportunities for farmers, who if ensured that excess produce would generate income, could then actively participate in the marketplace. As AU Commission chairperson Nkosazana Dlamini-Zuma noted: 'Industrialization cannot be considered a luxury but a necessity for the continent's development'.[38]
- There is need to enhance capacities in science and technology, engineering and technical skills, which are essential for the industrialisation of the continent, as well as to develop and enforce policies to retain trained professionals to prevent the ongoing 'brain drain' and ensure retention of technical skills for the continent.
- AU member states should pursue growth policies, with emphasis on pro-poor growth that creates employment. Future planning should aim for diversification of African economies. This would require balancing sound macro-economic policies with the need for social outcomes (such as reducing poverty), educating citizens to act accordingly (through such values as effective budgeting and hard work), and using 'coordinating councils' to bring together stakeholders to develop the sort of 'shared growth' envisaged.

- The AU should work with each member state to set up appropriate social, economic and political targets that can be easily monitored and fulfilled. In addition, the AU should develop a mechanism that can facilitate the transfer of knowledge, skills and expertise.
- The AU needs to find a way to mitigate and deal with climate change and its possible economic impact on Africa. This urgently requires the AU and member states to strengthen their engagement with the scientific community, so as to find solutions to some of the vexing challenges posed by climate change.
- To achieve greater and better-distributed growth and poverty reduction, AU member states need to increase their spending on agriculture and rural roads, direct complementary spending to sectors in need, such as education, carefully target public spending and coordinate spending among different levels of government.
- There is need for the AU and member states to move from the blame game of colonialism, though still acknowledging the legacies of the past, to confronting their developmental challenges head-on. Governments need to trim excess personnel in their bureaucracies and create viable democratic systems.
- There is need for improved communication among AU member states, especially on best practices and failures. African leaders must learn to share information and create regional corridors and infrastructural development that benefit their people.
- Public-private partnerships can work in appropriate circumstances. Governments should make available support for the private sector, to allow it to develop infrastructure and do things that governments cannot do – for the benefit of their countries. This includes closing the infrastructure gap. The state should focus on playing its rightful role in development, creating a conducive environment for the private sector to

thrive, investing in people, developing agriculture, promoting trade and investment and mobilising the much-needed financial resources to make all this happen.[39]

Conclusion

The African continent has the necessary resources to ensure the socio-economic well-being of its citizens. However, in order to achieve this it needs to develop models that are genuinely focused on enhancing the livelihood of Africans, and should resist the imposition of economic ideas and systems by external actors who are driven by their own geo-political agendas. To address its challenges, the African continent must accelerate its economic and political integration, which is the only basis upon which it can generate the necessary assertiveness to drive its own agendas. There are key sectors that are vital for enhancing the continent's transformation, including knowledge generation and skills improvement. These in turn form the basis to accelerate industrialisation and the beneficiation of the continent through effective utilisation of its natural resources to improve the lives of its peoples. Despite numerous failed models, implementation failures and a turbulent global economy, Africa can still chart a path forward and achieve its objectives, but this will require the urgent participation of all its citizens as active agents of change.

Notes

1. United Nations Economic Commission and Social Council (ECOSOC), Economic Commission for Africa (UNECA) and African Union (AU) Commission, *Report on Progress in Achieving the Millennium Development Goals in Africa* (Abidjan, 2013).
2. Food and Agriculture Organisation (FAO), International Fund for Agricultural Development (IFAD) and World Employment Program (WEP), *The State of Food Security Insecurity in the World: Strengthening the Enabling Environment for Food Security and Nutrition* (Rome, 2014).

3. Sara Turner, Jakkie Cilliers and Barry Hughes, 'Reducing Poverty in Africa: Realistic Targets for the Post-2015 MDGs and *Agenda 2063*', African Futures Paper no. 10 (Pretoria, 2014), http://www.issafrica.org/futures/papers/reducing-povertyin-africa-realistic-targets-for-the-post-2015-mdgs-and-agenda-2063 (accessed 2 December 2016).

4. African Peer Review Mechanism (APRM), *Country Review Report of the -Republic of South Africa* (Midrand: APRM Secretariat, May 2007) paras. 889–90, p. 276.

5. Terrence Corrigan, 'Socio-Economic Problems Facing Africa: Insights from Six APRM Country Review Reports', Occasional Paper (Johannesburg: South African Institute of International Affairs (SAIIA), 2009).

6. UNECA, 'A New Burst of Energy in Industrial Activity', *Africa Renewal*, August 2013, http://www.un.org/africarenewal/magazine/august-2013/new-burst-energy-industrial-activity (accessed 27 November 2016).

7. Ibid.

8. United Nations Conference on Trade and Development (UNCTAD), *Economic Development in Africa Report – Inter-African Trade: Unlocking Private Sector Dynamism* (Geneva, 2013), p. iv.

9. UNECA, 'Africa Can Take the Lead in Financing Its Infrastructure', *Africa Renewal*, 15 June 2014, http://www.un.org/africarenewal/news/africa-can-take-lead-financing-its-infrastructure (accessed 23 November 2016).

10. Mbaya Kankwenda, 'MDGs: A New Fashion of Development Goods', paper presented at a discussion forum at Free University of Brussels, 21 October 2010.

11. Charles Mutasa, 'Introduction: Millennium Development Goals in Africa', in Charles Mutasa and Mark Paterson (eds), *Africa and the Millennium Development Goals: Progress, Problems, and Prospects* (New York: Rowan and Littlefield, 2015), pp. 5–7.

12. Jocelyne Sambira and Kingsley Ighobor, 'Financing Africa's Development Agenda', *Africa Renewal*, December 2015, http://www.un.org/africarenewal/magazine/december-2015/financing-africa%E2%80%99s-development-agenda (accessed 27 October 2016).

13. African Centre for Economic Transformation (ACET), *Preview of the 2013 African Transformation Report* (Accra, 2013).

14. See website of the Comprehensive Africa Agriculture Development Programme (CAADP), www.nepad-caadp.net (accessed 11 November 2016).

15. Global Harvest Initiative, *2012 GAP Report: Measuring Global Agricultural Productivity* (Washington, DC, 2012), http://www.globalharvestinitiative.org/index.php/gap-report-index/2012-gap-report (accessed 5 December 2016).

16. Carlos Lopez, *Africa's New Agenda for Economic Transformation*, March 2015, https://www.chathamhouse.org/sites/files/chathamhouse/field/field_document/Carlos%20Lopes%20Transcript_kl_jm.pdf (accessed 3 December 2017).

17. Kingsley Ighobor, 'Sustainable Development Goals Are in Sync with Africa's Priorities', *Africa Renewal*, December 2015, http://www.un.org/africarenewal/magazine/december-2015/sustainable-development-goals-are-sync-africa%E2%80%99s-priorities (accessed 12 December 2017).

18. Sambira and Ighobor, 'Financing Africa's Development Agenda'.

19. Francis Nguendi Ikome, *From the Lagos Plan of Action (LPA) to the New Partnership for Africa's Development (NEPAD): The Political Economy of African Regional Initiatives*, PhD thesis, University of Witwatersrand, 2004 http://wiredspace.wits.ac.za/bitstream/handle/10539/196/mainthesis.pdf; jsessionid=88E01613E21479BDFBBAC813963CBB55?sequence=2v (accessed 19 December 2016).

20. Adebayo Adedeji, 'From the Lagos Plan of Action to the New Partnership for African Development and from the Final Act of Lagos to the Constitutive Act: Wither Africa?', keynote address at the African Forum for Envisioning Africa, Nairobi, 26–29 April 2002, p. 3, http://isites.harvard.edu/fs/docs/icb. topic1494737.files/Adebayo%20Adedeji%20Whither%20Africa.pdf (accessed 17 November 2016).

21. Claude Ake, *Democracy and Development in Africa* (Washington, DC: Brookings Institute, 2001).

22. Peter Hjertholm (ed.), *Foreign Aid and Development: Lessons Learnt and Directions for the Future* (London: Routledge, 2000).

23. Dambisa Moyo, *Dead Aid: Why Aid Is Not Working and How There Is a Better Way for Africa* (London: Farrar, Straus, and Giroux, March 2009).

24. William Easterly, Robert Levine and Dennis Rodman, 'Aid, Policies, and Growth: Comment', *American Economic Review* 94 (2004), pp. 774–80.

25. Moyo, *Dead Aid*.

26. UNECA, 'Appraisal and Review of the Impact of the Lagos Plan of Action on the Development and Expansion of Intra-African Trade; Conference of African Ministers of Trade Meeting, 11th session: 1990, 15–19 April: Addis Ababa, Ethiopia, http://repository.uneca.org/handle/10855/14129 (accessed 6 November 2016).

27. Bob Baulch and Edward Elgar (eds), *Why Poverty Persists: Poverty Dynamics in Asia and Africa* (Cheltenham: Edward Elgar, 2011, p. xiii).

28. UNECA and AU Commission, *Economic Report on Africa – Dynamic Industrial Policy: Innovative Institutions, Effective Processes, and Flexible Mechanisms* (Addis Ababa, 2014).

29. Richard E. Mshomba, *Africa in the Global Economy* (Boulder and London: Rienner, 2000).

30. NEPAD Secretariat, 'A Historical Overview of the New Partnership for Africa's Development (NEPAD)', background document (November 2001).

31. John Akokpari, Angela Ndinga-Muvumba and Tim Murithi, *The African Union and Its Institutions* (Johannesburg: Jacana Media, 2008).

32. AU, 'The Future We Want for Africa: About *Agenda 2063*', http://agenda2063. au.int/en/about (accessed 23 November 2016).

33. Bernama-Nnn-Ena, 'UNECA Chief Says Ethiopia to Be Africa's Major Economic Power by 2050', 31 December 2015, http://www.bernama. com/bernama/v8/wn/newsworld.php?id=1203421 (accessed 6 January 2017).

34. Suresh Chandra Saxena (ed.), *Africa Beyond 2000: Essays on Africa's Political and Economic Development in the Twenty-First Century* (Delhi: Kalinga, 2001).
35. Adebayo Alukoshi, 'Africa, from Lagos Plan of Action to NEPAD', *African Agenda* 5, nos. 2–3 (2002), pp. 8–9.
36. Sambira and Ighobor, 'Financing Africa's Development Agenda'.
37. UNECA, 'A New Burst of Energy in Industrial Activity'.
38. Sambira and Ighobor, 'Financing Africa's Development Agenda'.
39. Maxwell M. Mkwezalamba, AU Commissioner for Economic Affairs, opening remarks to the Committee of Experts of the Fifth Joint Annual Meetings of the AU Conference of Ministers of Economy and Finance and the UNECA Conference of Ministers of Finance, Planning and Economic Development (Addis Ababa, 22 March 2012).

CHAPTER 9

THE AFRICAN UNION AND ITS RELATIONS WITH SUB-REGIONAL ECONOMIC COMMUNITIES

Dawn Nagar and *Fritz Nganje*

This chapter reviews the relationship between the African Union (AU) and Africa's regional economic communities (RECs) against the backdrop of efforts towards the political and economic integration of the continent. There are currently about 19 regional and sub-regional organisations in Africa, with substantial differences in their objectives, capacities, level of functionality, and overlapping memberships. However, following concerns in the early 2000s about the proliferation of RECs, the AU Summit in Gambia in 2006 decided to recognise eight RECs as the building blocks of continental integration and placed a moratorium on the creation of new ones. The eight RECs are: The Economic Community of West African States (ECOWAS), The Common Market for Eastern and Southern Africa (COMESA), The East African Community (EAC), the Economic Community of Central African States (ECCAS), The Southern African Development Community (SADC),

The Intergovernmental Authority for Development (IGAD), The Arab Maghreb Union (AMU) and the Economic Community of Sahelo-Saharian States (CEN-SAD).[1]

One of the objectives of the AU as spelled out in its Constitutive Act of 2000 is to 'coordinate and harmonise the policies between the existing and future Regional Economic Communities for the gradual attainment of the objectives of the Union'.[2] An evolving normative and institutional framework has emerged since to give effect to this mandate across the different policy areas of the AU's integration project. However, as the following discussion demonstrates, while considerable efforts have been made to develop common policy frameworks and promote continent-wide initiatives that seek to bind the destiny of the different RECs to the political and economic integration agenda of the AU, the relationship between the AU and the RECs has been fraught with many challenges, contributing to the slow pace of regional integration in Africa. We begin with a brief overview of the historical antecedents of relations between the AU and RECs before analysing the dynamics of this relationships, first in the domain of economic integration, and then in the area of peace and security.

AU-REC Relations in Historical Context

The relationship between the AU and the RECs is rooted in the June 1991 Abuja Treaty, which identified the latter as the building blocks of the envisaged African Economic Community (AEC). Article 88 of the Abuja Treaty mandated the Secretariat of the Organisation of African Unity (OAU) (hereafter the Secretariat), which doubled as the Secretariat of the AEC, to strengthen the performance of RECs and create new ones, where they did not already exist. The Secretariat was also entrusted with the responsibility to work towards harmonising, coordinating and evaluating the activities of these regional blocs, with the support of member states, having in mind the economic integration objective envisaged in the Abuja Treaty.[3] In other words, the relationship between the OAU and RECs was to be informed by the six-stage roadmap for achieving continental integration over a period of 34 years from the date of entry into force of the treaty in May 1994.[4]

A Protocol on Relations between the AEC and the RECs was signed in February 1998. In addition to seeking to promote horizontal cooperation among the RECs, the 1998 protocol also provided an institutional structure to enable the Secretariat to support the RECs to achieve their respective mandates, while also coordinating and harmonising their policies, measures, programmes and activities to ensure that they did not duplicate or jeopardise efforts towards achieving the objectives of the AEC.[5] Importantly, the protocol committed the RECs to reviewing their treaties to identify the establishment of the AEC as their final objective and make provision for their eventual absorption into the African Common Market as a prelude to the full establishment of the AEC.[6]

The transformation of the OAU into the AU in 2000 added a new dynamic to the economic integration aspirations embodied by the AEC, and by extension relations between the AEC and RECs. With its overarching goal of fostering the Pan-African ideals of political unification and economic integration, and in addition to adopting an ambitious socio-political and economic agenda for Africa's development, the AU took over the regional integration programme of the Abuja Treaty, including the responsibility to strengthen, coordinate and harmonise the RECs for gradual continental integration. In principle, therefore, and by virtue of its Constitutive Act of 2000, the AU became the primary integration organisation in Africa, with all other integrating mechanisms, notably the RECs, expected to assume subordinate status to the AU, and being required to rationalise their agendas and operations to bring them in line with the common continental agenda driven by the AU.[7] This principle was upheld by the July 2001 Summit of the OAU Heads of State and Government, held in Lusaka, Zambia. This Summit reaffirmed the status of RECs as building blocks of the newly formed AU, and initiated a review process of the existing protocol between the RECs and the AEC, resulting in the adoption of the Protocol on Relations between the RECs and the AU in 2007. Among other provisions, the protocol required the RECs to align their policies, programmes and strategies with those of the AU.[8]

While the RECs were originally conceived as mechanisms to foster Africa's economic integration, their interface with the AU has evolved in the context of a broadened continental integration agenda, which requires coordination and harmonisation on a variety of policy frameworks and initiatives relating to governance, peace and security, as well as socio-economic development. As the subsequent discussion demonstrates, this changing context, coupled with the fact that the RECs are independent organisations with their own histories, mandates and capacities, has given rise to a complex relationship between the AU and the RECs. We will now proceed to examine the nature of this relationship in the area of economic integration before turning our attention to the dynamics of AU-RECs relations on peace and security.

The AU and the RECs on Economic Integration in Africa

This section provides an overview of the AU's economic agenda and a brief background, before examining its progress and achievements of economic integration.[9] Second, the section outlines the challenges in continental and regional economic integration and prospects for the advancement of socio-economic stability on the continent.

The pace of regional economic integration is dependent on benefits in the regional scheme. Regional economic integration over the past two decades has too heavily concentrated on tariff settings as a priority. Only recently has more attention been given to industrialisation, technology and research-driven integration. These areas must be made much more attractive for member states to have the drive to grow their economies, and for regional industries to be more involved in outputs of industrialisation and manufacturing. Enhancing regional value addition to industrialisation at the policy level must have smaller industries' input into larger economies' production base.

One of the main reasons for creating the RECs in Africa was to promote such structures with sustainable economic schemes to address the imbalance of weaker economies against stronger ones within regional clusters. The United Nations Economic Commission for Africa (UNECA) was designed as one of the frontrunners of the United Nations' socio-economic global strategy to 'force the pace of cooperation among African states in trade, transport, and industry through the mechanism of sub-regional coordinating bodies'.[10] In 1965, at a Lusaka meeting, Eastern African states met to harmonise industrial development and establish an Economic Community for East and Central Africa with a secretariat based in Lusaka. However, within two years it dissolved. The East African Community was created in 1967, comprising Kenya, Tanzania and Uganda, but this collapsed in 1977. The next attempt at regionalism, beginning in 1958, was the cooperative framework designed by the Economic Commission for Africa, which sought to promote regional economic cooperation on the continent that could eventually evolve into common markets through the establishment of multi-national programming and operational centres (MULPOCs) in Africa's five sub-regions. The funding of MULPOCs consumed an annual budget of approximately US $7 million over four years (1977–81) in financing projects in statistics, industry, national accounts, transport and communications and integration of women in development.[11] Through the MULPOC programme, the establishment of the Intergovernmental Authority for Drought and Development (IGADD) and the Eastern and Southern African Management Institute (ESAMI) was achieved. From 1977 to 1981, a series of multi-lateral negotiations among leaders from East and Southern Africa progressive development of the MULPOC programme. In 1981, these discussions also contributed to the establishment of the East and Southern Africa Preferential Trade Area (PTA).

The 1980's were beset by the persistence of chronic underdevelopment and the accumulation of debt, which meant that economic growth was negligible. This was one of the imperatives that drove the efforts to advance the pursuit of regional economic integration. The OAU, created in 1963, took more than three decades before transforming into its successor, the AU, in 2002. Further regional integration schemes were formed – and the AU's socio-economic programme, the New Partnership for Africa's Development (NEPAD), was created in 2001. Meanwhile, regional economic integration evolved independently from the continental body. In fact, even before UNECA had decided on a gradual integration strategy and division of Africa into five regions (North, Central, East, South and West), economic integration had commenced. For example, the Southern African Customs Union (SACU) had been created in 1910 and is still in existence, while the Kenya–Uganda customs union had been formed in 1917.

In assessing this disconnect between continental and regional economic integration, the African Union formulated several programmes, such as the AU Minimum Integration Programme of 2009, and also, more recently, in 2015, adopted its *Agenda 2063*. Few commodities are traded on the continent, with only 12 per cent of trade being intra-regional. Most African economies are peripheral, with five large core economies: Nigeria, Kenya, Egypt, Angola and South Africa. Africa's regions still lack regional integration policies viable for economic growth, such as government support for small, medium and micro-sized enterprises (SMMEs). Such businesses could grow industrialisation along with value-added production through intra-regional trade and manufacturing. These factors are important in fostering endogenous growth through the transfer of technology and skills to boost development, research and education supported by strong government policies.

Progress in Economic Integration

Achievements in regional free trade areas (FTAs) and customs unions has varied. These are important processes in creating a Continental Free Trade Area (C-FTA). Such processes find expression in continental accords of the Lagos Plan of Action and Final Act of Lagos (both of 1980), as well as the Abuja Treaty of 1991, mandating that regional economic communities should establish free trade areas and customs unions by the end of 2017 (see Mutasa in this volume). Four of the eight major regional economic communities have declared free trade areas, including COMESA, the EAC, ECOWAS and SADC. Two customs unions are recognised: the EAC and another in ECOWAS. SACU is not recognised as a regional economic community by either the Abuja Treaty or the AU. However, it is one of the regional mechanisms promoting economic convergence on the continent. Currently, SACU is in negotiations with all the larger markets with which SACU member states do not share an FTA, notably Egypt and Kenya.

Gradually the 19-member COMESA bloc also converged with the EAC of six member states (with South Sudan as its newest member), and with the 15-member SADC, and formed the COMESA-EAC-SADC Tripartite Alliance in October 2008. This alliance has a combined gross domestic product (GDP) of US$1.2 trillion and is seen as an important step by the African Union in reaching a C-FTA. In furtherance of this agreement, a meeting in June 2015, in Egypt, adopted the Tripartite Free

Trade Area, signed by 16 member states, mainly of the COMESA bloc.[12]

Most of SADC's member states (Botswana, Lesotho, Madagascar, Mauritius, Mozambique, South Africa and Zambia), and COMESA's member states (Ethiopia, Eritrea, and Libya), did not sign the Tripartite FTA in June 2015. Two SACU members signed the Tripartite FTA to secure national trade prospects in the region. Powerful economies have also impacted on the pace of Africa's economic integration. On its part, South Africa's stringent rules of origin have been viewed as an impediment to intra-regional trade for Southern Africa. As an illustration, Tshwane (Pretoria) has prohibited the importation of live animals from Namibia. As a result, costs to the Windhoek government were estimated at 30 billion South African Rands (US$2.2 billion) in establishing agro-processing schemes such as feed-loads and abattoirs to create an environment conducive to trade.

ECOWAS had adopted its customs union in January 2015, and by the end of April 2015, eight of its 15 member states had started the scheme's liberalisation process. It includes a 'common external tariff of zero per cent on essential social goods of 85 tariff lines; five per cent on goods of primary necessity [such as] raw materials, capital goods and specific inputs of 2,100 tariff lines; 10 per cent on intermediate goods of about 1,400 tariff lines; and 35 per cent on specific goods for economic development covering 130 tariff lines'.[13]

Progress in the other regional schemes has also varied. The five-member Arab Maghreb Union is finalising negotiations for an AMU free trade area; and in December 2014 the group created an intra-Africa trade initiative and readied itself for the C-FTA negotiations.[14]

Infrastructure

Regional infrastructure schemes have significantly taken off among Africa's five sub-regions. In March 2012, the Lamu Port Southern Sudan–Ethiopia Transport (LAPSSET) corridor was completed. In July 2013, at the 12th annual Ethiopian-Djibouti Joint Commission Ministerial Meeting, agreements on trade investment and infrastructure, as well as security and other issues, were reached. Agreements included rail and road infrastructural development, and new ports, power and water services. In Southern Africa, the Maputo Corridor, created in 1995, was further developed in 2014 by South Africa's Transnet for port and rail operators in Swaziland and Mozambique. The aim of the Maputo Corridor Joint Operating Centre (JOC) is to increase the Maputo Development Corridor (MDC) rail freight capacity. In March 2016 South Africa also provided Botswana and Swaziland with rail transport estimated between one and three billion South African rand (between US$74 and 200 million), among other railway schemes between the countries to improve regional transport for both goods and services.

Shadow Regionalism in Economic Integration
In ECCAS, shadow regionalism trumps economic integration. Although ECCAS has a free trade area, on average the region reduced only 34 per cent of tariff lines on intra-ECCAS tariffs to zero. The region also has the lowest share of intra-regional trade in terms of GDP of any of Africa's five sub-regions. Member states of ECCAS have been challenged by corruption and greed, and economic integration is thus progressing under acts of shadow regionalism. According to a United Nations (UN) report, 'illicit resources are mainly derived from deals in gold ($40 million to $120 million); timber ($16 million to $48 million); charcoal ($12 million to $35 million); 3T minerals (cassiterite [tin], wolframite [tungsten], coltan [tantalum]), cobalt and copper ($7.5 million to $22.6 million); diamonds, sourced mainly from outside of the Democratic Republic of the Congo (DRC) ($16 million to $48 million); and wildlife, including ivory and fisheries; local taxation schemes; cannabis; and other resources ($14.3 million

to \$28 million)'. Official estimates of DRC's gold produced and traded were 150.58 kg in 2014, and 180.76 kg in 2013, which is less than two per cent of the total gold produced. The remainder of the gold is smuggled and was estimated at ten tonnes (10,000 kilogrammes) in 2013 at a value of about US\$391 million to US\$418 million. In 2014, the DRC produced up to 40 tonnes (40,000 kilogrammes) of gold for the year, and illicit gold exports were estimated to be between US\$118 million and over US\$1.8 billion.[15] Moreover, 98 per cent of the net profits were from illegal natural resource exploitation, particularly of gold, charcoal and timber, which went to trans-national organised criminal networks operating in and outside the DRC. Armed groups retain around two per cent (approximately US\$13.2 million per year) of net profits from illegal smuggling, which also represents the basic subsistence cost for at least 8,000 armed rebel fighters per year.[16]

Negotiating the Continental Free Trade Area

There are many hurdles for the AU and its 54 member states before a continental free trade can be achieved and effectively supported by the RECs as the pillars of economic integration. The creation of an African Economic Community and a Monetary and Economic Union would need to address eight important AU areas:

- A detailed indicative roadmap on the negotiation and establishment of a C-FTA.
- All decisions within the C-FTA negotiation process to be by consensus.
- The application of the principle of reciprocity among member states.
- Multiple and overlapping memberships to be addressed.
- The gradual approach of integration and the principle of *acquis* whereby the C-FTA will build on previous existing agreements of member states within RECs.

- The principle of variable geometry, which provides flexibility for member states to reduce tariffs at different speeds in free trade agreements.
- The most-favoured-nation (MFN) principle, to be observed by member states to afford one another the MFN treatment under a C-FTA.
- National treatment for the regulation of domestic goods and services as well as internal taxes should apply to all African countries.[17]

Challenges

The AU has deployed a double-track process for achieving economic integration: one at the continental level and another at the regional level. Member states therefore need to comply with the integration approach and obligations thereof as expressed in the Abuja Treaty, as well as those defined by the RECs' integration schemes. The C-FTA is also based on the principle of *acquis*, which entails that previous agreements by RECs remain intact and include those concerning trade liberalisation frameworks reflective of open markets and agreements signed with external partners. However, trade liberalisation through bilateral trade agreements appears to contradict the principle of variable geometry, which is about incremental integration and trade protection, since the pace of integration varies between these two approaches: trade liberalisation and variable geometry. There is also the problem associated with membership overlap. Since the signing of the October 2008 Tripartite Agreement, several smaller economies have become dependent on other forms of securing economic growth to protect their industries and smaller businesses. For example, in SADC, several states with smaller economies have signed external trade agreements that could potentially protect smaller industries, resulting in the criss-crossing of trade agreements and overlapping of memberships with other states. At the regional level, Africa's governments need to revisit the treaties of RECs that allow for bilateral and multilateral relations of its member states,[18] and need to consider adding legally binding agreements that provide rules of engagement in bilateral and multilateral trade agreements.

Moreover, trade agreements that favour and protect regional trade in both goods and services must be negotiated, as the European Union (EU) has done by protecting its own industries through agricultural subsidies since the 1950s. Trade should expand across the continent and not for the sake of integrating regions. If more amicable relations with more intra-regional trade are to occur, then larger economies such as South Africa should relax stringent domestic industrial policies and trade protectionism.

The AU and the RECs on Peace and Security in Africa

As noted earlier, the AU has emerged as the primary vehicle for political and economic integration in Africa. However, given African leaders' preference for a gradual and pyramidal approach to continental integration, there has always been an acknowledgement of the critical role that RECs must play in this process. In this regard, the successful implementation of both the African Peace and Security Architecture (APSA) and the African Governance Architecture (AGA) depends on the involvement of the RECs. The focus of many of Africa's RECs has for the most part been on economic integration. However, with the growing recognition of the symbiotic relationship between security and development, and against the backdrop of intractable violent conflicts and instability in the different regions of the continent, almost all the eight RECs recognised by the AU would subsequently develop the institutional capacity to address issues of governance, peace and security in their respective neighbourhoods. Generally, the RECs have a mixed record of conflict management and peace-building. By their proximity to the theatres of regional conflicts, the

RECs tend to display a good understanding of the causes and dynamics of these conflicts. They also often have strong incentives to respond timeously to conflicts in their respective neighbourhoods. However, their peacemaking and peace-building efforts have sometimes been undermined by generally weak capacities, mainly in the domain of peace operations, but also regarding structural conflict prevention, preventive diplomacy and mediation. Additionally, the national interest considerations of powerful member states such as South Africa in Southern Africa, Nigeria in West Africa, as well as Ethiopia and Kenya in East Africa sometimes interfere with regional peace efforts, resulting in internal divisions and organisational paralysis, as well as biased interventions.[19] The regional peace and security initiatives of four of Africa's RECs – ECOWAS, SADC, IGAD and ECCAS – illustrate this assessment.

Although established in May 1975 primarily as a vehicle for economic integration in West Africa (albeit with a veiled security imperative),[20] ECOWAS played a major role in managing the conflicts in Liberia and Sierra Leone in the 1990s and early 2000s. In both cases, it was only after the regional body's vigorous diplomatic and military interventions, under the leadership of Nigeria, did ECOWAS Military Observer Group (ECOMOG) manage to stabilise the situation and paved the way for the United Nations to deploy peacekeeping missions.[21] Following this experience, ECOWAS would proceed to develop an elaborate and evolving normative and institutional framework to promote peace, security, human rights and democratic governance in the region.[22] This framework has formed the basis of a growing number of operational and structural interventions to promote shared political values, and prevent, manage and resolve conflicts in countries such as Côte d'Ivoire, Guinea-Bissau, Liberia, Mali, and Sierra Leone. ECOWAS's peace-building efforts in West Africa, which have taken the form of the deployment of peacekeepers, preventive diplomacy, electoral support and strengthening democratic institutions in its member states, have had mixed results. On the one hand, the organisation has contributed to bringing relative stability to a very volatile region, while also forging a regional consensus, although still tenuous, around democratic values and principles. On the other hand, Nigeria's declining capacity to underwrite regional initiatives and the continued interference in regional affairs by Western powers such as France have constrained the peace-making and peace-building role of ECOWAS.[23]

SADC, unlike ECOWAS, owes its origins to the politico-security alliance established by the Frontline States in 1976, and has since its establishment in 1992 identified the promotion of democratic governance, peace and security as central to its common agenda.[24] However, it was only following the adoption of the Protocol on Politics, Defence and Security Cooperation, in August 2001, that the organisation was able to articulate a clear normative agenda on, and progressively establish an institutional framework for, governance, peace and security in the region. At the centre of Southern Africa's architecture for political governance and security is the SADC Organ on Politics, Defence and Security Cooperation, whose Strategic Indicative Plan for the Organ (SIPO), adopted in 2004 and revised in 2010, aims to create an enabling environment for implementing the region's agenda on socio-economic development. To this end, SADC has developed a set of institutions, norms and guidelines to promote participatory governance and strengthen the conduct of democratic elections in the region, while also developing its capacity for peace-making and peacekeeping, including an electoral advisory council, a mediation unit, an early warning system and a standby force.[25] The peace-making and peacekeeping role of SADC has without doubt been instrumental in containing political conflicts and violence in Zimbabwe, the Democratic Republic of the Congo, Madagascar and Lesotho. However, a combination of an inordinate deference to national sovereignty, and inadequate technical and resource capacity, has seen SADC struggle to build sustainable peace in Southern Africa. SADC has been particularly weak in engendering regional consensus around shared political values as a prerequisite for the aspired-to security community.[26] Its capacity for post-conflict peace-building and reconstruction also remains underdeveloped.[27]

IGAD was created in 1986 as a regional mechanism to fight drought and promote development in the Horn of Africa. However, it was re-launched in 1996 with a mandate that included the prevention, management and resolution of conflict.[28] IGAD's peace and security architecture includes, among other components, its Conflict Early Warning and Response Mechanism (CEWARN), a mediation support unit, and liaison offices in different parts of the region. However, the institutionalisation of IGAD's peace and security framework has been limited; the organisation does not have a dedicated decision making organ in this area comparable to the AU's Peace and Security Council (PSC) or SADC's Organ. Decisions on peace and security are made at the level of heads of state and government, sometimes meeting informally. This is consistent with a broader ad hoc, pragmatic and less intrusive approach to dealing with issues of peace and security (compared to a REC like ECOWAS), which reflects strong mistrust and rivalries among IGAD member states, notably Ethiopia, Kenya and Uganda, in pursuit of their respective national interests in the region. A major consequence of this modestly institutionalised regional peace and security framework is that conflicts in the region have always attracted multiple and often poorly coordinated interventions, as was the case with the recent political crisis in South Sudan. This situation is exacerbated by the fact that in addition to the AU, which has a continent-wide peace and security mandate, IGAD also has to share the regional security space with the EAC and the East Africa Standby Brigade (EASBRIG), which it coordinates.[29]

ECCAS was established in 1983 to promote regional integration in Central Africa, but has since 1997 prioritised regional peace, security and stability as part of its agenda. However, it has remained a very weak regional peace and security actor. The peace and security structure of the ten-member REC is dominated by the Council for Peace and Security (COPAX), which is the primary decision making organ, although its decisions can be implemented only after they have been ratified by the Conference of Heads of State. COPAX is supported by the Commission for Defence and Security (CDS), the Central African Early Warning System (MARAC), and the Central African Multinational Force (FOMAC), the latter of which has been designated as the region's standby brigade for the African Standby Force (ASF).[30] However, this institutional framework has not functioned satisfactorily, owing largely to endemic governance deficits and political instability in the region, as well as regional rivalry and distrust. In this context, the organisation lacks the will and capacity for institutionalised engagement in preventive diplomacy and structural conflict prevention, and its response to conflicts such as that in the Central African Republic in 2013 tends to follow the preferences and initiatives of individual heads of state such as Chad's Idris Derby and Congo-Brazzaville's Denis Sassou-Ngeusso. ECCAS's weak peace and security capacity 'has been exacerbated by insufficient financial and human resources and a militarised view on security matters'.[31] The fact that ECCAS has overlapping member-ship with other regional and sub-regional organisations, notably the Economic and Monetary Community of Central African States (CEMAC), the International Conference on the Great Lakes Region (ICGLR), the EAC and SADC, has been both a function of, and a contributing factor to, its limited role in peace and security in the Central African region.

Dynamics of AU-REC Relations on Peace and Security
Article 16 of the 2002 Protocol Relating to the Establishment
of the AU Peace and Security Council recognised RECs as an
integral part of the continental peace and security architecture.
The protocol assumes the primacy of the AU in maintaining
peace and security in Africa, but calls on the PSC and the chair
of the AU Commission to work closely with the RECs to
harmonise and coordinate the activities of these regional
organisations. The ultimate goal of this partnership is to
ensure that the policies and activities of the RECs in these areas
are aligned with the principles and objectives of the AU.
In accordance with this requirement, a memorandum of
understanding (MOU) on cooperation around peace and
security was signed in January 2008 between the AU, the
RECs and the coordinating mechanisms of the regional
standby brigades of Eastern and Northern Africa. The MOU
enjoined the AU and the RECs to work together towards the
full operationalisation of the APSA and the maintenance of
peace, security and stability in Africa, based on the principles
of subsidiary, comparative advantage and complementarity.
It emphasised the imperative for information-sharing, regular
consultations, institutional presence and operational
cooperation between the AU and the RECs.

Its noble intentions notwithstanding, the MOU embodies
two weaknesses that have made effective coordination and
cooperation between the AU and RECs on matters of peace and
security largely elusive over the years. First, it is an agreement
between the secretariats of the respective organisations, and so
does not commit the PSC and similar decision making organs
in the RECs. Second, the MOU fails to provide an
authoritative interpretation of the concepts of subsidiarity,
comparative advantage and complementarity in this context.
If anything, by emphasising the principles of subsidiarity and
primacy in the relationship between the AU and the RECs,
the MOU inadvertently creates room for 'friction between

[these organisations] in crisis situations and inhibited policy and operational harmonisation in a range of areas, including the African Standby Force'.[32]

Subsequent to the signing of the MOU, a number of initiatives have been taken to strengthen the interface between the AU and the RECs on peace and security. Notably, the RECs have opened liaison offices at AU headquarters in Addis Ababa, and the AU has done the same at the headquarters of the different RECs. While these offices have improved communication between the AU and the RECs, their contribution to effective coordination between these organisations remains limited. The profile and mandate of liaison officers deployed to the AU has been such that they have not been able to engage with the substantive work of key AU organs such as the PSC. Coordination between the different components of the APSA and similar structures in the RECs has also been limited. On the one hand, the AU and the RECs have collaborated relatively well in operationalising the African Standby Force and the Continental Early Warning System (CEWS). Significant efforts have also been made to bring coherence to the activities of the AU Panel of the Wise and similar structures in the RECs, including through regular retreats and conducting joint missions under the aegis of the Pan-African Network of the Wise (Pan-Wise), established in May 2013. On the other hand, coordination between the policy and decision making organs of the AU, notably the PSC, and those of the RECs, is still under-developed. Although the PSC now holds regular retreats with the RECs, there are hardly any significant consultations between the Council and REC structures that make decisions on issues of peace and security such as the SADC Organ and the ECOWAS Mediation and Security Council.[33]

Against this backdrop, the interventions of the AU and the RECs to crisis situations on the continent have for the most part been defined by tension and competition rather than cooperation and division of labour. There have indeed been instances where the AU has deferred to or cooperated almost seamlessly with the RECs in peacemaking. As Tim Murithi and Aquilina Mawadza have pointed out, although the AU, through the PSC and the chair of the AU Commission, remained seized with the political crisis in Zimbabwe following the disputed elections in 2008, it in effect delegated responsibility for resolving the conflict to SADC in respect for the principle of subsidiarity.[34] A similar posture of delegation, cooperation and complementarity has to a large extent underpinned the AU and IGAD's response to the conflict in Sudan (before and after the signing of the Comprehensive Peace Agreement (CPA) in 2005) and South Sudan (since December 2013).[35] Most recently, the AU completely deferred to SADC's mediation and related intervention in Lesotho following an attempted coup in August 2014. However, most other peacemaking efforts have been characterised by tensions and competition between the AU and the RECs involved. Consider, for example, the diverging positions and rivalry between the AU and ECOWAS in Côte d'Ivoire in 2011, Mali in 2013 and Burkina Faso in 2015; or that between the AU and SADC in Madagascar in 2009, and the AU and ECCAS in the Central African Republic in 2013.

The September 2015 retreat of the PSC and similar organs of the RECs, held in Abuja, Nigeria, sought to address this coordination gap by adopting a formal consultative process that is expected to enhance collaboration and consultation between the Council and similar organs of the RECs. Among the measures agreed on was the participation of the RECs in PSC meetings when the Council is seized with an issue that is of concern to a particular REC, although it must be underscored that the RECs do not participate in the decision-making phase of PSC meetings. Moreover, while the Abuja retreat institutionalised the biannual meetings between the PSC and the RECs, it fell short of resolving the uncertainty and controversy over the interpretation of the principle of subsidiarity, only underscoring that 'the principles of subsidiarity, complementarity, and comparative advantage [will be applied] on a case by case basis, taking into account the peculiarities of each conflict situation/crisis'.[36] Earlier in 2014, a joint task force on strengthening relations between the AU and the RECs and regional mechanisms (RMs) in the area of peace and security had been established with the responsibility to 'develop a strategy and action plan for, among other things, implementing the commitments of the relevant legal instruments, developing modalities for collaboration and coordination at the strategic decision making level, and designing modalities for the implementation of the principles of subsidiarity, complementarity and comparative advantage'.[37] However, prospects for effective coordination and cooperation between the AU and the RECs in the area of peacemaking remain bleak in the context of fundamental legal, institutional and political challenges that are inherent in the relationship between these inter-governmental organisations.

Explaining the Weak Interface Between the AU and the RECs on Peace and Security

The preceding discussion points to endemic competition and tension between the AU and the RECs when it comes to responding to conflict situations that pose a threat to peace and security on the continent. This is the case even though these organisations serve the same member states, which have made commitments in various legal and policy instruments to work together towards the common goal of continental peace, security and development. Why then has effective coordination and cooperation eluded the relationship between the AU and the RECs in the domain of peace and security? There are many reasons that can be advanced to explain the dysfunctional relationship between the AU and RECs, but for the purpose of this chapter we will attempt to answer this question at the systemic and institutional level.

Regional Organisations as Instruments of Nation States in a System of Self-Help

The first explanation rests on the anarchic nature of the international system, which is still dominated by sovereign states with diverse interests and values, and which recognise no authority above them. From this perspective, inter-governmental organisations such as the AU and the different RECs should be seen primarily as vehicles through which states seek to promote their interests. Therefore, despite the legal and policy stipulations about the primacy of the AU in maintaining continental peace and security in Africa, and the centrality of the principles of subsidiarity, complementarity and comparative advantage in its relations with the RECs, the extent to which cooperation and coordination takes place within and between these organisations depends to a large extent on national interest calculations and the prevailing balance of power among member states. In any given conflict situation, states will prioritise the authority of either the AU or a REC not out of a careful assessment of the conflict dynamics and the capabilities of that organisation to respond appropriately, but mostly on the basis of which organisation affords them enough space to legitimise their preferred approach to resolving the conflict.[38] The organisational tension that is often observed between the AU and the RECs in peacemaking in Africa is sometimes symptomatic of the rivalry that arises when powerful states with interest in a particular conflict attempt to instrumentalise either of these organisations to impose competing ideas of how the conflict should be resolved. This challenge tends to be exacerbated by the existence of competing national interests within a given REC and the overlapping membership of these regional organisations, which gives rise to multiple and often diverging interests and initiatives in a single conflict situation.

The divergent positions adopted by ECOWAS and the AU during the political crisis that resulted from the April 2012 coup in Guinea-Bissau bear testament to this argument. Following the military takeover, the AU suspended Guinea-Bissau and called for the junta to return power to the legitimate civilian authorities. However, ECOWAS, acting against its own principle of zero tolerance of unconstitutional change of government, supported the creation of a transitional government by the perpetrators of the coup. It is believed that this position was influenced by the national interests of ECOWAS member states such as Nigeria, Côte d'Ivoire and Senegal, which were concerned about the presence of Angolan troops in Guinea-Bissau, and had secured the assurance of the junta that these troops would be asked to leave.[39] The influence of France in shaping and implementing ECOWAS's preferred response to the political crisis in Côte d'Ivoire in 2011 – which was frowned upon by some members of the PSC – further illustrates how the rivalry between the AU and the RECs in peacemaking can be exacerbated by external actors who attempt to use either of these organisations as entry points to promote their own interests on the continent.[40]

Shared Mandate, Multiple Centres of Power and Weak Institutional Linkages

Compounding this systemic obstacle to effective partnership between the AU and the RECs is the institutional dissonance that defines the AU's peace and security architecture. The protocol establishing the PSC recognises RECs as an integral component of the APSA, with the expectation that they will assume a key role in the implementation of the decisions of the PSC. However, the institutional design of the APSA fails to take into account the status of RECs as autonomous legal and political entities, to the effect that no binding provisions exist to give regional organisations an active voice in the decision-making processes of the PSC. As pointed out earlier, even the MOU that spells out the desired nature of the relationship between the AU and RECs on matters of peace and security is a technical instrument that places no obligations on the political organs of these organisations. Given the diversity of regional dynamics and state interests in Africa, the disconnect between the PSC and similar organs in the RECs forecloses opportunities for robust consultation and coordinated responses to conflicts, and has sometimes resulted in the RECs acting contrary to, and undermining, the position of the AU.[41] This was the case following what the AU considered to be an unconstitutional takeover of power in the CAR by the Seleka rebel group in 2013. The PSC called for the complete isolation of the perpetrators and imposed a travel ban on them. However, in defiance of the AU's stance, ECCAS went ahead to recognise Michel Djotodia as head of the transitional government in the CAR, while member states of the regional organisation as well as other French-speaking African countries allowed Djotodia to travel to their countries.[42]

Towards Greater Synergy Between the AU and the RECs on Peace and Security

It is evident from the preceding analysis that for if the processes of regionalisation in Africa continue to follow the logic of inter-govenmentalism, tension and competition cannot be avoided in the relations between the AU and the RECs. The member states that make up these organisations will always prioritise one of these bodies over the other, depending on which serves their national interests at any given time. Reducing the frequency of these frictions and mitigating their impact on the effectiveness of the continental peace and security architecture require institutionalised mechanisms for robust and regular consultation and coordination between the PSC and the organs of the RECs that are charged with making decisions on matters of peace and security. Additionally, efforts to promote greater synergy and complementarity between the policies and initiatives of the AU and the RECs on peace and security would benefit from an increased role of civil society and parliaments in defining the national security interests of the member states that make up these organisations. There is no gainsaying that, in many African states, the making of foreign and security policies is dominated by a few elites, whose narrow conception of the national interest is often the cause of the rivalry with other states, resulting in regional organisations being paralysed or pitted against one another.

Conclusion

In analysing the relationship between the AU and RECs through the prism of regional integration, trade, as well as peace and security, we see notable progress in the development of free trade areas within the African continent, in the lead up to the creation of a Continental Free Trade Area. In contrast, when it comes to peace and security the AU and the RECs are still struggling to harmonise and coordinate their efforts, due to a large extent to the self-interests of certain dominant countries. In order to overcome the paralysis experienced by both the AU and the RECs, African governments must gradually let their selfish interests recede and operationalise the principle of solidarity, which they deploy only rhetorically when it suits them. Africa's integration will continue to proceed at multiple levels, which means that the symbiotic relationship between the AU and the RECs will only increase in importance.

Notes

1. See African Union (AU), *Decision on the Moratorium on the Recognition of Regional Economic Communities*, Assembly/AU/ Dec.112 (VII), 2006.
2. *Constitutive Act of the African Union* (July 2000), art. 3(l).
3. *Treaty Establishing the African Economic Community*, art. 88.
4. *Treaty Establishing the African Economic Community*, art. 6.
5. *Protocol on Relations Between the African Economic Community and the Regional Economic Communities*, art. 3.
6. *Protocol on Relations Between the African Economic Community and the Regional Economic Communities*, art. 5.

7. See African Capacity Building Foundation (ACBF), *A Survey of the Capacity Needs of Africa's Regional Economic Communities* (Harare, 2008), p. 68; AU Constitutive Act of AU, Lomé, Togo (11 July 2000), http://www.achpr.org/files/instruments/au-constitutive-act/au_act_2000_eng.pdf (accessed 26 June 2017).

8. AU, 'Regional Economic Communities (RECs)', http://www.au.int/en/organs/recs (accessed 2 February 2016).

9. This section of the chapter is based on Dawn Nagar, *The Politics and Economics of Regional Integration in Africa, 1970–2015: The Case of COMESA and SADC*, PhD thesis, University of the Witwatersrand, Johannesburg.

10. Douglas Anglin, 'Economic Liberation and Regional Cooperation in Southern Africa', *International Organization* 37 (1983), p. 684.

11. Nagar, *The Politics and Economics of Regional Integration in Africa*.

12. The 16 member states and signatories to the Tripartite FTA included: Angola, Burundi (EAC), Comoros, the Democratic Republic of the Congo, Djibouti, Egypt, Kenya (EAC), Malawi, Namibia, Rwanda (EAC), Seychelles, Sudan, Tanzania (EAC), Uganda (EAC), Swaziland and Zimbabwe.

13. United Nations Economic Commission for Africa (UNECA), 'Assessing Regional Integration in Africa VII' (2016), p. 14.

14. UNECA, 'Assessing Regional Integration in Africa VII'.

15. United Nations Environment Programme (UNEP) and Mission des Nations Unies en République Démocratique du Congo (MONSUCO), 'Experts' Background Report on Illegal Exploitation and Trade in Natural Resources Benefitting Organized Criminal Groups and Recommendations on MONUSCO's Role in Fostering Stability and Peace in Eastern DR Congo', 15 April 2015. See also Promines Study, 'Artisanal Mining in the Democratic Republic of Congo' (June 2010), http://www.congomines.org/wp-content/uploads/2011/10/PACT-2010-ProminesStudyArtisanalMiningDRC.pdf (accessed 20 January 2015).

16. See UNEP and MONSUCO, 'Experts' Background Report on Illegal Exploitation and Trade' (2015).

17. UNECA, 'Assessing Regional Integration in Africa VII', pp. 11–14.

18. Nagar, 'The Politics and Economics of Regional Integration' (2016), p. 173.

19. Laurie Nathan, 'Will the Lowest Be First? Subsidiarity in Peacemaking in Africa', paper presented at the annual convention of the International Studies Association (Atlanta, 16–19 March 2016), p. 2.

20. Said Adejumobi argues that despite the declared focus on economic integration, the formation of ECOWAS was also motivated by Nigeria's interests in securing its immediate neighbourhood, following the experience of the Biafra War of 1967–70. For more on this, see Said Adejumobi, 'Region-Building in West Africa', in Daniel Levine and Dawn Nagar (eds), *Region-Building in Africa* (New York: Palgrave, 2016).

21. Gilles Olakounlé Yabi, *The Role of ECOWAS in Managing Political Crisis and Conflict: The Cases of Guinea and Guinea-Bissau* (Abuja: Friedrich-Ebert-Stiftung (FES), 2010), p. 10.

22. For detailed analyses of this framework, *see* Adejumobi, 'Region-Building', 2016, pp. 213–30. See also Yabi, *The Role of ECOWAS*, pp. 10–14.

23. See Adejumobi, 'Region-Building', 2016, pp. 213–30. Yabi, *The Role of ECOWAS*, pp. 52–5. See also Adekeye Adebajo, 'Pax Nigeriana Versus Pax Gallica: ECOWAS and UN Peacekeeping in Mali', paper presented at the Centre for Conflict Resolution (CCR) policy research seminar on 'Towards A New Pax Africana: Making, Keeping, and Building Peace in Africa,' Cape Town, 28–30 August 2013.

24. See Joao M.L. Ndlovu, 'The AU-SADC Interface on Peace and Security: Challenges and Opportunities', pp. 59–61.

25. Adekeye Adebajo, Dawn Nagar, Mark Paterson, Kudrat Virk and Jill Kronenberg, 'Governance and Security Challenges in Post-Apartheid Southern Africa' (Cape Town: CCR, September 2013); International Crisis Group (ICG), 'Implementing Peace and Security Architecture II: Southern Africa', Africa Report no. 191 (October 2012), https://www.africaportal.org/dspace/articles/implementing-peace-and-security-architecture-ii-southern-africa (accessed 26 June 2016).

26. Laurie Nathan, 'Synopsis of Community of Insecurity: SADC's Struggle for Peace and Security in Southern Africa', *African Security Review* 22, no. 3 (2013), pp. 181–9.

27. Adebajo, Nagar, Paterson, Virk and Kronenberg, '*Governance and Security Challenges*', p. 4.

28. See Adekeye Adebajo, 'The Peacekeeping Travails of the AU and the Regional Economic Communities', in John Akokpari, Angela Nding-Muvumba and Tim Murithi (eds), *The African Union and Its Institutions* (Auckland Park: Fanele, 2008), p. 151.

29. Bruce Byiers, *The Political Economy of Regional Integration in Africa: Intergovernmental Authority on Development (IGAD) Report* (Maastricht: European Centre for Development Policy Management (ECDPM), 2016), pp. 27–39.

30. See Adebajo, 'The Peacekeeping Travails', p. 150. See also Gabriella Ingerstad and Magdalena T. Lindell, 'Challenges to Peace and Security in Central Africa: The Role of ECCAS', Studies in African Security, *Swedish Defence Research Agency* (June 2015), p. 1.

31. Ingerstad and Lindell, 'Challenges to Peace', p. 4.

32. Nathan, '*Will the Lowest Be First?*', pp. 6–7.

33. See Alhaji Sarjoh Bah, Elizabeth Choge-Nyangoro, Solomon Dersso, Brenda Mofya and Tim Murithi, *African Peace and Security Architecture: A Handbook* (Addis Ababa: FES, 2014), pp. 69–74.

34. Tim Murithi and Aquilina Mawadza (eds), *Zimbabwe in Transition: A View from Within* (Auckland Park: Fanele, 2011), pp. 292–3.

35. See Byiers, *The Political Economy*, pp. 26–42.

36. AU, 'Retreat of the Peace and Security Council on Enhancement of Cooperation Between the African Union Peace and Security Council and the Regional Economic Communities and Regional Mechanisms for Conflict

Prevention, Management, and Resolution in the Promotion of Peace, Security, and Stability in Africa' (Abuja, September 2015).

37. Nathan, *Will the Lowest Be First?*', p. 7.
38. Ibid., pp. 2–3.
39. Institute for Security Studies (ISS), *Security Council Report* no. 56 (March 2014), p. 6.
40. See Adebajo, *Pax Nigeriana Versus Pax Gallica*'.
41. See Ndlovu, *The AU-SADC Interface*', pp. 63–7.
42. Solomon Dersso, 'The Best Option to Settle the CAR Crisis', *Al Jazeera*, 5 December 2013.

PART III

THE AU'S POTENTIAL HEGEMONS AND EXTERNAL ACTORS

CHAPTER 10

CAUGHT BETWEEN PAN-AFRICAN SOLIDARISM AND REALIST DEVELOPMENTALISM? SOUTH AFRICA'S PIVOTAL ROLE IN THE AFRICAN UNION

Chris Landsberg

This chapter is interested in the notion of South Africa as a pivotal state[1] in Africa and the republic's macro strategies vis-à-vis the African continent, with particular reference to the republic's interests, policies and strategies towards the African Union (AU) and some of the latter's organs such as the AU Commission, the Peace and Security Council, the New Partnership for Africa's Development (NEPAD) and the African Peer Review Mechanism (APRM), as well as its democratisation and peace diplomacy. The chapter seeks to assess and navigate the tensions between Pan-African good-neighbourliness and solidarism, and a self-interested paradigm pursued under the guise of 'developmental' integration. We are interested here in South Africa's grand strategies as much as we are interested in its specific functionalist interventions and policies. We can certainly apply a source-based, explanatory methodological approach as we seek to unpack and explain South Africa's AU strategies, including the decision to field in 2012 one of the most influential members of the ruling African National Congress (ANC), and former minister of health, former minister of home affairs, and former minister of foreign affairs, Nkosazana Dlamini-Zuma, to contest for the position of AU Commission chairperson.

We are interested here in unpacking the many pivotal strategies that South Africa had adopted to exert influence on the AU and the latter's work, programmes and organs. From a functionalist point of view, we are interested in how South Africa 'offered' to host the Pan-African Parliament (PAP), NEPAD and the APRM, and in what was behind South Africa becoming the largest funder of NEPAD[2] during the Thabo Mbeki years, even after NEPAD was technically located under the auspices of the AU.

Continental Policy Context

South Africa's agency and influence on the continent were also felt as it pushed ahead with its functionalist, developmental approach of building a Union of African States (UAS), not a United States of Africa (USAf), by emphasising the need to build strong institutions, shared and common norms and values, pro-growth developmental cooperation and a confederal approach to continental integration through which Africa's regional economic communities (RECs) are punted as the building blocks of continental union. Part of the strategy of pursuing a realist developmental approach, punted as Pan-African solidarism, was South Africa's role as what Deon Geldenhuys has called a 'norms entrepreneur'.[3] We are interested here in exploring, among other things, the South African policy of 'convergence of normative values' based on the officially stated notion that 'South Africa's leadership in Africa and globally partly derives from a unique and established role as an advocate of human rights, democracy and good governance'.[4] South Africa regarded itself as being 'at the forefront of setting up credible permanent institutions to serve Africa – most notably the New Partnership for Africa's Development (NEPAD) and the African Union (AU)'.[5] There is thus an implicit, if not explicit, exceptionalism in which it regards itself as a role-model in Africa, being emulated by others on the continent. At times, the pro-growth developmental strategy fuelled perceptions that South Africa was feeding 'sub-imperialist' interests in Africa.[6] All these assumptions must be tested. We will for example refer to South Africa's roles in South Sudan (even though under the AU mandate), the Central African Republic (CAR), the Democratic Republic of the Congo (DRC) and other African states.

Mandela and Africa as Foreign Policy Priority

As the 'new' South Africa broke with the apartheid era's ruffian and destabilising policies, a 1994 ANC foreign policy discussion document articulated a new national interest doctrine that would henceforth 'reflect the interests of the continent of Africa'.[7] The idea of South Africa as a 'norms entrepreneur' or norms subsidiser, through which South Africa would take a lead role in championing new norms and values for the continent and the AU, was very prominent during the Nelson Mandela years, from 1994 to 1999.[8] During these years, we witnessed the gradual emergence of what I have called elsewhere the 'Mandela doctrine', which was firmly based on the idea that human rights and democracy promotion lay at the centre of the republic's foreign policy, as boldly proclaimed in its opting for the 'canonisation of human rights' in diplomacy. Mandela argued that there was a need for the Organisation of African Unity (OAU) to move beyond old strictures of sovereignty and place human rights promotion firmly on the agenda. But there were also claims that 'Africa is our common home. Our destiny lies in Africa'.[9] Africa was by this time elevated to a position of priority in the republic's external strategy. Policy stated that 'under the Government of National Unity, Africa, particularly the southern African region, has become the centre-piece of South Africa's foreign policy'.[10] The policy statement continued that the continent and the region constitute 'the most important element in South Africa's external environment' and that 'geo-politically, emotionally and in terms of destiny, South Africa forms an inextricable part of Africa'.[11] Deputy president Thabo Mbeki also stated in 1995 that 'South Africa is committed to the interests of southern Africa and the African continent'.[12] So how would South Africa promote Africa's interests in practice?

In his address to the Foreign Affairs Portfolio Committee of Parliament on 14 March 1995, Minister of Foreign Affairs Alfred Nzo built on the pro-Africa statements as articulated by the president and his deputy when he articulated South Africa's foreign policy priorities: 'in terms of foreign policy, Africa is clearly to be a priority in the years ahead', and the 'promotion of economic development of the southern African region is of paramount importance as the economies of the countries in the region are intertwined to such an extent that, for South Africa to believe that it could enter a prosperous future in isolation without taking neighbouring countries with her, would be unrealistic and hazardous'.[13] Even under Mandela, South Africa saw the region and continent not just in progressive political terms. South Africa even at this time also saw the region as a market through its national developmental realism, as opposed to building regional industrial capabilities so that the region could move as one, with no one being the Big Brother – which is currently the case.

In a promissory note to the region, South Africa gave notice that it would be at the forefront of efforts to transform continental institutions as well as Southern African states, and identify the continent's premier continental body at the time, the Organisation of African Unity, as well as premier integration regional bodies like the Southern African Development Community (SADC), in their quest to transform themselves into 'regional blocs'.[14] Policy advisers also gave notice that, unlike the apartheid state with its aggressive and militant stance towards the region, a post-apartheid South Africa would not seek 'confrontation with other blocs but rather to develop mutually beneficial relationships'.[15] It would pursue the popular post-Cold War strategy of 'bloc formation', and while it conceded that such a challenge presented elements of both 'threat and opportunity', it tried to reassure fellow African states that it would at all times try to advance the interests of the SADC region and the broader continent. As such, South Africa set out to interact with the international community in ways that would yield benefits for the continent.[16]

Another strategy the Mandela government adopted vis-à-vis the continent was to engage its neighbours and fellow African states on the basis of the 'unity and solidarity' that 'join all of us together in a fraternal bond'.[17] It would not engage the continent on the basis of any coercive or hegemonic means, but would instead 'engage in pro-active confidence-building, preventive diplomacy, bridge-building and, above all, partnership'.[18] As part of this 'preventive diplomacy and posture and style', South Africa committed itself to 'continuously work towards a new consensus with fellow African states in order to find new and better ways for addressing problems facing our sub-continent'.[19] However, there is also the dimension through which South Africa had been aggressively pursuing its economic interests in the region, such as during the controversial 1998 intervention in Lesotho, whereby many believed South Africa was pursuing its own water interests. As a 2014 Centre for Conflict Resolution (CCR) report put it, 'South Africa's controversial intervention in Lesotho in 1998 was the earliest SANDF [South African National Defence Force] deployment in it's "near abroad" in the post-apartheid era, and was justified as a pre-emptive act to de-escalate as a "creeping coup".[20] Apart from the Lesotho debacle, President Mandela had a penchant for peaceful resolution of disputes and for diplomatic solutions to conflicts. Prior to the military intervention in Lesotho, Mandela tried but failed with quiet diplomacy to engage the Nigerian military junta and dictatorship in 1995 in a bid to convince the Nigerian ruling elite to spare the lives of Ogoni leader Ken Saro-Wiwa and eight others. These efforts failed, with Mandela eventually campaigning for the ostracism of Nigeria without much cooperation from other Africans and international actors farther afield.

President Mandela also engaged in personal diplomacy when he decided to intercede in 'Africa's first world war' in Zaire/DRC as he sought to broker a rapprochement between Mobutu Sese Seko and Laurent Kabila and pushed for a power-sharing arrangement in that country. Again, little came from this event, with other events overtaking the Mandela initiative as Mobutu was driven out of Zaire and Kabila moved into statehouse of the DRC in 1998.

Mandela went beyond the crafting of norms and values, and peaceful resolution of disputes, and also promoted cooperation between South Africa and its sub-continental and broader continental neighbours. 'With the barriers of apartheid broken down', South Africa's new foreign policy makers also saw 'new opportunities ... to share its technical and scientific know-how and experience, its financial and business acumen, as well as its recent and present experience in the resolution of conflict, democratic decision making and reconstruction and development, with other countries in the Southern Africa region'.[21] Very early in the post-settlement era, therefore, the functionalist, institutional leadership role of the republic comes through alongside a preference for quiet diplomacy and an activism in the promotion of human rights and democracy in Africa.

Mbeki's 'Africa First': Developmental Democratic Peace Doctrine

Thabo Mbeki came to display the traits of what Adekeye Adebajo called 'Africa's philosopher king',[22] and when he became president in 1999 he immediately started to display policy intellectual leadership by emphasising his 'Africa First' doctrine, which would be pursued under the ambit of what he called the 'African Renaissance' and the 'African Agenda'. We could highlight here a number of legacies of Mbeki's Africa First foreign policy project. Whereas President Mandela's doctrine was anchored mainly on human rights activism, the Mbeki doctrine made an explicit link between peace, development and democratisation and encouraged Africans to pursue these goals by themselves and not on the basis of the dictates of others. Former deputy minister of foreign affairs Aziz Pahad advanced the 'submission that peace, stability, security and sustainable development [are] dialectically inextricably linked to good governance, transparency, violations of human rights, lack of democracy, disempowerment of people, poverty, underdevelopment, corruption and foreign rapacious exploitation of our natural resources'.[23] As early as the turn of the century, Pahad went further, noting 'a new sense of confidence and belief that Africans must become determinants of our own destinies and that Africa's problems must be solved by Africans, albeit with support of the international community'.[24]

Thabo Mbeki engaged in deft diplomacy to ensure that the republic, which was barred from ever becoming a member of the OAU because of the pursuit of its racist and obnoxious apartheid policies, would not just become a member of the successor AU, but would also influence that organisation in major ways. By 2002, Mbeki and members of the 'African Renaissance coalition' spared little effort, having 'invested enormous amounts of political, financial and human resource capital in the establishment of formations like the AU and programmes like NEPAD and the APRM'.[25] He achieved the strategic goal of helping to transform the OAU into the AU when he became the first chairperson of the AU in 2002 after its launch in Durban. First, there was an emphasis on the African Renaissance – restoring African pride, dignity and strategic positioning.[26] Mbeki defined the African Renaissance as the need for Africans to determine who they are, what they stand for, what their visions and hopes are, how they do things, what programmes they adopt, whom they relate to and how. Mbeki also felt the need to sell the African Renaissance dream to Southern Africa and the rest of the continent. To be sure, while it was easy for Mbeki to sell the policy and visionary idea of an African Renaissance abroad, he found it much more difficult to do so domestically as his government struggled to build a Renaissance constituency at home, as evidenced by spates of xenophobic (read: Afro-phobic) attacks against fellow Africans.[27]

Whereas white apartheid governments had seen South Africa as an extension of Europe, Mbeki set out to assert the country as being in Africa, with Africa and as part of Africa, and with other forces in Africa for peace, democracy and reconstruction and development of the continent.[28] Notwithstanding the call by many that South Africa should act as some sort of African hegemon – the one that would lay down the laws to others through imposition and domination – Mbeki shunned such ideas and instead punted the notion of South Africa as equal partner on the continent and globally. African peace diplomacy occupied a special place on Mbeki's foreign policy agenda. He preferred to play the role of peacemaker and peacekeeper throughout Africa, acting through multilateral institutions: SADC, the AU and the United Nations (UN) Security Council.[29]

The 2004 ten-year review of government clearly stated that one of the most crucial elements of South Africa's preoccupation with Africa was the imperative of contributing to 'consolidating the AU and its institutions to ensure that they are operational, effective and efficient'. 'Having been established', policy determined, 'these institutions needed to function properly and optimally'. For example, since the establishment of the AU in 2002, the Mbeki chairpersonship made a point of ensuring that the new organisation hold ordinary and extraordinary summits, deliver key decisions and pass declarations. Wolfe Braude reminds us that policy was to engage the continent in three strategic ways, by

> strengthening Africa's institutions, regionally and continentally; supporting implementation of Africa's socio-economic development programme, the NEPAD; and improving bilateral political and socio-economic relations through dialogue and cooperation. From a system of 'racial capitalism' enforced through an oppressive apartheid regime, South Africa went through an exemplary peaceful transition to democracy.[30]

Under Mbeki's leadership, South Africa set out to lead by example, including in the area of assessed contributions and dues that would help to strengthen the continent's fledgling institutions; indeed, South Africa has been one of the five AU member states that 'have contributed the most to the AU budget and one of the few paying membership fees on time. South Africa makes a transfer of ZAR150–200 million to the AU annually'.[31] According to Brendan Vickers, this is about a 15 per cent contribution to the organisation's budget. These contributions also go to support the republic's institutional headship role by supporting the AU's subsidiary bodies, commissions and committees, and the hosts and sponsors the AU's Pan-African Parliament in Midrand, Johannesburg.[32]

Mbeki showed further policy intellectual leadership by championing the idea of 'strategic partnerships' based on the notions of 'mutual accountability' and 'mutual responsibility', as well as the idea of African ownership of the continent's own development agenda. In terms of the former,

Mbeki set out to be the 'intellectual architect'[33] first of the Millennium Africa Recovery Plan, which was merged with the Omega Plan into the New Africa Initiative (NAI) and finally became NEPAD – a modern development plan making the link between democracy and governance on the one hand, and peace and security, and infrastructural development and economic growth, on the other. But Mbeki always believed in building partnerships, and NEPAD was essentially a compromise plan between his Renaissance vision, Olusegun Obasanjo's Conference on Security, Stability, Development and Cooperation in Africa (CSSDCA), and Abdulaye Wade's Omega plan; Mbeki was also the chief architect of the APRM, together with his other like-minded partners in the African Agenda fraternity such as Obasanjo, Meles Zenawi, Wade and Abulaziz Bouteflika who shared in the club governance network strategy. The APRM, these leaders decided, was a governance promotion tool that would not rely on punitive measures to promote governance; it was to single out democracy and political governance, socio-economic development, economic governance and management and corporate governance. South Africa contributes more than half of NEPAD's financial budget, hosting its secretariat, based in Midrand, Johannesburg, and providing about ZAR35 million a year to this initiative, including to the APRM.[34] No other African state has invested so much in African institution building as does South Africa, and this is by far the largest contribution to the NEPAD-APRM programme, putting South Africa at the apex of appropriations to these programmes, at least from a financial point of view. Two-thirds of its contribution goes towards the NEPAD Planning and Coordinating Agency (NPCA), while one-third goes towards supporting the APRM initiative.[35] South Africa also hosts the NPCA, by providing equipment and tax exemptions to the agency and its staff. South Africa in the past provided high-level secondments to the NEPAD agency, including the first chief executive officer.[36] Between 2004 and 2006, the Mbeki government contributed US$6.9 million to the Development Bank of Southern Africa (DBSA) for support to the APRM.[37] This was more than half the total appropriation of US$12.6 million. During this time, Nigeria contributed only US$1.3 million.[38]

By the time of Mbeki's abrupt removal from office in September 2008, South Africa boasted a diplomatic presence in 47 of the continent's states, more than any other nation of the world, positioning it to be influential in Africa and elsewhere and thereby giving credence to the idea of an Africa First policy. As part of this policy, Mbeki was key to the founding of the AU and the negotiation and drafting of the AU's Constitutive Act of 2000. South Africa was never a proponent of the Kwame Nkrumah-esque 'United States of Africa'.[39] Instead, Thabo Mbeki, like Mandela, belonged to the gradualist school of African integration, and his vision was that of a continental functionalist project and an architecture of Afro-continentalism based on states living with common institutions, norms and values, and a rules-based common order, not that of Libya's Muammar Qaddafi, who favoured a federalist supra-nationalist USAf. Under the Mbeki functionalist approach there were five sub-regions, and a sixth extending to the African Diaspora.

Already as early as 2007, the Mbeki government put the idea of a developmental state and developmental integration firmly on the agenda. At its 52nd national conference in 2007, the ANC resolved 'to build the strategic, organizational and technical capacities of government with a view to a developmental state through building the technical capacity of the state to engage with, understand and lead the development of dynamic and globally integrated economic sectors'.[40] This was soon translated into government policy, and built into policy vis-à-vis the continent. As the 2009 Department of International Relations and Cooperation (DIRCO) document put it: 'Within the context of the Developmental state and the realization of the fact that South Africa's success is inextricably intertwined with that of the continent, the ANC (government) recognizes [that] the idea of building Partnerships for Development is a key element of its strategy in pursuit of a better Africa for all'.[41]

Further evidence of how ANC policy was translated is captured in the view from the Department of Trade and Industry (DTI): 'the South African government's approach to the continent is development oriented in nature and content'.[42] 'A development oriented approach', continued the DTI, 'means that "Development" is not defined solely in terms of economic, but as a "comprehensive" and multi-faceted "process", with social, cultural, political as well as economic elements'.[43] This highlighted the centrality of a developmental cooperation approach and anchored a pro-growth, and pro-institutions and norms, strategy.

The Mbeki government was aware that there was a price to pay for influence in Africa, including a monetary price, and continued to use rand diplomacy through the power of the purse. As an official strategic document put it: 'South Africa will be called upon to expend financial resources to bring peace and stability to affected regions'.[44] Mbeki has therefore long appreciated the power and influence of rand diplomacy. It was under his presidency that South Africa established the African Renaissance Fund (ARF), created by law in the year 2000, and set out to grant loans and financial assistance to other African countries, putting South Africa at the table with other donor nations; the ARF is now being transformed into a development agency. The ARF was a key instrument in service of *Pax-South Africana*. The preamble to the 2000 ARF Act states that 'the ARF was established to enhance cooperation between South Africa and other countries, in particular, African countries, through the promotion of democracy, good governance, the prevention and resolution of conflict, socio-economic development and integration, humanitarian assistance, and human resource development'.[45]

In terms of structure, the ARF was under the control of the director-general (DG) of foreign affairs. Funds for projects were disbursed after the approval of the DG or the minister of foreign affairs. The Department of Foreign Affairs (DFA) could also tap into its own resources and claim back such resources after approval had been sought from the minister of finance.

Loans or other financial assistance were granted in accordance with an agreement entered into with the country in question, and the South African minister of foreign affairs. Assistance granted was subject to terms and conditions as agreed upon by the country and the minister of foreign affairs, and in all cases in consultation with the minister of finance. An advisory committee was established to manage the ARF, and was also tasked with making recommendations to the ministers of foreign affairs and finance on the disbursement of funds through loans and other financial assistance.

So serious was Mbeki about playing at the strategic level that he and his government did not hesitate to use the power of the purse and a brand of open cheque-book diplomacy to provide funding, even exploring the idea of doubling aid to Africa by 2010, with a forward-looking goal of allocating as much as 0.7 per cent of annual income to aid by 2015.[46]

The purpose of the ARF included commitments in line with Peace and Security Council (PSC) prescripts, including the enhancement of socio-economic development and integration, the provision of humanitarian assistance, conflict prevention and the promotion of democracy and good governance.[47] Deon Geldenhuys found that, between 2003 and 2007, the fund financed projects totalling ZAR293 million in Burundi, Comoros, the DRC, Guinea, Lesotho, Liberia, Sierra Leone, Seychelles, Western Sahara and Zimbabwe.[48] In 2008, for example, South Africa contributed a further R300 million to Zimbabwe to help that country address its severe food shortages,[49] showing that it was willing to use financial leverages to help achieve its economic goals.

Mbeki played a key role in promoting a *Pax South Africana* and invested heavily in peace-making, peacekeeping and peace-building. On this score, Adekeye Adebajo described Mbeki as the 'pied piper of Pretoria' who 'piped the diplomatic tunes to which warlords, rebels and politicians danced as he led peace efforts in the DRC, Zimbabwe and Côte d'Ivoire'.[50] Mbeki showed that he was willing to commit funds to secure Africa, and supported peace initiatives in Burundi, the Comoros as OAU-mandated coordinator and the DRC; facilitated dialogue with Lesotho and Angola; helped train observes for peace processes in Ethiopia and Eritrea; provided logistical support for the peace process in Sierra Leone; supported UN-led processes in Western Sahara; provided support for Intergovernmental Authority on Development (IGAD) peace processes in Somalia; and provided assistance for de-mining. A 2014 Centre for Conflict Resolution (CCR) report observed in this regard 'South Africa has also played an active role in peacemaking and peacekeeping efforts on the continent, with the South African National Defence Force (SANDF) contributing significantly to the Mbeki government's peacebuilding agenda'.[51] Peacebuilding was an important priority area of focus under Thabo Mbeki's era. A CCR report reminds us that during Mbeki's era, 'SANDF has been deployed on a number of peace support operations (including security sector reform and peacebuilding activities throughout Africa, including Burundi (2001–2006 and 2007–2009); Central African republic (2007-present); Comoros (2001–2007); Cote d'Ivoire (2005–2006); the DRC (1999-present); Eritrea and Ethiopia (2000–2008); Liberia (2003–2005); northern Uganda and southern Sudan (2007–2009); and Sudan's Darfur region (2004–present)'[52]. What is significant about the above information and data is that, under Mbeki's leadership, South Africa had graduated from Africa's foremost destabilising and ruffian state to its pre-eminent peacemaker in Africa.

According to Mark Anthony Achonu-Douglasson, South Africa has provided untied development assistance to its Southern African neighbours including 'various forms of aid support to Zimbabwe, ranging from ARF-funded projects to an economic rescue package totalling US$88 million (R800 million). The latter involved a US$55 million (R500 million) credit line facility, the balance being budget support'.[53] Similarly, in 2011, a bailout loan of US$307 million tied to assistance was offered to the landlocked Kingdom of Swaziland, with conditions covering four areas for political and economic reforms.[54]

Another example of South Africa's untied development assistance and power-of-the-purse strategy is Lesotho, as another small, landlocked, least-developed country and largely dependent on the South African economy for survival. Through the ARF, development projects in infrastructures valued at US$12 million have been financed. However, despite the ARF's limitations, it can still be said that it has helped mobilise funds for regional priorities and become a tool for South Africa's foreign policy, especially in Africa. According to some observers, the ARF's operational existence has provided a wealth of knowledge and some skills for the proposed South African Development Partnership Agency (SADPA). But would SADPA actually take off, or is it merely an empty promise?

The Zuma Government, the AU, and 'African Advancement'

Let us now zero in on the Jacob Zuma administration's emerging foreign policy, that of 'continued prioritisation of the African continent'. As much as he has tried to distance himself from Mbeki's Africa strategies because of the *broedertwis* at Polokwane (fraternal battle), Zuma inherited a well-calibrated and consolidated set of policies and in the end felt duty bound to opt for continuity, not change.[55] In the words of Siphamandla Zondi, 'it is evident that the Zuma years marked continuity with the Mandela and Mbeki eras in respect of placing Africa at the centre of South Africa's international relations'.[56] Zondi asserted that Zuma set out to 'continue to prioritise the African continent by strengthening the African Union and its structures, and give special focus to the implementation of the New Partnership for Africa's Development'.[57] It appears that the 'Africa prioritisation' strategies of the Zuma government are being pursued under two broad themes: Africa continental, and improving political and economic integration of the SADC region.

We start here with the bilateral question, and in particular President Zuma's choice of Angola for his first state visit.[58] The idea of elevating South Africa–Angola ties to a more strategic plane was based on the rationale that there were bilateral benefits to be had economically.[59] At another level, however, the question arises as to whether this restoration of ties signals a geo-continental shift in policy away from the likes of Nigeria, Algeria, Ethiopia, Tanzania, Ghana, Mozambique and others, which were key allies in the club governance network. Angola was a curious choice to help play this role, for while it harbours the desire to be recognised as a regional hegemon, and seeks the status and prestige of the label, it is less clear whether Angola has a sub-regional and continental plan, let alone the will to execute it. The answer lies in the long-standing 'friendship' between Zuma and José Eduardo dos Santos dating back to the struggle days. There was also a lot in common among the new economy-driven, utilitarian foreign policy orientations of the Zuma and dos Santos regimes. The decision to anoint Luanda was also Zuma's way of staying within the set foreign policy framework, but also choosing a different strategy and proving that he was his own man instead of a lackey of friend-turned-foe Thabo Mbeki.

A 2009 Department of International Relations and Cooperation conceptual framework on identifying anchor states in the five geographical regions recognised by the African Union gave us an idea of this Africa First strategy when it stated that 'South Africa's foreign policy has since 1999 focused on consolidating the African agenda and strengthening bilateral relations with all African countries'.[60] The 2009 strategic document reinforced what I refer to here as a realist developmental approach when it stated: 'In pursuing the African agenda, South Africa has sought to assist in building the capacity of the continent to respond to and resolve continental crises, foster closer co-operation through regional integration, strengthen intra-African trade relations, and champion a common African developmental perspective, informed by the realities of underdevelopment and poverty on the continent'.[61]

Moving on to the next point, government has publicly committed itself to the establishment of SADPA, with the aim of promoting developmental partnerships. Neither the idea of SADPA, nor developmentalism, is novel, and here too several questions arise.

SADPA derives from the Mbeki presidency's decision to establish the ARF and South Africa effectively becoming an African donor country. As such, it was able to influence African politics in direct ways.[62] But with the promise of SADPA, government appeared to have promised more than it could actually deliver. The promise to establish this ambitious instrument coincided with the aftershocks of the 2008–09 global financial crisis and the shrinking economy and deteriorating social situation at home. South Africa's plummet into economic 'junk' status and poor economic growth rates of less than 1 per cent per annum by 2015 did not help, and meant that SADPA was postponed indefinitely.

In the wake of the SADPA setback it is fair to ask the question: What is the strategic orientation of the Zuma government's foreign policy? In the second-quarter edition of the policy magazine *New Agenda* in 2012, ANC stalwart Ben Turok asked the question: 'Is South Africa doing enough in Africa?'[63] President Zuma certainly believed that his government was doing enough. When another ANC stalwart, Essop Pahad, suggested to the president in *The Thinker* in 2014 that there appeared to be 'a perception in many countries in Africa that in recent years that the South African government and yourself are no longer deeply passionate and committed to African unity, cohesion, growth and development, or to the African Renaissance',[64] President Zuma responded emphatically, insisting that 'Africa has remained at the centre of our foreign policy. We have worked hard to strengthen support for the African Union, SADC and all continental bodies whose purpose is to achieve peace and security'.[65] President Zuma went further and vowed that South Africa will 'continue to support peacemaking and conflict resolution. In this regard', he insisted, 'South Africa will continue to support both regional and continental processes to respond to and resolve crises, promote peace and security, significantly increase intra-Africa trade and champion infrastructure development'.[66] The commander-in-chief was adamant that 'we have continued to advocate for strengthening of the structures of the African Union to enable the continent to address the challenges of conflict and unconstitutional changes of government'.[67] This stated commitment to continue to support African peace-support operations notwithstanding, in March 2013, 13 soldiers deployed in the Central African Republic were killed, prompting South Africa to withdraw its troops from that war-torn country.[68] South Africa also decided to withdraw the entire 797 contingent of its troops from its UN mission in Darfur in May 2016, further reinforcing perceptions that it was retreating from its continental responsibilities. President Zuma also gave notice that he was considering withdrawing from the intervention mission in the DRC under the auspices of SADC and the

United Nations, established in 2013 to end the military attacks and human rights violations committed by M23 rebels.[69]

The Zuma government tried hard to counter perceptions that it was turning its back on the continent, and it is important to say something here about the future of the APRM in this regard.[70] Government has come out in support of the implementation of the APRM, but Pretoria-Tshwane was aware of serious doubts about this governance instrument's future. This led President Zuma to remind us that, in 2014, South Africa submitted its third report to the APRM.[71] During the January 2016 AU Summit in Addis Ababa, South Africa's Eddy Maloka was appointed as the APRM's new chief executive officer in a clear attempt to counter perceptions that South Africa was not committed to the future of the mechanism. His appointment was also intended to bolster its influence in the programme.

While President Zuma's government did not always commit as much financial resources to continental institutions and programmes as did the Mbeki government, they did nevertheless continue with their assessed contributions. For example, for the 2017 financial year, the Zuma government contributed to the AU an amount of US$20,391,922[72]. In 2016, South Africa appropriated US$100,000 to the APRM, and contributed a further US$100,000 in 2017.[73] NEPAD received US$500,000 from South Africa in 2016, and another US$500,000 in 2017.[74]

The president also set out to refute the idea that South Africa distanced itself from NEPAD following the departure from office of Thabo Mbeki, claiming that South Africa not only supported the programme but also domesticated it. In the words of President Zuma, 'the Government of South Africa has ensured, over the years that the basic pillars of NEPAD that address sectoral priorities have been brought into our national development strategies. Synergies between NEPAD and our national plans include a focus on bridging the infrastructure gap, specifically with regard to

ICT [information communications technology], energy, transport, water and sanitation'.[75]

During Zuma's term, South Africa continued to position itself as something of a spokesperson or 'voice' for Africa and the AU, and the government committed itself to advancing AU–European Union (EU) relations by working on the first Africa–EU Action Plan implementation process. The Zuma administration can take a leaf from the book of its predecessor, which had learned some tough lessons from the Trade, Development and Cooperation Agreement (TDCA) negotiations with Europe, above all how not to go it alone. So, as government takes up the EU–Africa mentality, it has to take on board other Africans and their fears.

Policy stated that South Africa would, through continental and regional issues, work towards the entrenchment of democracy and respect for human rights on the African continent. Suffice it to point out here that the balance between a human rights and justice versus a peace, security and development approach has been a difficult one for this country to achieve in practice since the end of apartheid.

Under President Zuma, South Africa also championed the cause of African infrastructure development. Siphamandla Zondi reminds us in this regard that South Africa believed in the 'Africa Rising' narrative and 'the Zuma administration energetically championed NEPAD's infrastructure initiative with a specific focus on the idea of building a North-South corridor of transport and communications'.[76] President Zuma himself mentioned that 'the Programme for Infrastructure Development in Africa (PIDA) [and] the Comprehensive Africa Championing Initiative (PICI) ... are key AU/NEPAD programmes in which South Africa plays an active role'.[77] Zuma's emphasis on infrastructure development was in part driven by the utilitarian, instrumentalist 'Open for Business ... in a Big Way' strategy.

Nkosazana-Dlamini's Ascendancy to AU Commission Chair, and Foreign Policy

With South Africa having finished its stint as non-permanent member of the UN Security Council, the ANC decided to field Nkosazana Dlamini-Zuma to contest the position of AU chairperson, as it needed instruments of leverage in diplomacy, and the AU Commission position provided an ideal opportunity and platform to exercise influence not just on the continent, but also internationally with the aim of enhancing the republic's prestige abroad and bolstering its chances for a UN Security Council seat. Having Dlamini-Zuma at the helm in Addis Ababa was a great opportunity to achieve this goal.

South Africa needed extra leverage on the continent to realise its strategic goals. During the first five years of the Jacob Zuma presidency, South Africa's foreign policy developed an identity crisis between a commitment to Africa – a dedication to a so-called Africa First policy – and a deep tilt towards a new and crude *realpolitik* orientation and drive in its foreign policy. This tension played itself out during the calculated campaign to put Dlamini-Zuma forward to become the new AU Commission chairperson, no matter the price. But she was a reluctant redeemer, as she did not agree with the policy. She believed that such a decision would divide the continent, and she had to be persuaded to accept the decision.

Dlamini-Zuma was portrayed by the South African ruling ANC as some sort of paragon of efficiency and bold and astute leadership – a visionary and functional leader *par excellence*. Indeed, in Dlamini-Zuma, we have one of the ANC's most loyal servants, believing as she does in servant leadership, and she has also equipped herself in functional leadership, as she is very focused on strengthening institutions so that they can act on turning policies into tangible outcomes.

But by 2013 the issue around the elections had come and gone and Dlamini-Zuma had now won the prized position as new chairperson of the AU Commission, and the hard work started. The notion that the new chairperson would simply move into her new offices at AU Commission headquarters and just clean up the 'mess' left by Jean Ping was naive. She was always going to have her work cut out for her.[78] The further idea that she would walk into AU Commission headquarters and simply sort out the dysfunctional AU made a mockery of the realities of AU diplomacy; even though she had beat Jean Ping after four arduous and demanding rounds of voting, it meant that she had just scraped through, with her victory leaving lots of scars in the process.[79]

The new chairperson had to mend fences as she built a new team. She was also indebted to the many African states that had helped her secure her position as chairperson with their pledges of support. In putting together her executive team and cabinet, she had to reward some statespersons who had put their credibility on the line for her, and had to give them positions, especially Southern Africans. Given just how divided the continent and the AU in particular were, she was also duty-bound to reach out to civil servants from different African countries while simultaneously trying to weed out some dead wood. She had to reconcile relations with many states who had not voted for her, most notably Nigeria, Algeria and Ethiopia, and to show distance from Pretoria-Tshwane, lest she be regarded as an agent of South Africa, bent on trying to turn a continental position into an instrument of South Africa's crude national interests, rather than an instrument of the common continental interests. As Adekeye Adebajo put it: 'Dlamini-Zuma will need urgently to heal serious political divisions with Nigeria, central Africa and many Francophone countries. While she won an impressive 37 votes in the fourth round of voting, 17 other countries did not vote for her, suggesting that she had a lot of work to do to mend fences'.[80]

Dlamini-Zuma was portrayed as a functional leader *par excellence*, one who would transform the AU Commission from a moribund into a highly effective and efficient institution, and who would close the huge policy to implementation gap.

Building Credibility Through *Agenda 2063*

South Africa was concerned about a widely held perception that it was treating the AU Commission like an extension of its foreign policy. It wanted to give credence to the idea that Dlamini-Zuma was a visionary, functional leader, and she soon embarked on the expansive exercise of coming up with a new vision for the continent – *Agenda 2063*. Through this exercise in vision-building, Dlamini-Zuma again tried to restore her, and by extension South Africa's, continentalist credentials as she set out to 'revive' Pan-Africanism and promote continental integration. She latched on to the idea of Africa 'claiming the twenty-first century as the African Century' and that, under her leadership, 'Africa will promote peace, security, governance and economic development'. But there was of course little new and novel about these ideas. Since the end of the Cold War, and even before the formation of the AU, African leaders have and had placed these goals at the apex of their agendas.

But *Agenda 2063* was a highly ambitious, even unrealistic vision statement. The very idea of a 50-year-old vision statement is somewhat far-fetched. There is of course no gainsaying the idea that it is important for Africa to end all wars. But the statement that Africa should 'end all wars by 2020', without backing such a statement up with the necessary policy and institutional rigour, is almost meaningless.

Even the promise by *Agenda 2063* to speed up the idea of the Continental Free Trade Agreement is one that has enjoyed the attention of many policy makers since before the arrival of this new vision statement. What was needed was for the new AU Commission chairperson to show just how much political muscle she had and to try to extract commitment from political leaders to pool sovereignty to move the continent to deeper levels of integration. On this score, Dlamini-Zuma's greatest achievement has probably been to unlock a series of high-level talks between the AU Commission and Africa's regional economic communities such as SADC, IGAD, the Economic Community of West African States (ECOWAS) and the Economic Community of Central African States (ECCAS).

Now that we have revealed some of South Africa's tactics deployed to achieve its goal of achieving the prized position of AU Commission chair, we can proceed to unpack some of the republic's grand ambitions that underscored this decision. Officially, South Africa introduced the idea that part of its motivation for nominating Dlamini-Zuma was that it would use this position as one tool to help thwart – 'it would stop' – foreign encroachment on the part of Western powers in particular into Africa.

Self-interests have always been at play, as South Africa harbours very important – and very noble – goals in Africa, including African peace and stability, the continent's development and economic take-off, with the Zuma government under particular pressure to justify South Africa's status of the 'hegemon' in Africa, the 'gateway to Africa', the 'point person' (read: actor) for foreign powers in Africa; the 'spokesperson' for Africa; and the anointed one from whom external powers take their African cue.

Some observers were of the view that South Africa was bent on turning the AU Commission into an instrument of the republic's foreign policy, and the fact that Dlamini-Zuma spent a lot of time in South Africa, and regularly attended ANC meetings such as the National Executive Council (NEC) and National General Council (NGC) meetings, did not serve to dispel such perceptions. The AU Commission position served as a vehicle that would help South Africa punch above its weight, but this came at the cost of unity and cohesion among Africa's governments.

Conclusion

South Africa has long harboured global leadership ambitions, with playing a strategic role in African diplomacy, and peace and security and governance matters, seen as a means to bolster its global stature. Beginning with the end of apartheid in 1994, South Africa positioned itself as a reliable partner and peace-maker, and since Mbeki's ascendancy to power it has stressed peacekeeping and underwriting of peace processes through its financial and diplomatic resources.

South Africa never subscribed to the United States of Africa project, in which we would see the transcending of the African colonially inherited Westphalian nation state, or more properly state-nations. Instead, the republic was a proponent of the Union of African States project, the gradualist school of African graduation, through which common institutions would be created and built, norms articulated and agreed upon and hopefully transformed into 'shared values', and accelerated regional cooperation under the guise of so-called growth-driven developmental integration, but was no proponent of deep integration. Functionalism and institution building at regional and continental levels also featured prominently in the ANC-led government's African Agenda.

But we should also not underestimate the willingness of South Africa to play self-interested *realpolitik* in order to drive its agenda. Thus, when South Africa decided in 2011 that it would field a candidate for the AU Commission chair in 2012, it was embarking on a high-stakes game. It knew that there was nothing illegal about putting forward Dlamini-Zuma, but was also aware that this might be one of the most imprudent foreign policy decisions it could take. That decision, executed during the ANC's centenary commemoration year, served to divide the continent along regional, geopolitical and personal lines at the highest levels of government in Africa.

In short, South Africa has been a pivotal player in Africa since the dawn of democracy in 1994, and especially since the ascendency to the Presidency in 1999, and has played a key role in the establishment of the AU and its workings since around 1998, but this has not always been driven just by consideration of solidarity and solidarism. Self-interest has always been part of the consideration, with South Africa realising that its global stature derives from its pivotal role in Africa in political, military (read: peace and security), economic and even business interests, and its view that it is playing a pivotal role in Africa. It has been careful throughout not to overstate its avowed interests, but that those interests are at play is not in dispute.

Notes

1. See Chris Landsberg, 'South Africa: A Pivotal State in Africa', *Synopsis: Policy Studies Bulletin* 7, no. 4 (2004), pp. 1–4.
2. Deon Geldenhuys, 'South Africa's Role as International Norm Entrepreneur', in Walter Carlsnaes and Philip Nel (eds), *In Full Flight: South Africa's Foreign Policy After Apartheid* (Midrand: Institute for Global Dialogue, 2006), pp. 93–107.
3. Geldenhuys, 'South Africa's Role as International Norm Entrepreneur'.
4. Department of International Relations and Cooperation (DIRCO), *Conceptual Framework on Identification of Anchor States in the Five Geographical Regions Recognised by the African Union* (Pretoria-Tshwane, 29 October 2009), p. 17.
5. DIRCO, *Conceptual Framework*, p. 20.
6. Siphamandla Zondi, 'Africanity, Pan-Africanism, and African Renaissance: South Africa's African Agenda Under Mbeki and Zuma', in Lesley Masters, Siphamandla Zondi, Jo-Ansie van Wyk and Chris Landsberg, *South African Foreign Policy Review*, vol. 2 (Pretoria: Africa Institute, 2015), p. 114.
7. See African National Congress (ANC), *Foreign Policy Perspectives in a Democratic South Africa* (Johannesburg, December 1994).
8. Geldenhuys, 'South Africa's Role as International Norm Entrepreneur'.
9. Department of Foreign Affairs (DFA), 'Discussion Paper on South Africa's Foreign Relations', 4th draft (Pretoria, 1996), p. 25.
10. DFA, 'Discussion Paper', p. 26.
11. Ibid., p. 25.

12. Deputy President Thabo Mbeki, address to the Foreign Affairs Heads of Mission Conference, Cape Town, September 1995.

13. Minister of Foreign Affairs Alfred Nzo, address to the Portfolio Committee of Foreign Affairs, Cape Town, 14 March 1995.

14. Chris Landsberg, *The Diplomacy of Transformation: South African Foreign Policy and Statecraft* (Johannesburg: Macmillan, 2010), p. 101.

15. Landsberg, *The Diplomacy of Transformation*, p. 101.

16. Ibid.

17. DFA, 'Discussion Paper', p. 25.

18. Ibid., p. 27.

19. Ibid., p. 28.

20. Centre for Conflict Resolution (CCR), *Post-Apartheid South Africa's Foreign Policy After Two Decades*, policy research seminar report (Cape Town, June 2014), p. 13.

21. DFA, 'Discussion Paper', p. 25.

22. Adekeye Adebajo, *Thabo Mbeki: A Jacana Pocket Biography* (Johannesburg: Jacana Media, 2016).

23. Deputy Minister of Foreign Affairs Aziz Pahad, 'Conflict Resolution on the African Continent' (Pretoria, September 2000).

24. Pahad, 'Conflict Resolution on the African Continent'.

25. Chris Landsberg and Malcolm Ray, 'The OAU and the Liberation of South Africa: Lest We Forget We Are African!', *The Thinker* 51 (2013), p. 31.

26. Landsberg, *The Diplomacy of Transformation*, p. 140.

27. This view was expressed during a debate between A. Adebajo and C. Landsberg during the launch of the book Thabo Mbeki: The Rise and Fall of Africa's Philosopher King, University of Cape Town, South Africa, 13 May, 2016.

28. Landsberg, *The Diplomacy of Transformation*, p. 141.

29. Ibid., p. 145.

30. Wolfe Braude, cited in Mark Anthony Achonu-Douglasson, 'South Africa's Development Assistance Paradigm: Approach Towards Africa', MA diss. (University of Johannesburg, 2016), p. 55.

31. Wolfe Braude, cited in Achonu-Douglasson, 'South Africa's Development Assistance Paradigm', p. 55.

32. Brendan Vickers, 'Towards a new AID Paradigm: South Africa as African development Partner', Cambridge Review of International Affairs, Vol. 25: 4, 2012, pp. 535–56.

33. DIRCO, *Conceptual Framework*, p. 20.

34. See African Peer Review Mechanism (APRM), 'The African Peer Review Mechanism (APRM): Africa's Innovative Thinking on Governance', eighth gathering of the African Governance Forum, Berlin, 2–23 May 2007.

35. APRM, 'The African Peer Review Mechanism'.

36. Ibid.

37. Ibid.

38. Ibid.

39. See Chris Landsberg, 'Afro-Continentalism: Pan-Africanism in Post-Settlement South Africa's Foreign Policy', *Journal of Asian and African Studies* 47, no. 4 (2012), pp. 436–48.
40. ANC, 52nd National Conference Resolutions, Polokwane, 2007.
41. DIRCO, *Conceptual Framework*, p. 3.
42. Ibid.
43. Ibid.
44. Ibid., p. 17.
45. N. Besharati, South African Development Partnership Agency (SADPA): Strategic Aid or Development Package for Africa, South African Institute of International Affairs (SAIIA) Research Report 12, 2013.
46. Institute for Global Dialogue, *Framework 2008: Framework for South African Development Assistance* (Midrand, 2008).
47. Deon Geldenhuys, 'The Idea-Driven Foreign Policy of a Regional Power: The Case of South Africa', paper prepared for the first Regional Powers Network (RPN) conference at the German Institute of Global and Area Studies (GIGA), Hamburg, 15–16 September 2008, p. 17.
48. Geldenhuys, 'The Idea-Driven Foreign Policy of a Regional Power', pp. 17–18.
49. Ibid., p. 18.
50. Adekeye Adebajo, 'Rise and Fall of Africa's Philosopher King', *Sunday Independent*, 24 April 2016.
51. Centre for Conflict Resolution, Post-Apartheid South Africa's Foreign Policy after Two Decades, Policy Research Seminar Report, Cape Town, June 2014, p. 13.
52. Ibid.
53. Cited in Achonu-Douglasson, 'South Africa's Development Assistance Paradigm', p. 55.
54. Achonu-Douglasson, 'South Africa's Development Assistance Paradigm'.
55. See Chris Landsberg, 'South African Foreign Policy Formulation, 1989–2010', in Albert Venter and Chris Landsberg (eds), *Government and Politics in South Africa*, 4th edn (Pretoria: Van Schaik, 2011), p. 246.
56. Zondi, 'Africanity, Pan-Africanism, and African Renaissance', p. 113.
57. Quoted in Zondi, 'Africanity, Pan-Africanism, and African Renaissance', p. 105.
58. CCR, *Post-Apartheid South Africa's Foreign Policy After Two Decades*, p. 21.
59. Ibid.
60. DIRCO, *Conceptual Framework*, p. 3.
61. Ibid., p. 4.
62. See DFA, African Renaissance and International Cooperation Fund, *Annual Report 2007–2008* (Pretoria-Tshwane, 2008).
63. *New Agenda* 2012, The Editor, 'Is South Africa doing enough in Africa?', Issue 46 (Second Quarter), p. 9.
64. 'Dr Essop Pahad Interviews President Jacob Zuma', *The Thinker* 62 (4th Quarter 2014), p. 13.
65. 'Dr Essop Pahad Interviews President Jacob Zuma', p. 13.

66. 'Dr Essop Pahad Interviews President Jacob Zuma', p. 13.
67. Ibid.
68. Centre for Conflict Resolution, Post-Apartheid South Africa's Foreign Policy after Two Decades, op. cit., p. 13.
69. The Presidency, South Africa 1994–2014: Twenty Year Review, Pretoria, 2014, p. 158.
70. See APRM, *Republic of South Africa: Country Review Report* no. 5 (Midrand, September 2007).
71. 'Dr Essop Pahad Interviews President Jacob Zuma', p. 13.
72. DIRCO, South Africa's Contribution to the UN and AU 2016/2017 Financial Year, Pretoria, June 2017.
73. Ibid.
74. Ibid.
75. 'Dr Essop Pahad Interviews President Jacob Zuma', p. 13.
76. Zondi, 'Africanity, Pan-Africanism, and African Renaissance', p. 108.
77. 'Dr Essop Pahad Interviews President Jacob Zuma', p. 15.
78. Adekeye Adebajo, 'Dlamini-Zuma's Victory May Turn Out to Be a Pyrrhic One', *Business Day* (Johannesburg), 3 August 2012.
79. Ibid.
80. Ibid.

CHAPTER 11

THE AFRICAN UNION AND THE UNITED NATIONS: CRAFTING AN INTERNATIONAL PARTNERSHIP IN THE FIELD OF PEACE AND SECURITY

Ulf Engel

Beyond the rhetoric of the developmental partnerships that were entertained from the 1960s to 1990s, formalised multilateral partnerships between Africa and international organisations are a rather recent phenomenon. The African Union (AU) is maintaining two major partnerships, one with the European Union (EU),[1] and one with the United Nations (UN). They are based on the dialectics of changed perceptions of Africa's role in global politics on the one hand,[2] and more ambitious collective African aspirations on the other. First, in contrast to perceptions of marginalisation, crises and state-system frailty that characterised Africa's global role after the end of the Cold War,[3] at the beginning of the new millennium signs of African political and economic renaissance and 'encouraging developments' were registered.[4] And second, African states have discovered international 'partnerships' as a strategic answer, beyond the many bilateralisms, to deal with a multitude of political, economic and social challenges. This strategic 'inter-regionalism'[5] can be understood as a sovereignty-boosting strategy.[6]

Apart from renewed interest in Africa by China and other emerging powers as well as the West at large, and substantial economic growth rates across the continent in the first decade of the new millennium, the single most important game-changer in Africa's relations with the United Nations has been the transformation of the Organisation of African Unity (OAU) into the African Union, during 1999 to 2002. Collective African agency is not new, as the history of decolonisation or the anti-apartheid struggle demonstrates. But with the increasing institutionalisation and professionalisation of the AU Commission, Africa has become a more coherent actor in continental and global politics.[7]

This chapter focuses on the emergence and substance of the partnership between the African Union and the United Nations in one particularly important policy field – peace and security.[8]

Policies, Institutions and Routines

The AU–UN partnership dates back a decade. On 17 September 2007 the UN General Assembly stressed the need for closer cooperation and coordination between the UN and the African Union.[9] This position was detailed in 2008 in a Security Council report and in a Security Council resolution, and confirmed in later Security Council resolutions.[10] And in 2009 the UN Secretary-General discussed steps to strengthen the partnership with the African Union and the challenges of improving this and other strategic partnerships with regional organisations.[11] The African Union detailed its vision of the partnership in May 2010.[12]

Legally the partnership is based on Chapter VIII of the UN Charter and Article 17 of the Protocol Relating to the Establishment of the Peace and Security Council.[13]

The African Union's policy in this field is guided by its *Agenda 2063* and its flagship 'Silencing the Guns' project, to be achieved by 2020.[14]

It is within this framework that partnership is being operationalised. Since 2006, annual consultations have been held between the African Union's Peace and Security Council and the United Nations Security Council.[15] There are regular meetings between the UN Special Representative for the African Union and the AU Commissioner for Peace and Security. In addition, within this framework the Ad Hoc Working Group on Conflict Prevention and Resolution in Africa was established. In September 2010, the Joint Task Force on Peace and Security was launched to foster coordination and collaboration. In addition, there are the biannual desk-to-desk meetings. In New York, the UN Office of the Special Adviser on Africa organises an annual event held during Africa Week, every year in October, on the margins of the UN General Assembly's Debate on the Development of Africa. During the same period, along with the AU and its regional economic communities (RECs), the Office of the Special Adviser on Africa convenes the 'RECs Briefing' to UN member states 'in order to raise global awareness on the role and contributions of the RECs to Africa's peace, security, governance, and socio-economic development'.[16] Since 2009 the African Union has maintained a Permanent Observer Mission to the United Nations, and in July 2010 the UN established an Office to the African Union (UNOAU). Systematic communication and policy harmonisation between the New York and Addis Ababa structures of the African Union and also among member states remain a major challenge. In this respect, the establishment in 2015 of joint teams between the UNOAU and the AU Commission's Peace and Security Department to conduct horizon scanning and develop common positions on existing and emerging conflicts was a huge step forward.

In 2014 the UN and the AU established a joint framework for enhanced partnership in peace and security, and they are about to sign another joint framework for enhanced partnership in peace and security to guide their relation.[17] The latter was drafted on 17 November 2015, and was being finalised after the Security Council's open session on UN–AU cooperation held on 24 May 2016.[18] The framework highlights an increased common understanding of the causes of conflict in Africa and details areas of cooperation, such as early warning and conflict prevention (including the building of country- and region-specific UN-AU teams) as well as preventive diplomacy. It furthermore outlines various ways to jointly address conflict and engage in peacebuilding. Finally, four partnership review mechanisms are specified (the UNOAU-AU, the Joint Task Force on Peace and Security, desk-to-desk meetings and annual meetings of the Security Council and Peace and Security Council).

Peacekeeping Missions

The partnership plays a major role in peacekeeping in African conflicts. During the first decades after decolonisation, most UN peacekeeping missions were deployed in the Middle East and Asia. Since the end of the Cold War, however, the bulk of UN interventions have been on the African continent.[19] The history of UN peacekeeping operations in Africa started in 1960 with a mission in the Congo (UN Secretary-General Dag Hammarskjöld died on 18 September 1961 in a plane accident en route to Northern Rhodesia). Today there are nine missions and one support office in Africa.[20] Following Norrie Macqueen's typology, one can identify four different types of UN peacekeeping missions in Africa.[21] First are missions related to state disintegration or situations of likely state disintegration, for example in the Congo (ONUC, 1960–4) and Somalia (UNOSOM, 1992–5);[22] second are missions related to accompanying, monitoring and legitimising interventions by regional multilateral forces, for example in Liberia (UNOMSIL, 1993–7), Sierra Leone (UNAMSIL, since 1988), and the Central African Republic (MINURCA, 1998–2000);[23] third are missions with a view to implementing peace agreements 'that had been reached to end internal conflicts within African states', for example in Angola (MONUA, 1991–9) and Mozambique (ONUMOZ, 1992–4);[24] and fourth are missions with 'oversight of international agreements affecting the international relations of established states', for example the decolonisation of Namibia (UNTAG, 1988–91).[25]

In addition are the more recent hybrid missions, such as the 2007 joint UN–AU operation in Darfur (UNAMID) – in the case of Darfur there was also a joint UN–AU conflict mediation effort.[26] Some missions have been transferred from the AU to UN, such as the transition in 2013 in Mali from AFISMA to MINUSMA, or in 2014 in the Central African Republic (CAR) from MISCA to MINUSCA. However, in Somalia, the initial vision of the African Union of transitioning AMISOM to a UN peacekeeping operation has not yet taken place.

Based on a 24 September 2003 joint declaration on UN–EU cooperation in crisis management, some division of labour has emerged between the UN and the EU. They agreed to set up a joint consultative mechanism with a view to planning, training, communication and best practices. This has played out in particular in the cases of the CAR, Chad, the Democratic Republic of the Congo (DRC) and Mali, despite the fact that there was 'great reluctance to get involved comprehensively'.[27]

Initially there was a legal tension between Article 53(1) of the UN Charter, which states that 'no enforcement action shall be taken under regional arrangements or by regional agencies without the authorization of the Security Council',[28] and Article 4(h) of the Constitutive Act of the African Union, which authorises AU interventions in 'grave circumstances' such as genocide, war crimes and crimes against humanity[29] – without mentioning the need to obtain approval of the UN Security Council. However, the problem was later reconciled.[30]

In September 2014 the Joint Task Force on Peace and Security undertook a lessons-learned exercise on transitions from AU peace support operations to UN peacekeeping operations, based on the cases of the CAR and Mali. The exercise highlighted the need for joint action and close collaboration between both organisations throughout the planning stages of a peace operation.[31] In October 2014, a High-Level Independent Panel on Peace Operations (HIPPO) was appointed to carry out a comprehensive assessment of the state of UN peace operations in light of emerging needs. The African Union contributed to this process by developing a common African position on the UN Review of Peace Operations: 'In the light of the centrality of Africa for United Nations peace operations, the Panel called for a stronger United Nations–African Union strategic partnership guided by a division of labour that is based on comparative advantages'.[32] Following the so-called new horizon process on UN peacekeeping,[33] the Secretary-General, in his 2015 report *The Future of UN Peace Operations*, reiterated the UN's plea for stronger global-regional partnerships.[34]

Finance and Capacity Building

The African Union's activities in the field of peace and security are heavily under-financed. Member states contribute less than three per cent of all funding to ongoing activities in this area.[35] Thus, dependency on donors (or 'international partners') is particularly high. The two most important external sources of finance for the Union in the area of peace and security are the United Nations and the European Union.[36]

The UN, according to its scale of assessment, is putting up the bulk of resources for nine current peacekeeping missions in Africa – in the fiscal year 2015–16 a record US$6.8 billion, or 83 per cent of all UN expenditure on peacekeeping (in the previous five fiscal years, the budget for Africa averaged at US$5.5 billion).[37] However, in principle the UN Security Council 'recognizes that regional organizations have the responsibility to secure human, financial, logistical and other resources for their organizations'.[38] The African Union, however, called on the UN 'to address in a systematic manner the issue of the predictability, sustainability and flexibility of the funding of AU peace support operations'.[39] On 9 January 2012, the Peace and Security Council

> reiterate[d] the AU's strong conviction of the need for the AU and the UN, building on the progress already achieved and lessons learned, to develop a stronger partnership, based on an innovative, strategic and forward-looking reading of Chapter VIII of the UN Charter, in order to more effectively promote peace, security and stability in Africa, particularly in view of Africa's evolving security landscape and the complexity of the challenges at hand, the development by the AU and its RECs/[regional mechanisms] of a comprehensive normative and institutional framework for dealing with peace and security issues, and their proximity and familiarity with the challenges facing their Member States.[40]

In addition to bankrolling peacekeeping operations, the UN engages in capacity building around peace and security. A joint declaration on enhancing the UN–AU cooperation framework for capacity building was signed on 16 November 2006.[41] It was superseded by a renewed UN–AU partnership on Africa's integration and development agenda for the period 2017–27, adopted by the 25th AU Assembly in June 2015.[42]

Contested Issues

Structurally, there is a tension between the African Union and the United Nations when it comes to representation and in this context, the reform of the UN Security Council. In the so-called Ezulwini Consensus of 7–8 March 2005, AU member states agreed to strive for no less than 'full representation' of Africa in all UN bodies.[43] With regard to the Security Council, this meant no fewer than two permanent seats, with all the prerogatives and privileges of permanent membership including the right of veto, and five non-permanent seats.[44] And even though Africa 'is opposed in principle to the veto, it is of the view that so long as it exists, and as a matter of common justice, [the veto] should be made available to all permanent members of the Security Council'.[45]

Politically, the AU–UN partnership has not always been an easy one, when permanent members of the Security Council have pursued narrow national interests.[46] In the cases of Libya in 2011 and Mali in 2013, political contradictions between the African Union and members of the Security Council became obvious. After the Security Council, had approved a no-fly zone in Libya (with all three African members concurring), the conflict escalated further.[47] The African Union's mediation plan was subsequently undermined by the North Atlantic Treaty Organisation (NATO), which intervened in Libya based on the Security Council's resolution. And in Mali the transition from AFISMA to MINUSMA 'generated a series of tensions between the United Nations and the African Union and was further complicated by the political involvement of some regional States'.[48]

Already in the Tripoli Declaration of 31 August 2009, the African Union had noted 'valued international partnerships':

> At the same time, we reiterate our determination to ensure that these partnerships are fully based on Africa's leadership, because without such leadership, there will be no ownership and

sustainability; because we understand the problems far better than those who come from far away; because we know which solutions will work, and how we can get there; and because, fundamentally, these problems are ours, and we will live with their consequences.[49]

Responding to the revolutions unfolding in northern Africa in 2011, the chair of the AU Commission noted 'the reluctance of members of the international community to fully acknowledge the AU role in the promotion of peace in the continent and their selective application of the principle of ownership'.[50] In this particular respect the AU's international partnerships should be 'fully based on Africa's leadership'.[51] In a follow-up report on the partnership, the AU Commission chair noted in 2013 the need for greater coherence by, among other things, working towards a more flexible and innovative interpretation of Chapter VIII, enhancing consultations between the AU's Peace and Security Council and the UN's Security Council, organising closer consultation between the UN Secretariat and the AU Commission and 'addressing effectively and in a systematic manner the issue of predictable, sustainable and flexible funding of AU-led peace support operations undertaken with the consent of the Security Council'.[52]

A final problem, operationally, is the conduct of UN peacekeeping missions, as sexual and gender-based violence committed by UN peacekeepers has strained AU–UN relations.[53]

Conclusion

The international partnership between the African Union and the United Nations represents a form of strategic inter-regionalism with a view to boosting the continent's sovereignty, and in this respect the partnership is a win-win situation for all parties concerned. Given the wide range of peace and security challenges the African continent is facing, the partnership tends to become ever broader. Thus, the AU has suggested enlarging the scope of its partnership with the UN from traditional threats to peace, security and stability, to a series of threats perceived to be new, including governance-related intra-state conflicts and violence, terrorism and transnational crime, piracy on the east and west coasts of Africa, border disputes and the effects of climate change and environmental degradation.[54]

However, there are at least seven fundamental challenges to the partnership. First, working towards closer horizontal integration of the African Peace and Security Architecture (APSA) and the complementary African Governance Architecture (AGA) in all fields of preventive diplomacy, peacemaking, peacebuilding and post-conflict reconstruction and development; second, increasing the capacity of the African Union's structures in New York (the Permanent Observer Mission to the UN, the Africa Group and the A3 – the three African non-permanent members of the Security Council); third, promoting vertical integration within the partnership, including the RECs and regional mechanisms; fourth, increasing the financial contribution of AU member states towards peace and security activities and enhancing African ownership of APSA; fifth, addressing the lack of political will of some AU member states when it comes to the organisation's own standards in terms of structural conflict prevention and the interlocking of short-term peace-making with long-term peace-building through promoting democracy, governance and human rights; sixth, accepting African leadership in the formulation of solutions to African problems by the P3 (the three Western permanent members of the Security Council); and finally, addressing the question of how best to create synergies between the African Union's partnership with the United Nations and its partnership with the European Union.

Postscript (June 2017)

In 2015 and 2016 the African Union finally took far reaching decisions on its finances and member states' contributions to UN peacekeeping operations. In January 2015 the AU Assembly of Heads of State and Government decided that in future member states should contribute 25 per cent of the funding to UN peacekeeping operations (as opposed to a combined 2.2 per cent according to the UN scale of assessment); and in June 2016 the AU Assembly decided that additional finances for the African Union's operations should be raised through a 0.2 per cent levy on eligible imports in order to increase ownership of the new institutions and policies and also to reduce dependency on international partners and donors. This model was suggested by the UN Economic Commission for Africa and the African Development Bank. In the mid-term it remains to be seen whether the African Union and her member states have the political will and technical capacity to implement these decisions.[55] If so, the international partnership between the African Union and the United Nations may see some fundamental changes in terms of African ownership and commitment, but also in terms of a deepening of the various forms of cooperation – as already indicated in the 2017 Joint Framework for Enhanced Partnership in Peace and Security.[56]

Notes

1. See Andrew Sherriff and John Kotsopoulos, 'Africa and the European Union: An Assessment of the Joint Africa-EU Strategy (JAES)', in Tim Murithi (ed.), *Routledge Handbook of Africa's International Relations* (Abingdon: Routledge, 2014), pp. 305–15; Stefan Gänzle and Sven Grimm, 'The European Union (EU) and the Emerging African Peace and Security Architecture', in Hany Besada (ed.), *Crafting an African Security Architecture: Addressing Regional Peace and Conflict in the 21st Century* (Farnham: Ashgate, 2010), pp. 73–88; Toni Haastrup, 'Africa-EU Partnership on Peace and Security', in Jack Mangala (ed.), *Africa and the European Union: A Strategic Partnership* (New York: Palgrave Macmillan, 2013), pp. 47–67.

2. See William Brown, 'A Question of Agency: Africa in International Politics', *Third World Quarterly* 33, no. 10 (2012), pp. 1889–1908; Sophie Harman and William Brown, 'In From the Margins? The Changing Place of Africa in International Relations', *International Affairs* 89, no. 1 (2013), pp. 69–87; Lesley Blauuw, 'African Agency in International Relations: Challenging Great Power Politics', in Paul-Henri Bischoff, Kwesi Aning and Amitav Acharya (eds), *Africa in Global International Relations: Emerging Approaches to Theory and Practice* (London and New York: Routledge, 2016), pp. 85–107; Jo-Ansie van Wyk, 'Africa in International Relations: Agent, Bystander, or Victim?', in Bischoff, Aning and Acharya, *Africa in Global International Relations*, pp. 108–20.

3. John W. Harbeson and Donald Rothchild (eds), *Africa in World Politics: The African State System in Flux*, 3rd edn (Boulder: Westview, 2000), p. 17.

4. John W. Harbeson and Donald Rothchild (eds), *Africa in World Politics: Reforming Political Order*, 4th edn (Boulder: Westview, 2009), p. 3.

5. Tânia Felício, 'Multilevel Security Governance: Reinventing Multilateralism Through Multiregionalism', *Human Security Journal* 5 (2007), pp. 50–61.

6. Conceptually this builds on John Agnew, *Globalization and Sovereignty* (Lanham: Rowman and Littlefield, 2009); and Fredrik Söderbaum, 'Modes of Regional Governance in Africa: Neoliberalism, Sovereignty-Boosting, and Shadow Networks', *Global Governance* 10, no. 4 (2004), pp. 419–36.

7. See Ulf Engel, 'The Changing Role of the AU Commission in Inter-African Relations: The Case of APSA and AGA', in John W. Harbeson and Donald Rothchild (eds), *Africa in World Politics: Engaging a Changing Global Order*, 5th edn (Boulder: Westview, 2013), pp. 186–206.

8. Though there is also the Africa Partnership Forum between the Group of Eight (G8) and African states, established in 2003 under the G8-Africa Partnership. This goes back to the G8 Action Plan, issued in response to the 2001 New Partnership for Africa's Development (NEPAD). See Patrick Hayford and Adolf Kloke-Lesch (assisted by Christoph Hosang), *Africa Partnership Forum: Evaluation Report – A Forum Puts Itself to the Test* (London: Africa Partnership Forum, 2013). On the history of relations between the Organisation of African Unity (OAU) and the United Nations (UN), see Berhanykun Andemicael, *The OAU and the UN: Relations Between the Organization of African Unity and the United Nations* (New York: United Nations Institute for Training and Research, 1976); Edmond Kwam Kouassi, 'Africa and the United Nations Since 1945', in Ali A. Mazrui and Christophe Wondji (eds), *Africa Since 1935* (Paris and Oxford: United Nations Educational, Scientific and Cultural Organisation (UNESCO) and Heinemann Educational, 1993), pp. 871–905; Edmond Kwam Kouassi, 'OAU-UN Interaction over the Last Decade', in Yassin el-Ayouty (ed.), *The Organization of African Unity After Thirty Years* (Westport and London: Praeger, 1994), pp. 139–46; Michael Njunga Mulikita, 'The United Nations Security Council

and the Organisation of African Unity: Conflict or Collaboration?', *African Security Review* 11, no. 1 (2002), pp. 27–39.

9. UN General Assembly, Resolution 296 on cooperation between the United Nations and the African Union, A/RES/61/296, adopted 5 October 2007. In detail see also Malte Brosig, *Cooperative Peacekeeping in Africa: Exploring Regime Complexity* (Abingdon: Routledge, 2015), pp. 50–60. For prior relations between the UN and the OAU/African Union (AU), see Margaret A. Vogt, 'Conflict, Resolution, and Peace-Keeping: The Organization of African Unity and the United Nations', in Gunnar M. Sørbø and Peter Vale (eds), *Out of Conflict: From War to Peace in Africa* (Uppsala: Nordiska Afrikainstitutet, 1997), pp. 57–78; Margaret A. Vogt, 'The UN and Africa's Regional Organisations', in Adekeye Adebajo (ed.), *From Global Apartheid to Global Village: Africa and the United Nations* (Scottsville: University of KwaZulu-Natal Press, 2009), pp. 251–68.

10. UN Security Council, *Report of the Secretary-General on the Relationship Between the United Nations and Regional Organizations, in Particular the African Union, in the Maintenance of International Peace and Security*, UN Doc. S/2008/186, 7 April 2008; UN Security Council, Resolution 1809 on cooperation between the United Nations and regional organizations, S/RES/1809, adopted 16 April 2008; UN Security Council, Resolution 2033 on the importance of developing effective partnerships between the United Nations and regional organizations, in particular the African Union, S/RES/2033, adopted 12 January 2012; Security Council UN, Resolution 2167 on cooperation with regional and sub-regional organisations in matters relating to the maintenance of peace and security, S/RES/2167, adopted 28 July 2014.

11. UN, *Support to African Union Peacekeeping Operations Authorized by the United Nations: Report of the Secretary-General*, UN Doc. A/64/359-S/2009/470, 18 September 2009; UN, *Implementation of the Recommendations of the Special Committee on Peacekeeping Operations: Report of the Secretary-General*, UN Doc. A/64/573, 22 December 2009, para. 52.

12. AU Commission, *The UN-AU Partnership on Peace and Security: Towards Greater Strategic Coherence: Report of the Chairperson of the African Union Commission* (Addis Ababa, 2010).

13. UN, *Charter of the United Nations*, Chapter VII, http://www.un.org/en/sections/un-charter/chapter-viii/index.html (accessed 6 July 2016); AU, *Protocol Relating to the Establishment of the Peace and Security Council* (Durban, 2002).

14. AU, *50th Anniversary Solemn Declaration*, adopted by the 21st Ordinary Assembly of Heads of State and Government, Addis Ababa, 26 May 2013 (mimeo); AU Commission, *Agenda 2063: The Africa We Want*, 2nd edn (Addis Ababa, 2014).

15. See http://www.un.org/en/africa/osaa/partnerships/au.shtml (accessed 6 July 2016). For the modalities of the partnership, see Dawit Yohannes Wondemagegnehu, *AU-UN Collaboration in Peace and Security in Africa: Re-Spacing Security Governance in the New Millennium?*, PhD thesis submitted

to the Institute for Peace and Security Studies, Addis Ababa University, and the Global and European Studies Institute, University of Leipzig, 2016.

16. See http://www.un.org/en/africa/osaa/partnerships/au.shtml (accessed 6 July 2016).

17. See http://www.un.org/undpa/africa/un-au-cooperation (accessed 6 July 2016).

18. UN Security Council, 'Statement by the President of the Security Council on Cooperation Between the United Nations and Regional and Subregional Organizations in Maintaining International Peace and Security', UN Doc. S/PRST/2016/8, 24 May 2016.

19. For comprehensive overviews, see Adebajo, *From Global Apartheid to Global Village*; Adekeye Adebajo, *UN Peacekeeping in Africa: From the Suez Crisis to the Sudan Conflicts* (Boulder: Rienner, 2011); Joachim Koops, Norrie Macqueen and Thierry Tardy (eds), *The Oxford Handbook of United Nations Peacekeeping Operations* (Oxford: Oxford University Press, 2015).

20. UN, 'Current Peacekeeping Operations', http://www.un.org/en/peacekeeping/operations/current.shtml (accessed 6 July 2016).

21. Norrie Macqueen, *United Nations Peacekeeping in Africa Since 1960* (Harlow: Pearson Education, 2002). *See also* UN, 'Past Peacekeeping Operations', http://www.un.org/en/peacekeeping/operations/past.shtml (accessed 6 July 2016); Arthur Lee Burns and Nina Heathcote, *Peacekeeping by UN Forces from Suez to Congo* (London: Pall Mall, 1963).

22. Macqueen, *United Nations Peacekeeping*, p. 28.

23. Ibid., p. 29.

24. Ibid.

25. Ibid., p. 30.

26. Representative of many reports, see AU Peace and Security Council (PSC), *Progress Report of the African-Union High-Level Implementation Panel for Sudan and Southern Sudan*, PSC/PR/2 (CDLVI), Addis Ababa, 12 September 2014. See also UN and AU Commission, *Special Report of the Secretary-General and the Chairperson of the African Union Commission on the African Union–United Nations Hybrid Operation in Darfur*, UN Doc. S/2016/510, 8 June 2016; Alex de Waal, 'Sudan: Darfur', in Jane Boulden (ed.), *Responding to Conflict in Africa: The United Nations and Regional Organizations* (New York: Palgrave Macmillan, 2013), pp. 283–306.

27. Brosig, *Cooperative Peacekeeping in Africa*, pp. 224 (for an overview on cooperation in the cases of Somalia, the Central African Republic, and Mali, *see* pp. 175–240). Introducing many case studies, see also Thierry Thardy and Marco Wyss (eds), *Peacekeeping in Africa: The Evolving Security Architecture* (London and New York: Routledge, 2014). See also David Curtis and Gilbert Nibigirwe, 'Complementary Approaches to Peacekeeping? The African Union and the United Nations in Burundi', in Besada, *Crafting an African Security Architecture*, pp. 109–27; Youssef Mahmoud, 'Partnerships in Peacebuilding in Burundi: Some Lessons Learned', in Besada, *Crafting an African Security Architecture*, pp. 129–41; Giovanna Bono, 'The Impact of the Discourse of the

"Politics of Protection": The Case of the EU and UN Policing and Military Missions to Chad (2007–2010)', *African Security* 5, nos. 3–4 (2012), pp. 179–98.

28. UN, *Charter of the United Nations*, Chapter VII.

29. OAU, *Constitutive Act of the African Union* (Lomé, 2000), para. 4(h).

30. UN, *Report of the Secretary-General on the Relationship Between the United Nations and Regional Organizations*, para. 7. See also UN, *A Regional-Global Security Partnership: Challenges and Opportunities – Report of the Secretary-General*, UN Doc. A/61/204-S/2006/590, 28 July 2006.

31. UN, *Causes of Conflict and the Promotion of Durable Peace and Sustainable Development in Africa: Report of the Secretary-General*, UN Doc. A/70/176-S/2015/560, 24 July 2015, para. 30.

32. UN, *Causes of Conflict*, para. 31; AU PSC, *Report of the Chairperson of the Commission on Follow-Up Steps on the Common African Position on the Review of United Nations Peace Operations*, PSC/AHG/3 (DXLVII), New York, 29 September 2015.

33. UN Department of Peacekeeping Operations and Department of Field Support, *A New Partnership Agenda: Charting a New Horizon for UN Peacekeeping* (New York, 2009).

34. UN, *The Future of United Nations Peace Operations: Implementation of the Recommendations of the High-Level Independent Panel on Peace Operations – Report of the Secretary-General*, UN Doc. A/70/357-S/2015/682, 2 September 2015, paras. 28–32. See also UN, S/PRST/2014/27, statement by the president of the UN Security Council on cooperation between the United Nations and regional and sub-regional organisations in maintaining international peace and security, 16 December 2014; Security Council Report, *The Security Council and UN Peace Operations: Reform and Deliver* (New York, 2016), http://www.securitycouncilreport.org/atf/cf/%7B65BFCF9B-6D27-4E9C-8CD3-CF6E4FF96FF9%7D/research_report_peace_operations_may_2016.pdf (accessed 6 July 2016).

35. Ulf Engel, 'The African Union Finances: How Does It Work?', Working Paper no. 6 (Leipzig: Centre for Area Studies, 2015).

36. See European Commission, *African Peace Facility. Annual Report 2014* (Luxembourg: Publication Office of the European Union, 2015).

37. See Engel, 'The African Union Finances', p. 20. Missions include MINURSO for Western Sahara; MINUSCA in the Central African Republic; MINUSMA in Mali; MONUSCO in the Democratic Republic of the Congo; UNAMID in Darfur/Sudan; UNMIL in Liberia; UNMISS in Sudan; UNISFA in Abyei; UNOCI in Côte d'Ivoire; and UNSOA as support for the AU's AMISOM in Somalia.

38. UN, S/PRST/2009/3, statement by the president of the UN Security Council on 'Peace and Security in Africa', 18 March 2009, p. 1.

39. AU PSC, PSC/PR/COMM (CCCVII), communiqué on the AU-UN partnership, Addis Ababa, 9 January 2012.

40. AU PSC, PSC/PR/COMM (CCCVII), communiqué on the AU-UN partnership, para. 6.

41. UN, A/61/630, letter dated 11 December 2006 from the UN Secretary-General addressed to the president of the General Assembly, 12 December 2006.

42. UN, *The Future of United Nations Peace Operations*, p. 28.

43. AU Executive Council, *The Common Position on the Proposed Reform of the United Nations: 'The Ezulwini Consensus'*, Ext/EX.CL/2 (VII), 7th Extraordinary Session, Addis Ababa, 7–8 March 2005.

44. AU Executive Council, *The Common Position*, para. C(e)2(i–ii).

45. AU Executive Council, *The Common Position*, para. C(e)2(iii).

46. A point well argued by Adebajo in *UN Peacekeeping in Africa*.

47. UN Security Council, Resolution 1973 on a no-fly zone in Libya, S/RES/1973, adopted 17 March 2011.

48. UN, S/2014/879, concept note for the Security Council open debate on the theme 'Peace Operations: The Partnership Between the United Nations and the African Union and Its Evolution', 16 December 2014; UN, annex to letter dated 8 December 2014 from the Permanent Representative of Chad to the United Nations addressed to the UN Secretary-General, 9 December 2014, p. 6. See also Thomas G. Weiss and Martin Welz, 'The UN and AU in Mali and Beyond: A Shotgun Wedding?', *International Affairs* 90, no. 4 (2014), pp. 889–905.

49. AU, *Tripoli Declaration on the Elimination of Conflicts in Africa and the Promotion of Sustainable Peace*, special session of the AU Assembly on the consideration and resolution of conflicts in Africa, Tripoli, SP/ASSEMBLY/PS/DECL (I), 31 August 2009, para. 21.

50. AU Commission, *Report of the Chairperson of the Commission on Current Challenges to Peace and Security on the Continent and the AU's Efforts: Enhancing Africa's Leadership, Promoting African Solutions*, EXT/Assembly (A//2 [01.2011]), Extraordinary Session of the AU Assembly, Addis Ababa, 25–26 May 2011, para. 48.

51. AU Commission, *Report of the Chairperson of the Commission on Current Challenges*, para. 48.

52. AU PSC, *Report of the Chairperson of the Commission on the African Union–United Nations Partnership: The Need for Greater Coherence*, PSC/AHG/3 (CCCXCVII), New York, 23 September 2013, para. 23. See also AU PSC, PSC/AHG/COMM/1 (CCCXCVII), communiqué on the situation between the Republic of Sudan and the Republic of South Sudan and other related issues, New York, 23 September 2013; Arthur Boutellis and Paul Williams, *Peace Operations, the African Union, and the United Nations: Toward More Effective Partnerships in Peace Operations* (New York: International Peace Institute, 2013); Paul D. Williams and Solomon A. Dersso, *Saving Strangers and Neighbors: Advancing UN-AU Cooperation on Peace Operations* (New York: International Peace Institute, 2015).

53. UN Security Council, Resolution 2167, para. 27. See also Gabrielle Simm, *Sex in Peace Operations* (Cambridge: Cambridge University Press, 2013).

54. Pierre Buyoya, 'Statement by the AU High Representative for Mali and the Sahel to the UN Security Council', New York, 16 December 2014 (mimeo). See also UN, S/PV.7343 on cooperation between the United Nations and regional and sub-regional organizations in maintaining international peace and security, New York, 16 December 2014.

55. AU Assembly, 'Decision on the Report of Alternative Sources of Financing the African Union'. 24th Ordinary Session. Assembly/AU/Dec. 559 (XXIV), Addis Ababa, 30–31 January 2015; and AU Assembly, 'Decision on the Outcome of the Retreat of the Assembly of the African Union', 27th Ordinary Session. Assembly/AU/Dec.605 (XXVII), Kigali, 17–18 July 2016, respectively.

56. UN/AU, *Joint United Nations-African Union Framework for Enhanced Partnership in Peace and Security*, New York, 19 April 2017.

CHAPTER 12

THE AFRICAN UNION–CHINA PARTNERSHIP: PROSPECTS AND CHALLENGES

David Monyae

The Africa–China relationship can be traced back over several centuries. However, the current relationship was formalised multilaterally through the African Union (AU) and exists at a bilateral level on a state-to-state basis. In 2006 the Chinese government declared that China will 'unswervingly carry forward the tradition of China-Africa friendship, and, proceeding from the fundamental interests of both the Chinese and African peoples, establish and develop a new type of strategic partnership with Africa'.[1] China formally recognised the AU, alongside the European Union (EU) and the Association of Southeast Asian Nations (ASEAN), among the international confederations of states named as strategic partners.

This chapter assesses the African Union's evolving relationship with China, informed by the current 'New Strategic Partnership' formalised under the relationship in 2006. In analysing the development of this relationship, the chapter assesses whether it is a relationship based on a mutual beneficiation or whether it is asymmetrically biased towards China. The African Union's strategy in this partnership is compared to the Chinese strategy, with a view to enumerating a range of suggestions for how the AU can better engage Beijing on the way forward.

From Bandung to FOCAC: A Historical Background

At the height of the Cold War, China established a tradition of developing cooperative frameworks and strategic partnerships. For example, in 1955, at the Bandung Conference, China adopted its 'Five Principles of Peaceful Coexistence' together with India. Subsequently, similar frameworks were established with 29 Asian and African countries. The agreement established the following principles: 'Mutual respect for sovereignty and territorial integrity; mutual non-aggression; non-interference in each other's internal affairs; equality and mutual benefit; and peaceful co-existence'.[2]

Since the 1950s, China's strategy towards its Africa relations has since evolved from 'confrontation to co-operation, from revolution to economic development and from isolation to international engagement'.[3] In 2000, the launch of the Forum on China-Africa Cooperation (FOCAC) formalised a new kind of relationship. This relationship culminated in the construction of a China-financed state-of-the-art building for the African Union headquarters in Addis Ababa, which was billed as a gift from the People's Republic of China. This is perhaps the most powerful representation of the ongoing trajectory of the Sino−African relationship. However, prior to assessing the current Sino−African relationship, it is worthwhile to trace its trajectory and evolution.

FOCAC was established on 11−12 October 2000 at a meeting hosted by Beijing. It was attended by representatives of 44 African countries, with a total of 80 ministers participating. At the time, the engagement focused on enhancing relations between China and Africa through investments, financial cooperation, debt relief and cancellation, agricultural cooperation, natural resources and energy and multilateral cooperation. The forum has since been held tri-annually, in China (2000), Ethiopia (2003), China (2006), Egypt (2009), China (2012) and South Africa (2015). The outcome agenda and activities of the FOCAC initiative in Africa have been reviewed every three years, according to expectations and demands.

In November 2006, President Hu Jintao officially formalised the China–Africa strategic partnership at FOCAC's Beijing summit.[4] At the time, China not only pledged to double its assistance to the African continent by 2009, but also pledged to provide preferential loans of at least US$3 billion, and preferential buyer credits of US$2 billion. China also committed to cancelling debt in heavily indebted poor African countries. This meeting was significant because it illustrated China's strategy towards its relations with Africa, which included economic development and strategic partnerships. In effect, the initial 1955 Bandung Conference was an important reminder of the common interests that Africa and China share. This historic gathering by the so-called Third World countries was a watershed event for the relationships that would follow. Egypt established the first known diplomatic ties with China in 1956, marking the first formalised bilateral relationship between an African state and China.[5] The majority of African states followed suit after attaining independence, with the exception of Burkina Faso. Some African countries have experienced fluctuating relationships with both China and Taiwan, depending on their policy orientation towards either Beijing or Taipei.

Since the establishment of the Organisation of African Unity (OAU), in 1963, and the creation of its successor, the African Union (AU), in 2002, African states multilaterally have maintained fairly cordial relationships with Beijing.

It is important to note that at the inception of the Bandung Conference, China was at some stage in the relationship as under-developed and impoverished, with sectors of its population living in poverty, as a significant number of African countries. The Bandung Conference was a crucial step towards the formation of the Non-Alignment Movement (NAM), in which African states and Asian states played a pivotal role. The NAM became instrumental for African states to position themselves in an increasingly bi-polar global order dominated by the interests of the Soviet Union and the United States (US). The Cold War had resulted in instability in the periphery of the US and Soviet spheres of influence, marked by proxy wars and hostile relationships.

The NAM provided African countries with a moderate degree of neutrality in the context of the raging Cold War. However, a number of African countries also leveraged their membership in the NAM to advance their liberation movements. For example, by utilising the considerable influence achieved by the United Nations (UN) General Assembly's Group of 77 (G77) plus China, as well as drawing the UN's Africa Group, created in 1954, countries like Zimbabwe, Namibia and South Africa were able to engage a wide range of strategic partners to pursue their agenda for liberation.[6] China supported African liberation movements through military training, provision of weapons and financial assistance. The support that Beijing rendered to Africa at that time has since transformed into the ongoing partnership between the two actors in the post–Cold War era. A key principle that has typified the Sino–African relationship has been one premised on solidarity, particularly in the struggles against colonialism and imperialism, the call for the transformation of the institutions of global governance, collective security, development and economic growth and cultural and people-to-people diplomacy.

Adekeye Adebajo notes 'that as a result of pressure of a determined Southern majority, including twenty-six African states and led by Tanzania's formidable permanent representative at the UN, Salim Ahmed Salim, the People's Republic of China took its permanent seat on the UN Security Council in 1971, in the face of strong opposition from Washington, solid African backing also helped China secure the 2008 Olympics Games'.[7] African states have also received material benefits from their relationship with Beijing. China's foreign direct investment (FDI) into Africa has progressively taken an upward trajectory, and recently overtook that of traditional Western investors. In 1950, China's total investments in Africa stood at US$12 million, which increased to US$35 million in 1955 and US$125 million in 1965. China's 'Open Up and Reform Policy' in the 1970s resulted in an unprecedented 3.6 per cent average annual increase in investment into Africa, a phenomenon that further increased dramatically throughout the 1980s. The 1990s were marked by an additional surge in bilateral exports and imports between China and Africa. By 2000, China recorded over US$10 billion worth of FDI into Africa, and by 2008 this figure had reached an impressive US$107 billion, despite the global economic crisis that defined that year.[8] As of 2017, Africa is again at centre stage of China's growth and expansionist ambitions with the launch of Beijing's Silk Road initiative, also known as the One Belt One Road (OBOR) initiative, and the launch of the twenty-first century Marine Route initiative. The Silk Road initiative focuses on development through energy, security and markets. The Silk Road was a historical trading route between China and Europe between third century B.C.E. and the fifteenth century C.E., a time during which China was a powerful player in terms of trade. The renewed emphasis on the Silk Road is meant to emphasise China's goals towards becoming a world power and consolidating its status as such. The New Silk Road Economic Belt and the 21st Century Maritime Silk Road will be consolidated with a US$40 billion fund, supported by the Chinese-led Asian Infrastructure Bank

(AIIB) and the New Development Bank (the latter of the BRICS bloc, comprising Brazil, Russia, India, China and South Africa).[9]

More recently, in 2015, the sixth FOCAC meeting was the first dialogue since President Xi Jinping became the head of state of China. Xi emphasised that AU–China relations continued to be mutually beneficial, citing how China had led efforts towards fighting the 2014 Ebola epidemic, which affected several countries across the African continent. Conversely, Africa has regularly come to the assistance of China when it the latter been affected by natural disasters. Furthermore, Xi reiterated that China–Africa relations were based on the understanding the partners stood on equal footing, 'treating each other as equals' and being 'good friends, good partners and good brothers'.[10] This emphasis is particularly important because China's strategy towards Africa has been characterised as having neo-imperialistic overtones, due to the asymmetrical nature of the investment flows into the continent. Subsequently, President Xi pledged a development package of US$60 billion, but the specificities of how it will be used remain unknown.

Economically, the African Union and its constituent members have benefited by China's engagement. On 12 July 2006, the secretariat of the Chinese Follow-Up Committee signed a memorandum of understanding on strengthening consultation and cooperation with the New Partnership for Africa's Development (NEPAD).[11] In 2006, China sponsored NEPAD's Pan-African Infrastructural Development Fund (PAIDF) with an infusion of US$625 million. At the fifth FOCAC summit, in 2012 China and its African partners noted:

> The two sides highlighted the important role of the New Partnership for Africa's Development (NEPAD) in promoting African development and integration and applauded the

cooperation between FOCAC and NEPAD. The Chinese side will increase exchanges and expand cooperation with the NEPAD Planning and Coordinating Agency in a joint effort to promote economic and social development and regional economic integration in Africa.[12]

Thus there is a general willingness by the Chinese to deepen their cooperation with the African Union and its constituent members by strengthening the capacity of the latter.

China's Instrumentalisation of Strategic Partnerships

China's strategic partnership with Africa has obtained mostly been through economic and security relations, although its commitment towards the latter remains questionable. Festus Aubyn argues that China's non-interference posture towards Africa needs to be re-assessed, especially considering the amount of money China has invested in some countries and given the potential for these funds to be utilised to repress societies. For example, China has invested at least US$7 billion into Sudan's oil sector through China's National Petroleum Corporation (CNPC). These resources are invested into a government that is also embroiled in conflicts in Darfur and the Nuba provinces. In the long run, conflicts in countries from which resources are being extracted are not in the long-term interests of these affected countries, and stain China's reputation on the continent. China has engaged in efforts to support peace initiatives in Sudan through the UN in a multilateral engagement, with the AU through regional initiatives and with support to Africa's regional economic communities (RECs) and sub-regional interventions. China has also engaged directly with the government in Khartoum, but with limited success in influencing Sudan's posture towards the persistence of conflicts in its territory.[13]

China's economic approach towards Africa has been described as an 'aid for oil strategy'.[14] China has also employed a non-interference approach to the internal affairs of African states, expecting other countries to reciprocate this stance when it comes to its own internal affairs. The principle of non-interference, especially in relation to African states, was established through the China's Principle of Peaceful Coexistence that stresses mutual respect for sovereignty and territorial integrity, mutual non-aggression, non-interference, equality and mutual benefit.[15]

China relies on the support of Africa countries at the UN. The Africa Group, which includes 54 countries, comprises almost a quarter of the UN General Assembly. China has been able to align itself with Africa and this has on a number of occasions assisted in positioning China politically in the UN. Recently, China relied on the support of Africa during its proposal to host the Olympics when the issue of human rights was raised. One of the most significant issues that China has remained consistent on is its approach to Taiwan and its reiteration of its One China Policy. China has even gone so far as to sever ties with African countries that have openly challenged this policy.[16]

Assessing Africa's Strategic Partnerships with China

The ever-increasing costs of commodities fuelled by the rapid industrialisation in the global South is supposedly promoting a new 'scramble' for Africa. This new scramble is limited not only to Africa's natural resources but also to voting support in major multilateral bodies like the United Nations and World Trade Organization (WTO). China's exponentially growing trade and diplomatic courtship with African states has generated interest and concern in the West. The relationship is welcomed by many who see Chinese economic growth as a wave that Africa must ride to escape its under-development and poverty trap. Equally, the relationship has come under serious scrutiny, with some critics going as far as likening the relationship to that of European colonialism. Because of the debates around the Sino–African relationship, it is crucial to analyse whether China is a colonial power or an equal partner that can be trusted in trade and diplomatic matters.

In order to debunk the argument that China is colonising Africa, one has to critically analyse key elements of the relationship. The first important element of the Sino–African relationship is political equality. In a departure from the practices of the continent's former colonial powers and Cold War patrons, Africa has been elevated by China to the status of an equal trading partner. This is contrary to the traditional 'charity case' narrative reproduced by the political and business elites of Western states. Therefore, the Western-driven narrative of describing China – Africa as a 'new scramble for Africa' must be out rightly be dismissed. Beijing had previously criticised the West for suddenly taking an interest in Sino–African engagement when in the past it chose to ignore it. Africa has been providing natural resources, including oil and minerals, to the West; therefore the growing demand for African natural resources by China is a threat to established status quo. China has also changed the rules of engagement set by the West – often paying for natural resources with infrastructural investments that Africa direly needs. Consequently, Africa sees its engagement with China as a strategic partnership that is in the continent's interests.

Sino–AU Peace and Security Initiatives: An Appraisal

It should be noted that since the establishment of the AU–China strategic dialogue mechanism, there have been a few strategic dialogues around peace and security. Because of these dialogues, the AU has benefited immensely, for example with its plan to 'Silence the Guns' by 2020 to soon become a reality. China's support for Africa in the arena of peace and security can be seen in the following African initiatives, like the African Union Mission in Somalia (AMISOM) and the United Nations–African Union Hybrid Operation in Darfur (UNAMID). Furthermore, China has gradually increased its financial support for Africa through the UN's Department of Peacekeeping Operations.

These developments are welcomed by the African Union, particularly due to China's willingness to provide boots on the ground for peacekeeping missions. Unlike the African Union's traditional Western sponsors, China has proved to be a partner prepared to risk its own personnel in peace operations on the continent. The Chinese strategy has provided tangible results. The successful combating of Somali pirates in the Gulf of Eden can be attributed to Chinese naval vessels patrolling the waters. Of all the five permanent members (P5) of the United Nations Security Council, China is presently contributing the largest number of boots on the ground for UN peacekeeping operations on the African continent. Few developed states are willing to risk their troops to silence guns on the African continent, but China has proved to be a reliable partner in helping the AU realise it goal of pursuing and promoting peace and security.

Comparing Chinese and African Union Strategies of Engagement

The Chinese Strategy

Many political actors are reluctant to engage the African Union when dealing with African states. They resort to using bilateral relations rather than the more complicated multi-lateral route. Beijing has been pushing a pragmatic approach that favours bilateral relations pursed within the multilateral framework of FOCAC. China has increasingly started to show willingness to involve the AU in its business in Africa. China has elevated the African Union from being an observer at the

FOCAC summit to being a full participating member. Furthermore, Beijing has clearly stated:

> China appreciates the significant role of the AU in safeguarding peace and stability in the region and promoting African solidarity and development. China values its friendly cooperation with the AU in all fields, supports its positive role in regional and international affairs and stands ready to provide the AU assistance to the best of its capacity.[17]

The studies of China's Africa strategy (or lack thereof) have overwhelmingly focused on China's economic interests in Africa, the role played by the Chinese government and Chinese companies, and the economic and social impacts of such activities on the ground.[18] The relationship between China and Africa is operationalised at both the domestic and the multilateral level. China, like all actors in the arena of global international relations, is driven by its own national interests. As a result, Beijing has advanced its national interests while dealing with the African Union. Politically, the One China Policy is an issue that Beijing prioritises. Economically, Beijing has used Africa as the source of natural resources and markets for its products. The economic investments and vast Chinese personnel on the African continent have resulted in security becoming a major interest. Beijing seeks to sell its 'China model' as an ideological alternative to African states that have been struggling to implement Western ideals. Sino–African relations have been relatively smooth and free of major disturbances due in part to the shared sense of historical victimisation by Western colonial powers and a common identity/affinity as developing countries.[19]

China's rise has been labelled a peaceful one. Indeed, China has managed to become a world power, rising from humble beginnings as a third-world country to the status of a global power to be reckoned with, without any major confrontation with other states. Beijing's foreign policy has been particularly consistent, predicated on pursuing its interests while minimising its confrontation with the United States. The strategic partnerships it shares with major powers and multilateral organisations, including the AU, constitute an approach that has served Beijing in an array of issues, including its One China Policy, human rights, military cooperation, anti-terrorism, non-proliferation and people-to-people exchanges. These and other important strategic interests are included in Beijing's joint declarations.[20]

The Chinese are often misunderstood, and their engagement with Africa has been distorted in the West's anti-ascendancy rhetoric. Thus, distorted discourses surrounding the Sino–African relationship have surfaced, typically claiming that China is interested in Africa only for natural resources; that China is exaggerating its financial assistance to Africa; that Chinese businesses employ only their own nationals; that Chinese aid and finance are a vehicle for securing natural resources; and that China is land-grabbing Africa's territory for its own agricultural purposes. The basis of these myths is imbedded in the West's agenda to discredit China's continued support for Africa. The strong presence of China in Africa consequently upsets the traditional relationship that Western states have had with Africa. There is also a genuine competition between China and Western countries for Africa's resources. Africa regrettably has not developed a strategy to leverage its relationship with China to its advantage and to securing its own economic future.

In the final analysis, China's strategy has been to use Africa mainly for economic reasons and diplomatic purposes. China's economic boom meant that the country needed to access additional natural resources, for which Africa is a prime and rich source. As well, China has been able to engage and leverage its influence over Africa to ensure voting outcomes in its favour within multilateral organisations.

China's Africa strategy is evident in the establishment of FOCAC in 2000. China's 2006 Africa policy document further highlighted Beijing's priorities in its engagement with Africa: sincerity, friendship and equality (the political angle of the relationship); mutual benefit, reciprocity and common prosperity (the economic angle of the relationship); mutual support and close coordination (the international dimension); and mutual learning and common development (the cultural dimension). Beijing has achieved several these outcomes with varying degrees of success.

The African Union Strategy

Regional integration can be viewed as a normative strategy for managing external developments but also a defensive approach to containing the forces of globalisation.[21] It is argued that the succession from the Organisation of African Unity to the African Union was an attempt by African states to strengthen economic cooperation, stabilise the African security landscape and form a vehicle for collective bargaining. The latter is what the African Union has been attempting to achieve in its engagements with China. External factors are not just a catalyst for regional cooperation but also a necessary condition for regional integration in the global South.[22] The AU's improved relationship with China can be seen with its growing role in the FOCAC initiative. The new strategic relationship is the fulfilment of the hypothesised argument that external influence is necessary for stronger regionalism.

Do Africans understand China? For Africans to engage in fruitful partnership with China, they need to comprehensively understand how China operates and the grand Chinese plan for Africa. The director of the Institute of Economic Affairs (IEA) of Ghana, Charles Mensa, argued that 'Africa has to catch the tail of the huge dragon of China this time, because when China takes off, Africa will also be lifted'.[23] Africa has elaborated *Agenda 2063* as its developmental blueprint, and it is crucial to investigate how the Sino–African relationship fits into this ambitious agenda. Frank discussions should be held to analyse how the relationship can industrialise Africa and help it escape its economic problems.

One of the biggest challenges that the African Union faces is lack of capacity, resulting in shortcomings especially when dealing with a vast country like China. China has a strong bureaucracy that is well funded compared to the African Union, which struggles with funding. The FOCAC summits are a good reference point. Who sets the agenda for FOCAC, and who captains the chairing of the summits? Without capacity to control the important decision making apparatus of the relationship, Africa will always expose itself to exploitation in its engagements with China. This could result in Africa becoming dependent on China, which Africa should of course avoid given its debilitating historical experience with European powers.

So far, African states lack a coordinated response mechanism, and most the continent's political actors interact with China on an individual basis, pursing different national interests. A collective bargaining approach for the AU is a viable option for FOCAC members for them to synchronise their negotiating with Beijing. Equally, China will benefit from an acceleration of the desired outcomes through a unified AU, because this will reduce negotiations with different political actors.

The AU has seen significant progress in the gradual development of its security architecture through the establish-ment of collective security mechanisms. He Wenping from the Institute of West Asian and African studies notes that there has been a shift from the non-intervention posture of the Organisation for African Unity to identifying cases such as genocide, gross violations of human rights, instability in countries that threatens broader regional stability and unconstitutional changes of government.[24] There is significantly much more work to be done to enhance the capacity of Africa's inter-governmental organisations. The current crisis in Burundi, for example, illustrates the weakness of the AU's capacity to intervene in regional conflicts.

Criticism of China

Relations between China and Africa have not been as equal as the Chinese insist. It is evident that an over-riding concern for China in initiating its relationship with Africa was to pursue its national and geo-political interests. China is also relatively economically and politically stronger than Africa, and through FOCAC it is able to influence Africa and advance its interests on the continent. China has also explicitly stated its commitments towards Africa through the Beijing Declaration and FOCAC's action plans. These do not reflect Africa's ideas towards China and rather illustrate the continent's passive approach towards its relationship with China.[25]

For the most part, China has maintained its approach of non-interference towards Africa. China's political engagement with Africa is limited. It consistently deals directly with African countries, and thus engagement through the AU has its limitations. China's approach to Africa has been on a case-by-case basis, depending on the internal affairs of countries and how this can advance China's interests.

Criticism of the African Union

'Win-win development' is an important outcome and the point of reference when analysing African Union–China engagement. But will Africa continue to win as Beijing's commodity-driven economy slows and transitions to a more consumer-centred one? Africa must soon diversify its trade relationship with China, but the AU seems to have no concrete long-term strategic plan for China. What the AU needs is a carefully thought-out and comprehensive roadmap on how to deal with increased Chinese engagement. The AU should not be side-lined but should rather be at the centre of advising on and establishing concrete policies for member states to follow.

China has been criticised for focusing more on bilateral agreements with African states rather than on sub-regional or regional engagement. China is a state with a strong, disciplined bureaucracy that is well staffed and well-funded, while the African Union's coordination mechanisms are barely functional. It is therefore imperative for the African Union to understand its shortcomings when its member states deal with China bilaterally and multilaterally simultaneously. The AU has often rhetorically called for common positions and collective approaches for its member states when dealing with foreign affairs.

A parasitic relationship will forever result in other states and organisations undermining Africans and their goals. Minor issues like having one's headquarters donated by China paint a poor picture of the African Union's ability to achieve self-reliance. Currently, member states are not contributing as much as they should when it comes to African Union programmes. How will 'African solutions to African problems' be implemented when the African Union can barely fund its own programmes? All AU member-states contribution currently go towards operational costs. All programmes are donor-funded, which therefore means that only those programmes that donors want are implemented.

Recommendations to Improve Africa's Relationship with China

In the field of peace and security, it should be acknowledged that China must avoid the mistake of militarily intervening in internal African conflicts. Only in cases where the African Union calls upon China to assist should Beijing engage in Africa's internal battles. The Sino–African relationship should prioritise capacity building, and post-conflict humanitarian assistance and reconstruction. When Beijing is dealing with

African conflicts, it should prioritise conflict prevention methods under AU principles. 'African solutions to African problems' remains a cornerstone for Africa's engagement with external partners, and should be respected.

The China–Africa Think Tank Forum (CATTF), founded in October 2011, has been linking Chinese and African think tanks as well as scholarly activities with interests in Sino–African relations. Zhejiang Normal University and the China–Africa Business School together constitute the forum's standing secretariat. Such developments should be welcomed. Information and skills transfer between China and the AU should be a priority. More student exchange programmes should be in place to increase the number of African students and professors in Chinese universities and vice versa. The Confucius Institutes in South African and other African universities should equally advance Pan-African interests as much as they advance Chinese culture and language.

China needs to revisit its non-intervention policy, particularly when posed with peace and security challenges in Africa. Already one can see the early phase of Chinese Africa policy shift when it comes to peace and security. In the case of South Sudan, China appears to be intervening to enforce the AU's and UN mandates.

The AU has entered endless strategic partnerships with many countries and regional bodies such the EU, Japan, Turkey, the US, Germany and South Korea. It is imperative for the AU to accord these partnerships some sort of ranks to ensure that it priorities the most important partners. It should therefore measure tangible benefits accrued from any partnership it enters with any country or body. Where Africa benefits in terms of increased fair trade and assistance in key areas of its developmental needs, the AU should pay more attention to the partner. In cases where relationship exist only on paper without clear benefits to the continent, the AU ought to abandon such strategic partnership. Chinese companies should contribute meaningfully as part of their social responsibility in grassroots activities to strengthen people-to-people relations between Chinese and Africans. Providing community services like healthcare, education and clean water is an important step towards building trust and breaking stereotypes. Through Chinese universities, Beijing could invest more in 'soft' infrastructure such as joint research in areas of Africa–China relations in partnership with African universities. The AU–China relations have reached maturity stage, hence sensitive questions such as illegal poaching of endangered African animals like rhinos and elephants should be discussed within the FOCAC. Other worrisome matters that both the AU and China could put on the table are the questions of migration and the treatment of Africans in China and Chinese in Africa.

Conclusion

South–South cooperation mechanisms can be strengthened by an improved Sino–African relationship. For the African Union to succeed in its efforts to spur economic growth in Africa and foster political integration, it needs to rise to the occasion. To revive and develop its basic infrastructure, Africa needs China. The African Union needs Beijing to improve its infrastructure on a continental scale, especially in building good roads, reliable telecommunications and power generation. If managed well, the Sino–African strategic partnership has the potential to help realize Kwame Nkrumah's vision of a United States of Africa. Lessons should be taken from the Chinese on how to manage similar relations. For instance, the China–EU relationship should be a major lesson for the AU. To do so, the AU ought to devote significant resources to researching and better understanding China. Until the hurdles of political and economic division, as well as disease and war, are overcome, Africa will not achieve its dream of meaningful political and economic integration.

Acknowledgements

I would like to acknowledge Matsie Molope and Lennon Monyae for their extensive comments and invaluable suggestions for this chapter.

Notes

1. Chinese Ministry of Foreign Affairs, *China's African Policy*, 2006, http://www.fmprc.gov.cn/eng/zxxx/t230615.htm (accessed December 2016).

2. Judith Van de Looy, *Africa and China: A Strategic Partnership? ASC Working Paper 67/2006*, African Studies Centre, Leiden, The Netherlands.

3. Kossi Ayenagbo, Wang Rongcheng, Chen Xueting, Ajibike Omolola Lawani, Tommie Njobvu, and Desire Bessan, 'Sino-African Economic and Trade Relations: Its Impact and Implications on the African Continent', *African Journal of Business Management*, Vol. 6 (21) (2012), pp. 6420–7.

4. Feng Zhongping and Huang Jing, 'China's Strategic Partnership Diplomacy: Engaging with a Changing World', Global Partnership Grid Series, Working Paper no. 8 (Brussels, European Strategic Partnerships Observatory, June 2014).

5. Zhang Chun, 'The Sino-Africa Relationship: Toward a New Strategic Partnership', 2013, https://www.lse.ac.uk/IDEAS/publications/reports/pdf/SR016/SR-016-Chun.pdf (accessed 25 November 2016).

6. Sally Morphet, 'Multilateralism and the Non-Aligned Movement: What Is the Global South Doing and Where Is It Going?', *Global Governance* 10 (2004), pp. 517–37.

7. Adekeye Adebajo, *The Curse of Berlin: Africa After the Cold War* (Durban: University of KwaZulu-Natal Press, 2010), p. 164.

8. Huang Meibo and Qi Xie, 'Forum on China – Africa Cooperation: Development and Prospects', *African East Asian Affairs*, 2012, p. 15.

9. Teresa Fallon, 'The New Silk Road: Xi Jinping's Grand Strategy for Eurasia', *American Foreign Policy Interests* 37 (2015), pp. 140–7.

10. President Xi Jinping's speech at the African Union Summit, Johannesburg, January 2015.

11. Zezhong Zhang, 'Promoting FOCAC More Maturely in the Next Decade'.

12. *FOCAC Declaration*, 2012.

13. Festus Aubyn, 'Featured Analysis: Key Factors Shaping the Interest of China in Africa Security Issues', *Africa Conflict Monthly Monitor* (July 2013), pp. 8–13.

14. Sergei Troush, 'China's Changing Oil Strategy and Its Foreign Policy Implications', Working Papers, CEAP, Visiting Fellows, Wednesday, 1 September 1999.

15. Aubyn, *'Featured Analysis'*.

16. Yun, *Africa in China's Foreign Policy* (Washington, DC: Brookings Institution, 2004).

17. See www.focac.org, December 2016.
18. Yun, *Africa in China's Foreign Policy.*
19. Ibid.
20. Ibid.
21. Julie Gilson, *Asia Meets Europe: Inter-Regionalism and the Asia-Europe Meeting* (Cheltenham: Edward Elgar, 2002).
22. Samuel Makinda and Wafula Okamu, *The African Union: Challenges of Globalization, Security, and Governance* (London: Routledge, 2008).
23. Professor Liu Hongwu, Reply to the Washington Post's Questions On the Relations of China – Africa, Embassy of the People's Republic of China in the Republic of Botswana, http://bw.china-embassy.org/eng/zt/zfhz/t623449.htm (accessed 15 June 2017).
24. He Wenping, 'Understanding China's Engagement with Africa & How the UK Can Build Relationships with China in Africa', 23 June 2009 – 25 June 2009, Centurion Lake Hotel, Pretoria, Conference Report, DFID & Centre for Chinese Studies, 2009, http://www.ccs.org.za/wp-content/uploads/2009/11/DFID_Conference_Report-RE-PDF.pdf. (accessed 15 June 2017).
25. Ambrose du Plessis, 'The Forum on China-Africa Cooperation Ideas and Aid: National Interest(s) or Strategic Partnership?', *Insight of Africa* 6, no. 2 (2014), pp. 122–3.

CONCLUSION

THE AFRICAN UNION IN TRANSITION: SUSTAINING THE MOMENTUM

Tim Murithi

This book is important and timely due to the pressing need to ensure that the African Union (AU) becomes 'fit for purpose' as recommended by the 2017 Kagame Panel report titled *The Imperative to Strengthen Our Union.*[1] The book's authors have interrogated and deliberated on where the African Union stands in terms of its efforts to advance the interests of its people in a world that is currently in flux due to the upheavals created by identity politics and upward surge of globalisation. Kuruvilla Mathews and Molefi Asante have appealed for a re-interpretation of the notion of Pan-Africanism in order to make it more contextually relevant for the twenty-first century. Khabele Matlosa, Hesphina Rukato, Amos Sawyer, Afeikhena and Mutasa have argued that the AU and its departments and agencies need to complement and enhance their collective interventions in order to achieve the objectives of the AU, namely a peaceful and prosperous Africa. As Kasaija Apuuli has discussed in the book, a security approach is necessary, but not sufficient, for the gradual stabilisation of war-affected regions across the continent. The challenging work of winning the hearts and minds of local populations through the transformation of societies is equally important and a vital complement to the security initiatives in these war-affected regions. The cyclical nature of conflict points to the critical need to move beyond the temporary stalemates and ceasefires, peace-keeping deployments and military operations that are so common in this era, towards a regional policy informed by intentionally confronting the underlying grievances that have fuelled decades of autocracy, animosity and violence on the continent. As Chris Landsberg notes, a key challenge is that African governments continue to seek national solutions or inward-looking state-centric solutions to problems that require adoption of a more expansive regional and continental perspective.

In addition, David Monyae and Ulf Engel have argued here that in the absence of a dedicated framework for intervening and robustly securing countries and regions, the continent will continue to remain beholden and subservient to the prevarications and infiltration of global powers. Consequently, there is a strong Pan-Africanist argument to find a way to push through the political, diplomatic and financial obfuscation that is stalling, and threatening to undermine, the cooperation between the numerous components of the African Union.[2] As Dawn Nagar and Fritz Nganje have argued in their chapter, the AU Commission, in partnership with Africa's regional economic communities, and African civic organisations, needs to scale up its advocacy agenda for promoting greater synergy between its various thematic interventions. In the absence of a genuine commitment across the entire AU system to facilitate and enable synergy, the pursuit of the Pan-African vision of a peaceful and prosperous continent will remain an elusive aspiration.

Africa's Leadership Deficit

To a large extent, efforts to ensure sustainable peace, security, governance and development in Africa have always been undermined by the dominant international and geo-political agendas of the day. After colonialism, it was the Cold War; and in the post–Cold War world the pressures of globalisation are impacting on Africa's peace and development efforts. However, the continent's ability and capacity to promote peace have also been undermined by Africa's leaders and their failure to find ways to address their differences and hold one another accountable. Africa's leadership deficit leaves the continent extremely vulnerable to internal fissures and external penetration and exploitation. For example, the fuel that adds to the flame of conflict in Africa is the role that globalisation plays in perpetuating and sustaining wars. The biggest challenge in trying to resolve disputes in Africa is to effectively deal with the role of international actors in fuelling conflict. Africa's experience with misrule is evident in the willingness of the continent's so-called leaders to collude with foreign governments and trans-national corporations to extract mineral resources, and these resources are being used to finance endless wars and withhold health, educational and infrastructural services to the continent's citizens. Examples of this include multi-national oil companies extracting oil and gas from South Sudan, Angola and Mozambique; global diamond cartels excavating in Zimbabwe and Congo-Brazzaville; timber conglomerates culling and extracting trees in Sierra Leone and Liberia; and industrial giants extracting copper, chromium and coltan from the Democratic Republic of the Congo (DRC) and the Central African Republic (CAR). Africa's leadership deficit is evident in this continued collusion with these global predators. The issue of whether these natural resources are exploited by a corrupt government that is often not legitimate, or by a militarised group, adds fuel to the fire of autocracy and conflict, and feeds into illegal trading of small arms and drug-dealing networks that make the situation difficult for one country to control or manage by itself. This reality has been made possible or easier by the emerging global networks of trade and instant financial transactions that allow the ability to shift huge amounts of capital at the click of a button to off-shore accounts beyond the investigative reach of unsuspecting citizens and civil society organisations, as has now been revealed by the infamous Panama Papers. Private military companies, or what were once called 'mercenaries', flourish in this new environment and can operate undetected and unidentified. The first order of protection of the interests of African citizens has to be its leaders. The inverse remains the case across the continent as leaders connive with insidious external actors. The point is that the promotion of peace, security and development in Africa is no longer the task of an individual leader or nation state, in the context of globalisation. This is at the very least a continent-wide challenge. At the very most, it is a global responsibility that implicates the citizens and governments where these multi-national companies are registered, specifically in Europe, America, China, Russia and India, which make profits from the exploitation and misery of people in war-affected and under-developed parts of Africa. This global responsibility also invokes the need for active citizenship in confronting these corrupt practices where they persist, and for holding Africa's so-called leaders to account through the self-ascribed promotion of civic leadership, both in Africa and around the world.

Addressing the Limitations of the AU's Internal Processes

The AU inherited a cumbersome bureaucracy from its predecessor, the Organisation of African Unity (OAU), which it has struggled to transcend. Consequently, there are remnants of the 'OAU way' of doing things that continue to hamper the AU in its daily management and administrative processes. The persistence of this culture of bureaucracy has serious implications when it, for example, creates a situation in which peacekeepers in Somalia are not paid in a timely manner for their sacrifice in what is a challenging conflict situation. This is only one example of many that continue to afflict the operations of the African Union in supporting peace, security, but also governance process across the continent.

There are also archaic management practices that foster attitudes of territoriality in the control and distribution of service provision goods across the AU. In particular, this is evident in the Union's recruitment processes, which remain encumbered and mired in bureaucratic inertia. A tangential effect of this bureaucratic system is the nefarious manifestation of 'office politics' between the office of the chairperson of the AU Commission and the individual commissioners, who sometimes behave as though they have an 'independent' mandate to run the affairs of their own commission, as though they did not belong to a larger whole that needs to function in a seamless and coordinated manner. This phenomenon replicates itself at the level of the directors of departments, some of whom are less inclined to enhance inter-departmental cooperation and collaboration.

The African Union at 15 Years: Sustaining Momentum for Change

African continental integration is not yet a concrete reality, remaining a promise to be fulfilled. As the AU advances into the next 15 years of operations the key challenge will be to sustain the momentum for constant change and improvement. In particular, the centrality of a coordinated approach will remain vital if the AU is to achieve its objectives as an organisation. Specifically, even though the link between peace processes, governance, development and trade interventions is self-evident at the conceptual level, this does not necessarily translate into concrete inter-organisational complementarity on the ground as far as AU initiatives are concerned.

As a number of contributors to this book have argued, the state-centric approach to dealing with crisis in Africa is now anachronistic and self-defeating. Political violence has real spill-over effects to neighbouring countries, and armed militia that are resisting the authority of a particular state are inevitably camped out in neighbouring countries, illustrating the inefficacy of dealing with 'national' crises. There is a need to adopt a regional lens when promoting peace, security and governance, whether it be in the Horn of Africa, the Great Lakes region, the Mano River Union or the Sahel. On this basis, the notion of 'regional reconciliation' is an important framework through which the nexus between security, governance and development can be enhanced and further elaborated.[3] The idea is that crises are addressed through regional forums that bring together the leaders of neighbouring states to address a particular crisis in a formal setting. By extension this calls for government-to-government collaboration at a regional level, to complement the people-to-people interventions that are already common in situations such as the one in the eastern DRC. The African Union can provide the overall framework through which its departments and agencies can co-jointly pursue early warning, early intervention, peacekeeping, peacebuilding, reconciliation and development to ensure that the phenomenon of cyclical violence is once and for all expunged from the continent of Africa.

In addition, the AU has a central role in promoting and advancing the operationalisation of the Continental Free Trade Area. This development will be vital in increasing intra-African trade and opening up the continent to the free movement of people through the issuing of a continent-wide African Passport. The private sector has an essential role to foster entrepreneurship and development of businesses in order to draw more Africans, particularly the youth, into the workforce. The AU is in a unique position to act as a catalyst for supporting the processes geared towards enhancing entrepreneurship by establishing coherent policy frameworks and holding its member states to account for upholding the principles of integrity in guiding their societies towards improved livelihoods.

This book has engaged in a broad-ranging discussion of the African Union's efforts to improve the lives of its citizens. In terms of the future prospects for the AU, the organisation has all the necessary policy institutions to function as an effective international actor on behalf of the continent. It is necessary to continue to articulate the political incentives of improved continental integration and intra-African trade, particularly to some of the errant African leaders who are still pursuing agendas that serve only themselves, their families, and cronies. In order to achieve this it will be necessary for African citizens to continue to mobilise and empower themselves to hold their governments to account for their actions and practices. In addition, African leaders can exert peer pressure on fellow leaders to ensure that they uphold the principles and norms that they have signed up to, as well as maintain their unified positions in global forums.

In terms of security and governance, the interventionist stance adopted by the African Union in its past 15 years is an appropriate one for the continent going forward. African conflict situations cannot be allowed to escalate, because they will continue to have a much more destructive effect on their people and citizens of neighbouring states. Consequently, there is a need for the notion of regional reconciliation to gain currency, anchored by deepening collaboration between the AU, its institutions and its partners, if these cyclical conflicts are to be extinguished permanently. The advent of a more pronounced synergy in effect serves to re-define the processes of peace, security, governance and trade in Africa. The security and governance of one can only be achieved by ensuring the security and governance of all. Every African is every other African's keeper, which reaffirms the notion of

Pan-African solidarity. Without a genuine commitment across the entire AU system to facilitate and enable synergy, the pursuit of the Pan-African vision of a peaceful and prosperous continent will remain an elusive aspiration.

Notes

1. Paul Kagame, *The Imperative to Strengthen Our Union: Report on the Proposed Recommendations for the Institutional Reform of the African Union* (Addis Ababa, 29 January 2017).
2. Jide Okeke and Tim Murithi, 'The "Toolbox" of African Rapid Intervention Strategy: Beyond the ASF, RDC, and ACIRC', in Festus Aboagye (ed.), *A Comprehensive Review of African Conflicts and Regional Interventions* (Addis Ababa: African Union and African Peace Support Trainers Association (APSTA), 2016), pp. 75–84.
3. Tim Murithi, *Regional Reconciliation in Africa: The Elusive Dimension of Peace and Security*, presentation at the Annual Claude Ake Lecture, Nordic Africa Institute and Department of Peace and Conflict Research, Uppsala University, Sweden, 26 October 2016.

SELECT BIBLIOGRAPHY

Abegunrin, Olayiwola, *Africa in Global Politics in the Twenty-First Century: A Pan-African Perspective* (New York: Palgrave Macmillan, 2009).

Aboagye, Festus (ed.), *A Comprehensive Review of African Conflicts and Regional Interventions* (Addis Ababa: African Union and African Peace Support Trainers Association, 2016).

Abrahamsen, Rita (ed.), *Conflict & Security in Africa* (Suffolk: Currey, 2013).

Adebajo, Adekeye (ed.), *From Global Apartheid to Global Village: Africa and the United Nations* (Scottsville: University of KwaZulu-Natal Press, 2009), pp. 251–68.

——, *The Curse of Berlin: Africa After the Cold War* (Durban: University of KwaZulu-Natal Press, 2010).

Ake, Claude, *Democracy and Development in Africa* (Washington, DC: Brookings Institute, 2001).

Akokpari, John, Angela Ndinga-Muvumba and Tim Murithi (eds), *The African Union and Its Institutions* (Johannesburg: Jacana, 2008).

Andemicael, Berhanykun, *The OAU and the UN: Relations Between the Organization of African Unity and the United Nations* (New York: United Nations Institute for Training and Research, 1976).

Asante, Molefi K., *An Afrocentric Manifesto* (Cambridge: Polity, 2007).

——, *Speaking My Mother's Tongue: Introduction to African American Language* (Fort Worth, TX: Themba Hill, 2010).

——, *The History of Africa*, 2nd edn (New York: Routledge, 2015).

El-Ayouty, Yassin (ed.), *The Organization of African Unity After Thirty Years* (Westport, CT and London: Praeger, 1994).

Bah, Alhaji Sarjoh, Elizabeth Choge-Nyangoro, Solomon Dersso, Brenda Mofya and Tim Murithi, *The African Peace and Security Architecture: A Handbook* (Addis Ababa: Friedrich Ebert Foundation, 2014).

Baulch, Bob and Edward Elgar (eds), *Why Poverty Persists: Poverty Dynamics in Asia and Africa* (Cheltenham: Edward Elgar, 2011).

Besada, Hany (ed.), *Crafting an African Security Architecture: Addressing Regional Peace and Conflict in the 21st Century* (Farnham: Ashgate, 2010).

Bischoff, Paul-Henri, Kwesi Aning and Amitav Acharya (eds), *Africa in Global International Relations: Emerging Approaches to Theory and Practice* (London and New York: Routledge, 2016).

Booth, David and Diana R. Cammack, *Governance for Development in Africa* (London: Zed Books, 2013).

Boutellis, Arthur and Paul Williams, *Peace Operations, the African Union, and the United Nations: Toward More Effective Partnerships in Peace Operations* (New York: International Peace Institute, 2013).

Brosig, Malte, *Cooperative Peacekeeping in Africa: Exploring Regime Complexity* (Abingdon: Routledge, 2015).

Daniel, Donald, Patricia Taft and Sharon Wiharta (eds), *Peace Operations* (Washington, DC: Georgetown University Press, 2008).

Esedebe, Olisanwuche, *Pan Africanism: The Idea and Movement, 1776–1991* (Washington, DC: Howard University Press, 1994).

Forster, Bankie and Viola C. Zimunya, *Sustaining the New Wave of Pan Africanism* (Windhoek: National Youth Council of Namibia, 2011).

Geiss, Immanuel, *The Pan-African Movement* (London: Methuen, 1974).

Green, Reginald Herbold and Ann Willcox Seidman, *Unity or Poverty: The Economics of Pan-Africanism* (Harmondsworth: Penguin, 1968).

Grudz, Steven and Yarik Turianskyi (eds), *African Accountability: What Works and What Doesn't* (Johannesburg: South African Institute for International Affairs, 2015).

Harbeson, John and Donald Rothchild (eds), *Africa in World Politics: The African State System in Flux*, 3rd edn (Boulder, CO: Westview, 2000).

Hjertholm, Peter (ed.), *Foreign Aid and Development: Lessons Learnt and Directions for the Future* (London: Routledge, 2000).

Hugh, Thomas, *The Slave Trade: The History of the Atlantic Slave Trade, 1440–1870* (London: Picador, 1997).

Huntington, Samuel, *The Third Wave: Democratization in the Late Twentieth Century* (Norman, OK: University of Oklahoma Press, 1991).

Hyden, Goran and Michael Bratton (eds), *Governance and Politics in Africa* (Boulder, CO: Rienner, 1992).

James, Cyril Lionel Robert, *A History of Pan African Revolt* (New York: PM, 2012).

Jerome, Afeikhena, *An Appraisal of the African Peer Review Mechanism (APRM)*, mimeo (Oxford: St. Anthony's College, Oxford University, 2006).

Klein, Herbert, *The Atlantic Slave Trade* (Cambridge: Cambridge University Press, 2010).

Levine, Daniel and Dawn Nagar (eds), *Region-Building in Africa: Political and Economic Challenges* (Cape Town and New York: Palgrave Macmillan, 2016).

Makinda, Samuel and Wafula Okumu, *The African Union: Challenges of Globalization, Security, and Governance* (London: Routledge, 2008).

Maloka, Eddie (ed.), *A United States of Africa?* (Pretoria: Africa Institute of South Africa, 2001).

Mangala, Jack (ed.), *Africa and the European Union: A Strategic Partnership* (New York: Palgrave Macmillan, 2013).

Masterson, Grant, Kojo Busia and Adele Jinadu (eds), *Peering the Peers: Civil Society and the African Peer Review Mechanism* (Johannesburg: EISA, 2010).

Mazama, Ama, *The Afrocentric Paradigm* (Trenton: Africa World, 2003).

Mazrui, Ali and Christophe Wondji (eds), *Africa Since 1935* (Paris and Oxford: United Nations Educational, Scientific, and Cultural Organisation and Heinemann Educational, 1993).

Moyo, Dambisa, *Dead Aid: Why Aid Is Not Working and How There Is a Better Way for Africa* (London: Farrar, Straus and Giroux, March 2009).

Mshomba, Richard E., *Africa in the Global Economy* (Boulder, CO and London: Rienner, 2000).

Muchie, Mammo (ed.), *The Making of the Africa-Nation: Pan-Africanism and African Renaissance* (London: Adonis and Abbey, 2003).

Murithi, Timothy, *The African Union: Pan-Africanism, Peacebuilding, and Development* (Aldershot: Ashgate, 2005).

———— (ed.), *Routledge Handbook of Africa's International Relations* (London: Routledge, 2014).

Murithi, Tim and Aquilina Mawadza (eds), *Zimbabwe in Transition: A View from Within* (Johannesburg: Jacana, 2011).

Mutasa, Charles and Mark Paterson (eds), *Africa and the Millennium Development Goals: Progress, Problems, and Prospects* (New York: Rowan and Littlefield, 2015).

Ndulo, Muna and Mamoudou Gazibo (eds), *Growing Democracy in Africa: Elections, Accountable Governance, and Political Economy* (Cambridge: Cambridge Scholars Publishing, 2016).

Nkrumah, Kwame, *Africa Must Unite* (New York: Panaf, 1963).

Saxena, Suresh Chandra (ed.), *Africa Beyond 2000: Essays on Africa's Political and Economic Development in the Twenty-First Century* (Delhi: Kalinga, 2001).

Sharamo, D. Roba and Chrysantus Ayangafac (eds), *The State of Human Security in Africa: An Assessment of Institutional Preparedness*, (Addis Ababa: Institute for Security Studies, 2011).

Sherwood, Mammo, *Origins of Pan Africanism: Henry Sylvester Williams, Africa, and the African Diaspora* (New York: Routledge, 2014.)

Sørbø, Gunnar and Peter Vale (eds), *Out of Conflict: From War to Peace in Africa* (Uppsala: Nordiska Afrikainstitutet, 1997).

Thardy, Thierry and Marco Wyss (eds), *Peacekeeping in Africa: The Evolving Security Architecture* (London and New York: Routledge, 2014).

Walters, Ronald W., *Pan Africanism in the African Diaspora: An Analysis of Modern Afrocentric Movements* (Detroit, MI: Wayne State University Press, 1997).

Williams, Paul D. and Solomon A. Dersso, *Saving Strangers and Neighbors: Advancing UN-AU Cooperation on Peace Operations* (New York: International Peace Institute, 2015).

Williams, Paul D., *War & Conflict in Africa* (Cambridge: Polity, 2011).

Zizwe Poe, Darly, *Nkrumah's Contribution to Pan Africanism: An Afrocentric Analysis* (New York: Routledge, 2003).

INDEX

Page numbers in *italics* refer to figures, those in **bold** refer to tables.
Italic text is used for titles of publications.

www.ingramcontent.com/pod-product-compliance
Lightning Source LLC
Chambersburg PA
CBHW071834270326
41929CB00013B/1987